Cities as International Actors

Tassilo Herrschel • Peter Newman

Cities as International Actors

Urban and Regional Governance Beyond the Nation State

Tassilo Herrschel
University of Westminster
London, United Kingdom

Peter Newman
University of Westminster
London, United Kingdom

ISBN 978-1-349-67945-4   ISBN 978-1-137-39617-4   (eBook)
DOI 10.1057/978-1-137-39617-4

Library of Congress Control Number: 2016956481

Cover illustration: © HAWKEYE / Alamy Stock Photo

Printed on acid-free paper

This Palgrave Macmillan imprint is published by Springer Nature
The registered company is Macmillan Publishers Ltd.
The registered company address is: The Campus, 4 Crinan Street, London, N1 9XW,
United Kingdom

PREFACE

This book results from our long-term interests in city and regional governance and the ways in which apparently 'borderless' challenges—a globalised economy, climate change, migration—have come to dominate the concerns of the policy-makers we talk to. Faith in the ability of national institutions and governments to respond and look after their cities and regions has declined. Cities have been among the first to realise the declining ability—or inclination—of nation states to maintain economic cohesion and comparable conditions of life and opportunities for all. And a rising anti-globalist, cultural nationalism also challenges the legitimacy of international organisations, from the G20 to the EU and the UN. Working at both levels—the global and the local—we became more and more interested in how sub-national actors are responding.

We also became aware of the enthusiastic case for cities and regions to take to the international stage being made by lobbying networks such as UCLG, and some academics such as Benjamin Barber's notion of a global 'parliament of mayors'. On the other hand, our conversations with urban and regional policy-makers over the last decade or so suggested to us that city and regional actors were not so much concerned with the big picture of defining a 'new global governance', but much more concerned with effective day-to-day management of the impacts of the global on the local. And, whilst some 'global cities' were envisioning their global 'leadership', many other actors in less glamorous locations were increasingly thinking and acting internationally to better their chances of survival in a globalised world. City and regional actors were telling us about their new international alliances, joining lobbying groups, or exploring new possibilities of joining up with the private sector. This prompted us to try to understand the growing variety and complexity of these new activities in the international/global arena. So, we became interested in how all the newly engaging, different types of sub-national governments were responding, and what shaped their decisions and strategies: local, regional, national or international factors? And how did they relate to each other and gain influence?

We set on the objectives of both giving an overview of these changes and collecting evidence of the detail of city and regional activities. As we found out from the many discussions we had with policy-makers over the last 10–15 years in different cities across Europe and North America, local factors, such as economic success, political culture and leadership, all combine to a particular—greater or lesser—local impetus to 'go international'. But this was just one side of the coin. We discovered that nation states continue to matter as they set the conditions under which cities and regions can, and feel the need to, engage internationally, facing either support or obstacles for such action, and that international organisations were increasingly keen to recruit sub-national 'partners' to increase the efficacy of their own policies.

Over the past few years, this has involved extensive and often repeated conversations with policy-makers in a large number of localities and government agencies. The international (Swedish–Danish) region of the Øresund has been a particularly inspiring example of such dynamics, illustrating the increasingly more independent role of some of the main cities, the emergence of a division between cities as actors and the 'rest' of the administrative regions involved (such as Skåne), the resulting political tensions about responsibilities, loyalties and legitimacies of policies and, last but not least, the continued responsibilities and more or less cogent influence of the nation state. Policy-makers in Malmö, Skåne, Ystad, Landskrona, Helsingborg, Kristianstad, Copenhagen and other locales have over the last 15 or so years provided fascinating insights into the international ambition—and thus increasingly multi-scalar dimension—of local and regional policies, their rationales and challenges. And here, Cecilia Gyllenkrok and Pontus Tallberg need to be mentioned in particular. Similarly, on the other side of the world, the Pacific Northwest has demanded our ongoing attention as the local and the international are tied together ever more closely. Portland, Tacoma, Seattle, Victoria and Vancouver have all been places of repeated encounters and inspirational discussions with policy-makers and fellow academics, with particular thanks going to Brian Walisser, Gary Paget, Janet Young and Peter Holt, and, among colleagues, Ethan Seltzer, Yonn Dierwechter and Emmanuel Brunet-Jailly. They all have been part of ongoing discussions and reflections on city-regional governance in a globalising world and the tensions, challenges and opportunities for policy-makers and politicians that spin from that.

We also need to thank those academic colleagues who have listened to these developing ideas in meetings and conferences and who have responded to earlier presentations of some of the main ideas. Coming from within spatial sciences and also outside, they have been instrumental in sharpening our rationale and conceptual argument underlining the book through critical questions, repeated stimulating and enjoyable discussions during workshops and also joint projects. In particular we would like to mention Frands Pedersen, Igor Calzada, Gerd Lintz, Manfred Kühn, Marius Guderjan and Magnus Lindh, and, at the end of a conference in Bristol, John Keane. Particular thanks go also to colleagues at the Vrije Universiteit, who provided a most helpful sounding board for our developing ideas during Tassilo Herrschel's stay as research fellow there during 2015: Bas van Heur, Stefan de Corte and Nicola Dotti. And while in Brussels, fascinating insights were gained from many discussions at the international Brussels representations of cities, regions and their networks.

There are many others who have provided critical and encouraging support to a developing theme of the 'conceptual gap' between Urban Studies and International Relations, encouraging us to step out of our own disciplinary comfort zones. We are grateful to all those who have helped us clarify what we meant by this gap (not least the often quizzical colleagues in our own Politics and IR Department), and we have made the academic challenge of interdisciplinary learning a major theme of the book. Our view is that across the disciplines there is much to learn from other perspectives in the ongoing challenge of developing and refining our understandings of urban and regional governance beyond the nation state.

We have benefited from some very helpful comments from readers of drafts of the manuscript. And we must put on record our appreciation to our editorial team, Christina Brian and Amber Husain, for their support and continuing patience with slipping deadlines, while maintaining sufficient pressure to keep the project 'on the road'.

Thanks to all.

Tassilo Herrschel
Peter Newman
London, UK
June, 2016

CONTENTS

LIST OF FIGURES

CHAPTER 1

Cities Joining States as International Actors

This book is about the increasing presence as actors in their own right of cities and regions in international policy-making and governance. The book is also about the 'conceptual gap' exposed by the presence of sub-national actors between the concepts of internationality developed by the two main relevant disciplines International Relations and Urban Studies. Both recognise the emergence of new international actors, but largely fail to step out of their respective disciplinary confinements. The book thus seeks to address and investigate the ways in which cities reach across spatial and institutional scales and get themselves directly involved in the international arena. But what have the two disciplines have to say about this from their different analytical and discursive traditions? Are the narratives and conceptualisations complementary in what they have to say, or contradictory? And can the two broad disciplines with their particular engagement with, and explanation of, the governance of the international arena learn something from each other and thus provide a more complete narrative of the new international arena? What can we learn from such a cross-disciplinary perspective about the forces behind this sub-national challenge to the traditional concept of the sovereignty of nation states as the predominant international actors? Traditional views presume that states and 'national interest' are coterminous, each between a set of equally clearly defined borders. Yet, reality is no longer as clear-cut, if ever it was established conceptualisations of 'state', 'sovereignty' and 'national interest' require revisiting, as new sub-national actors are adding complexity and agency to the picture.

© The Author(s) 2017
T. Herrschel, P. Newman, *Cities as International Actors*,
DOI 10.1057/978-1-137-39617-4_1

1

In adopting a broad, cross-disciplinary view, this book identifies three main ways in which cities are becoming international actors: (1) building or joining networks for collective engagement, (2) lobbying, and engaging with, existing international organisations (IOs) to also act on their behalf (rather relying on nation states), and (3) directly engaging as individual actors with own agendas vis-à-vis states and IOs as the established forces ordering the international realm. We locate our analysis within wide-ranging debate in Urban Studies and International Relations as the two primary disciplines addressing the two main subjects of this book: the city-region and 'internationality' respectively. Based on this, one of our intentions is to encourage more debate across disciplinary boundaries. The book examines the different analytical and conceptual lenses and points to a 'conceptual gap' that the changing nature of the international realm and its governance is exposing. Established disciplinary comfort zones and conceptual demarcation lines no longer can offer satisfactory answers to an increasingly dynamic and uncertain international environment. Accustomed certainties of structure, order and representational responsibility no longer seem to hold in the face of a world that seems increasingly disorderly and beyond the reach of traditional concepts and responses.

The book sets out to explore the broadening range of international action by looking in depth at a range of illustrative cases in different national settings and global contexts, with the primary focus on Europe and North America. In so doing, we acknowledge the impact of national context—in the form of traditions, structures and values–concerning the organisational nature and institutional role of the state across the different scales from the local to the international. The role of local factors, such as economic structure and success, institutional capacity and political capability, are clearly important in shaping policies that recognise and seek to address proactively the developmental prospects of a city or city-region by stepping out into the international or global economic realm. Through the illustrative cases we explore the interdependency between these factors on the ways in which local political and economic actors work together, and seek to shape local fortunes through individual and/or collective policies across spatial scales. Our cases do not attempt to provide a comprehensive account of the many varieties of possible combinations of contextual factors and forms of international action, but, rather, we aim to point to linkages and interdependencies, as well as gaps, between existing concepts and interpretations of these processes and thus encourage further research.

Through this approach, we identify the main challenges facing sub-national actors as the 'new kids on the block', as they enter the realm of states, IOs and other cities and regions, and thus add to the evolution of a more complex, and as yet unsettled, global governance which will continue to demand further explorations. What this book seeks to do is point to the analytical and conceptual gains to be drawn from making links between Urban Studies and International Relations about the role and functioning of the state as an expression of institutional traditions, power relations and democratic constructs, and how that shapes governance across scales. We explore how established views of the state as a holistic, legal entity, with internationally accepted and agreed powers and responsibilities, including the notion of sovereignty, can gain from taking a more differentiated look at the internal agency of a state, with varying relationships and uneven access to, and distribution of, power and so more accurately capture theoretically the role and workings of the 'nation state' in the international arena.

Over the past twenty years or so, there has been rapid growth of city and regional networks as new vehicles to protect and promote local and regional interests in a globalising, yet politically still largely state-centric, world. As a consequence, nation states and their territories come into sharper focus, as their borders lose the function of protecting and maintaining an image of a sovereign, cohesive entity in the international arena. Instead, the picture is becoming more detailed and differentiated, with a growing number of sub-national entities, cities, city-regions and regions, becoming more visible in their own right, either individually, or collectively as networks, by, more or less tentatively, stepping out of the territorial canvas and hierarchical institutional hegemony of the state. Prominent and well-known cities, and those regions with a strong sense of identity and often a quest for more autonomy, have been the most enthusiastic, as they began to be represented beyond state borders by high-profile city mayors and some regional leaders with political courage and agency. While some have ventured out individually with confidence, such as the mayors of the main 'global cities', others have invested time and resources in networking with like-minded others, and with the United Nations (UN) and other IOs, to gain the necessary capacity and desired impact which, individually, they felt lacking. Variations in economic success, and thus associated confidence and sense of self-reliance, matter here, too. They have created platforms for the voice of cities and regions to be heard at growing numbers of international conferences and elsewhere on the international stage, raising awareness of the fact that states are not merely undifferentiated 'black boxes', but the composite of sub-national entities with their own dynamics, interests and agendas.

Sub-national actors have been gaining a foothold in international policy-making and developing a growing confidence in articulating their own political agendas beyond the borders of their nation states. This novel international activity includes finding new partners beyond nation states and their established, formal governmental representations, either at the sub-national level—in the form of local/regional governments or business actors from other countries—or supra-nationally, in the shape of IOs, such as the UN. And these new partners are then to be used as policy levers to gain more influence on the international arena next to the nation states as the established dominant actors. In turn, IOs can have more direct influence on urban and regional policy. The result is an increasingly complex international web of opportunity-seeking by a growing range of actors and their interconnections vertically and horizontally. These interrelationships and strategic engagements criss-cross, as they connect a range of individual local and regional actors both within and between state territories.

As a result, the international realm now looks very different from the static mosaic of nation states that defined international relations during the Cold War years. For some, this may be worrying, as we can see in the rapid rise of right-wing populism in Europe and North America, promising to resurrect the 'reliable' world order of yesteryear, while for others it offers a more progressive scenario of carving out new opportunities in more fluid arrangements which offer opportunities to other actors than foreign ministries and offices. The Cold War arrangement was focused exclusively on the relationships between sovereign nation states within their respective geo-ideological alliances around the two superpowers, producing an, in essence, frozen structure. Initially, the ability of sub-national actors to work with others across national borders may have been limited to a few economically or politically powerful cities—such as the 'world cities' identified in the mid-twentieth century by Peter Hall (1966). For others, such ventures very much depended on an explicit encouragement, or, at least, toleration, by the respective nation states. One example is the Sister Cities International programme initiated by US President Roosevelt to reach out to (at first) Europe as a step to rebuild political bridges in the aftermath of the Second Wold War. In a similar vein, the French and German governments, through the two leaders Charles de Gaulle and Konrad Adenauer, pushed their respective municipalities into *jumelages* (or *Partnerschaften*) across the border as a low-key, grassroots approach to support reconciliation efforts between the two 'arch enemies', as the official discourse went until 1945. This, then, became part of the much bigger political project of the European Union (EU), which has offered a particularly supportive environment for international engagement by—and among—sub-national governments as part of its inherent integrationist agenda.

Now, economic globalisation is a dominant force driving international action by sub-national actors concerned about 'losing out' in the race for increased competitiveness for new, or continued, foreign direct investment. As borders surrounding nation states have become less effective as barriers to the movement of goods, capital and people, national economies transformed from state-based forms of mercantilism to an increasingly open global market with - increasingly - unhindered free trade. Cities and regions thus found themselves much more exposed, as state protection from the harsh winds of international competition lost its effectiveness. The much increased range of direct competitors around the world, rather than merely those within a country, has caused cities and regions to be concerned about the wisdom of continuing to rely on the notion of an inherently favourable home market compared with the global 'outside'. With states no longer being able and/or willing to take care of the interests of 'their' localities and regions, sub-national actors sought to develop greater independence and stronger own feet to stand on in the global market of investment and economic opportunities.

A growing effort has thus been directed towards attracting internationally mobile capital by sharpening and advocating the city and regional profiles of states more proactively and visibly, rather than relying on a conventionally expected trickle-down effect from national economic development and policy. The economic rise of the Asian city, and the leading cities of the BRIC countries (Brazil, Russia, India, China) raised the spectre of increased competition from a wider range of locational profiles, state structures and policies, and economic conditions. One result is an enlarged field for connections and alliances between subnational actors, as well as, of course, head-on competition and rivalries. The growing importance of direct connections and interrelations as part of a global division of economic activity in an increasingly febrile and rapidly changing market also means that it is an advantage to have a finger on the (economic) pulse, so as to be quick enough in responding effectively to changing circumstances and opportunities. Losing these connections, or being bypassed by them, reinforces existing, and produces new, marginalities and exclusions with correspondingly deteriorating prospects. Cities and regions have thus increasingly ventured out into the global arena of economic flows in the hope of identifying, creating and utilising opportunities for successful competition. Nation states may have been weakened by this multiplication in new competitive forces and economic crises and related loss of opportunities and competitive advantages. They thus may have been unable to respond in sufficiently specific and differentiated ways, so as to enhance effectively competitive opportunities for individual locales. As a result, some cities and regions, especially those with fewer independent means and capacities to act, may feel worse off by losing the support and protection they once had, while not feeling sufficiently empowered, resourced or confident to take independent steps onto the international arena of competitive capitalism to boost their own prospects for economic development.

At the same time, the demand for effective collective responses to the challenges of climate change has also created space for non-nation state actors in diverse forums to create new and complex international relationships both horizontally within networks and with other local and regional actors, and vertically, with IOs. Other global issues, for example the struggle for natural resources and international migration, also create a need for cities and regions to add their voice to inter-'national' debate to promote their interests beyond economic opportunity. In Europe, the EU provides incentives and institutional frameworks for multiple new forms of city and regional networking and lobbying, including at the international EU level. But a growing number of cities and regions also seek to 'go it alone' by establishing their own representations in Brussels, either individually or in shared accommodation, as the base for European lobbying. So, in Europe, and especially there, but also increasingly beyond, sub-national governments find themselves engaged in various networks with other sub-national actors, and with private sector, civil society groups, and national and international bodies, in developing policy responses to economic, environmental and other challenges that cross borders and demand collective solutions. This, in turn, demands both taking a broader, holistic perspective at the international or even global level, while also allowing for a more specific, detailed view that takes on board place- and institution-specific circumstances and ways of doing things. It is a seeming contradiction that the term 'glocalisation', introduced by Eric Swyngedouw in the early 1990s (Swyngedouw 1992, see also 2004), tries to capture. While such glocalism was first developed as an economic concept—just as globalisation was initially seen first and foremost as economically driven—policy responses have had to attempt to follow, so as to remain relevant and effective. The outcome of 'political glocalisation' can be seen as manifested in the growing engagement of the 'local', i.e. cities and regions, with the 'international/global', all in the pursuit of achieving more locally effective and successful responses to the challenges of globalism.

The forces of globalisation may be seen as a crisis of 'statism', as neoliberal responses dominate global policy (Curtis 2014). But that does not automatically mean that public policy is powerless, and the state a mere bystander, as globalisation unfolds. Rather, political responses and governmental policy-making have faced the need to find new ways of working and being effective. As a consequence, cities and regions find themselves having to navigate ever more complex webs of networks of formal and informal relationships—webs which they themselves increasingly contribute to building, crossing established territorial scales and institutional areas of responsibility along the way. For academic analysis and interpretation to be able to capture this process adequately, conceptual responses are needed that draw on a greater number of accounts of broader-based studies of these fundamental structural changes in attempts to govern globalism. New networks, new voices, new perceptions of local–global relationships seem to present a 'messy empirical complexity' (Moran 2010, p. 42). And understanding the roles of new global players and new relationships across policy fields, institutional sectors and operational scales, presents a challenge for analysts of how to break out of the 'territorial trap' reflected on by Agnew at first in the mid-1990s, and then, again, more recently (2009). This 'trap' restricted—and in several ways continues to do so—our understanding of international policy and politics to a world of states as fixed, single scale, cohesive territorial entities. In this understanding, no other actors really matter, nor are any sub-nationally visible. This concern with solely the scale of the nation state ignores emerging sub-national actors as relevant players in the arena of political-economic international relations. Yet, the growing intermingling of sub-national actors, especially powerful and confident cities and regions, with international and global matters, raises question marks over the salience of such a conceptual head-in-the-sand approach, as states face—potentially existential—challenges 'from within'. Growing inequalities as a result of neo-liberal globalism, such as between the successful cities and the less successful, struggling, often peripheral, cities and regions, produce rising political discontent, such as we are now facing across Europe and in the

United States as populist accusations of self-serving metropolitan elitism. Claims for more nationalist, anti-globalist and protectionist approaches, or explicit demands for devolved responsibilities and even outright independence, undermine established political certainties and notions of nationality, which fundamentally shape the ways in which states can work and operate internationally. Ignoring such processes reduces the potential relevance of messages and explanations offered by academic disciplines.

Analytical responses, however, have varied already, with several attempts at addressing the nature of 'governing' the global, such as in International Relations (IR) or International Political Economy (IPE). This is the case especially in terms of promoting international free trade, or securing peace in a geo-political setting with inherent contestations for influence. IOs were created to take on that role of bringing some order to a presumed inherently anarchic internationality (Brown et al. 1995). They were put in place by collective agreement between nation states as, from a traditional 'realist' IR perspective, it is only states that are relevant actors in organising the international realm. And so IOs are, in essence, viewed as agents controlled by, and working on behalf of, nation states. Meanwhile, and separate from that, economic perspectives recognised the importance of intra-state variations in production factors and comparative advantage, and thus a variable scope for market-based competition for new investment. Yet, while some regions gained more attention as important 'entrepreneurial' actors in economic development, e.g. in the example of Emilia-Romagna as the Third Italy (Cooke 1996), or the state of Baden-Württemberg in southern Germany (Staber 1996), the local level was associated much more with the image of more or less passive locales as stages where international/global capitalism acted itself out. The localities studies in the early 1980s (Cooke 1989), viewing cities and other localities as places which got 'restructured', illustrate this view. Only later, cities were seen as also strategic actors with 'urban entrepreneurialism' and 'urban boosterism' (Harvey 1989). Yet, such ideas generally located cities and regions in their national contexts, rather than on the international stage. Fig. 1.1 illustrates the analytical and conceptual foci of the different approaches to the issue of cities in a globalising (economic) world.

Our aim in this book is therefore to understand how and why subnational actors are developing more agency and are increasingly engaging in international policy and politics more directly. To do that, we need to explore how the academic disciplines that deal with the urban and the international scales are responding to the demands for a new

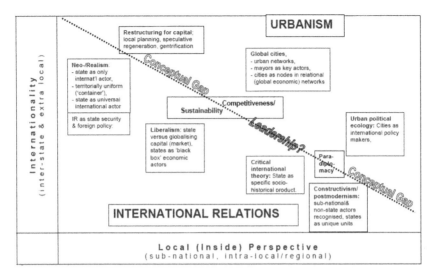

Fig. 1.1 Changing perspective of internationality as state and urban spheres of engagement

global governance that recognises and incorporates actors over and above sovereign nation states. We need to understand the forces pushing cities, regions and other sub-national actors onto the global stage, and need to develop the conceptual tools to make sense of the increasingly complex and changing relationships of the international realm in which cities and regions now find themselves.

Taking a look back, such a role for individual cities and regions is not in itself a novelty. It appears so only in the context of the legacy of nineteenth-century nationalism and imperialism, and the ascent of the territorially defined nation state as primary international actor. Networks of internationally powerful cities existed before the forging of nation states and an imperial international order. Some academics, for example Agnew (2009), argue that the supreme authority of the nation state as sovereign actor was, in fact, never complete. Other analysts suggest that new global realities are guiding the world back to the pre-Westphalian era, when networks of trading cities—the ancient Silk Road, the medieval Hanseatic League—provided the platform for relationships of mutual benefit and exchange (Katz and Bradley 2013). One needs to remember that then, as now, city actors had to engage with other powers to secure their interests. Going it alone was not always the best strategy to achieve that. The merchants of the Hanseatic League, for instance, enjoyed substantial trading privileges as a result of inter-city diplomacy and collective agreements within the networks (Lloyd 2002), as well as with larger powers, such as states. That way, the League could negotiate 'extra-territorial' legal spaces with special privileges, such as the 'German Steelyard' in the port of London (Schofield 2012). This special status was granted and guaranteed by the English king as part of an agreement between the state and a foreign city association. If there are lessons from previous eras, then they include the need to look beyond the post nineteenth-century fixation on the construct of the 'nation state' and at the historic precedence of a much more varied, cross-scalar picture of relationships between cities—both individually and as collective networks—IOs and states.

Despite the fixation on the nineteenth-century construct of the Westphalian nation state, there is growing, and strong, evidence that they no longer are the only actors that matter in shaping the international realm. Instead, we need to consider the rise in importance of cities and regions alongside changes within nation states, as well as the roles of IOs, all leading to a greater 'thickness' and, some may say, disorder in international governance. These roles come into play in response to the two different scales of 'regions'—supra- and sub-national respectively. The former includes macro-regional associations of states, such as the EU or ASEAN (Association of Southeast Asian Nations), while the latter looks at a lower scale and embraces groups of internationally oriented cities that seek to lobby, and work with, IOs, such as in the global platform and actions of UN Habitat, and its joint meetings with global networks of municipalities such as the umbrella organisation UCLG (United Cities and Local Governments). To understand these complex international relations, different approaches are required that not only develop the new interests of urban scholars in the international/global arena, but also address the need to make connections across disciplinary boundaries. This is needed to understand how IR as the discipline focused most of all on the international sphere, views the potential for sub-national actors on the global stage. On the other hand, looking to the second main relevant academic field, what are the conceptual challenges of these new urban engagements for urban theory in particular, and political science more generally?

Arriving at these challenges from different disciplinary backgrounds, some scholars have recently begun to raise questions about the importance of the work of cities beyond national borders. For instance,

McCarney et al. (2011) point to the 'underrepresentation of cities and sub-national regions as sites of governance or partners in global governance' (pp. 219–220). Meanwhile, McCann and Ward (2011) collect a number of perspectives on urban policy in the face of globalisation, and Scott (2012, p. 12) looks at the responses of some US metropolitan areas, concluding that 'in this emerging world, the logic of urban and regional development can no longer be meaningfully described in terms of purely national models but must be analysed directly in the context of an insistent process of globalization in which metropolitan areas in many different countries are increasingly caught up in an overarching system of competition, collaboration and social interaction'. Earlier, Sassen (2006, p. 347), talking about regulation of a 'post nation state', considers interactions between state and non-state actors, specifically global finance and cross-border activist politics. In this context, she points out that 'the cross-border network of global cities emerges as one of the key components in the architecture of "international relations"'. More recent work shares this emphasis on the special place of global cities as they assert themselves on the global stage (for example, Lee 2014; Ljungkvist 2016).

The emphasis on global cities, of course, excludes the activities of numerous 'lesser' cities, and regional and sub-regional groupings, that have forged cross-border international alliances to respond to global economic forces as a form of 'self-help'. As a consequence, there is wide acknowledgement of a global urban system that goes beyond the boundaries of national state territories (Krätke 2014). Academic interest grows in the economic power of, and challenges faced by, 'macro-regions', 'mega-cities' and 'city-regions' (Harrison and Hoyler 2015). Alongside the driving force of competition, other authors have been developing new analytical perspectives on the 'transnational politics' around climate change (for example, Bouteliger 2013; Bulkeley 2012; Bulkeley et al. 2013, 2014). Global climate governance is increasingly understood in polycentric terms: undertaken by a variety of actors, as they operate across multiple scales, utilising diverse forms of authority and rule-making. In this context, 'the growing urgency and complex politics of governing the environment, across borders of multiple sorts and in more democratic and representative ways, are eroding or transforming state-centred conceptualisations of sovereignty, territoriality, and representation' (McCarthy 2007, p. 190).Yet, such trans-scalar and cross-border perspectives are much less prevalent in economic policies, where competitive rationality counteracts collective action. As cities are pushing their claims across conventional borders and boundaries, they challenge issues of democratic legitimacy and control, especially when less visible, informal networks and lobbying are concerned. For example, what happens in the network C40 Cities (Global Leadership on Climate Change) (see Chap. 3) matters to the whole world, as this grouping brings together the largest and globally most influential (also in terms of environmental costs) cities (http://www.c40.org/about). In the continued absence (at least until the recent COP 21 Paris Summit in December 2015) of tangible outcomes from intergovernmental efforts to reduce greenhouse gas (GHG) emissions, it is increasingly significant that mayors of some of the largest cities, which claim a stake in international politics, are taking concrete actions that demonstrate that preventing catastrophic climate change is possible (C40 Cities; ARUP 2014), while also responding to the criticism that it is cities that are at the forefront of detrimentally affecting sustainable development.

The analysts and policy-makers whose arguments we have discussed here, are approaching the questions about cities as international actors largely from the perspectives of the 'urban' disciplines, i.e. political geography, urban and regional studies, and urban politics. The urban perspective has much to say about the drivers pushing sub-national actors into the international realm as a way of boosting their developmental prospects and interests. Yet, when it comes to understanding more about the nature of the international arena and the mechanisms and logics of engagement found there, this work has much less to say. For instance, questions need exploration and answering that address the ways in which the international realm works, how IOs interact with states, and how international networks operate. It is at that point that the resources of other academic disciplines—political science and IR in particular—need to be drawn upon as these have a well-established track record of conceptualising and analysing 'internationality', albeit from a predominantly heavily state-centric vantage point. Yet, there are more signs within IR, in particular in its constructivist and post-modernist theoretical interpretations, of greater appreciation of the growing evidence of a more complex composition of the international arena beyond the nation state. Thus, if in the past IR was fixed on relations between sovereign nation states almost to the exclusion of considering sub-national actors altogether, now there is much more work from a range of theoretical perspectives, from traditional realist to more recent constructivist interpretations. And there are aspects of Global Political Economy that aim to understand the work of IOs as well as transnational businesses, non-governmental organisations

(NGOs) and states as a diverse combination of multi-scalar interests and politics. The analysis and discussion in this book draws on the diverse perspectives and agendas of the institutions entering the international arena, and rules and norms that appear to manage and guide international politics and governance. Responding to those developments, IR now perceives the contemporary international political system as more of a complex open system, rather than a 'flat' nation state-only arena of actors, which displays 'emergent properties' (Sol et al. 2013) and degrees of 'organized complexity' (Jessop 1998).

Sub-national actors need to navigate in this increasingly complex web of networks of actors, interests and relationships, and this may well include needing to project and/or protect their interests on the international arena through more immediate action—either through collective action with other, like-interested actors, or individually on the basis of held confidence and institutional capacity. Some IOs, such as the UN, encourage, or even co-opt, sub-national 'partners' to increase the reach and effectiveness and not least the legitimacy, of their own interests and policy actions. Cities and regions, rather than ceding power to IOs, may sense greater advantages to be gained from networking with, rather than being 'subordinate' to, them. This, they try to achieve through boosting their own international presence directly, and increase their bargaining power—both politically and economically. But how can these two major developments—direct individual, and indirect international engagement—be analytically conceptualised as a dual process of urbanisation of the 'international', and internationalisation of the 'urban', respectively?

A major ambition in this book is to explore the potential of IR theories to help explain the emerging 'new international' with its growing degree of 'urbanisation' in terms of both the prevalence of urban actors and the growth of urban agendas in the international arena of defining and making policies. How, given this urban input, can urban theories be extended into the international sphere to help conceptualise the new urban(ised) 'international'? From both disciplinary perspectives, there is a need to take sufficient account of the complexities, discrepancies and conflicts between a slow-in-response state administrative structure and progressively more fluid communicative, and functional relations between a growing number of actors inside and outside government. They increasingly find themselves tied to, and positioned between, urban centres as connectors between the intra- and extra-national political agendas and policy processes.

1.1   Conceptualisations of 'City' and 'Internationality' from an Urbanist and IR Perspective

The following diagram Fig. 1.1 illustrates the positions of some of the main theoretical approaches to analysing and discussing globalisation in terms of its implications for the roles of cities and regions on the one hand, and a nation state-centric understanding of 'internationality' on the other. This is placed in a matrix defined by two analytical perspectives: 'Internationality' as the dominant focus of interests, with a primary interest in relationships and interaction between nation states, and a 'local perspective' looking primarily at the sub-state level of localities and (intra-state) regions. The role of these two analytical and theoretical foci is then associated with the two primary disciplines of interest here—'urbanism' and 'International Relations'. A diagonal notional division distinguishes two triangular halves (not necessarily following a straight line), depicting at the top left, a view that focuses exclusively on states as sole players of relevance in the international arena with no attention given to any sub-national players. This contrasts with the opposite scenario, at the bottom right of the diagram, where much attention is given to sub-national factors and conditions in their likely impact on a state's international engagement, both through direct, individual action, and indirectly, through IOs or networks.

The bottom left triangle is shown as shaped by an IR perspective of internationality, whereas the 'opposite' top right triangle depicts the growing role of local perspectives as favoured by 'urbanism'. 'Urbanism' stands here for urban-centric analyses with an inherent recognition of the city as an important place of political, economic and cultural development and articulation, and subsequent action. In scalar terms, this includes in the majority of cases a locally focused perspective, reaching to a regional dimension in the instances of large metropolises and city-regional conurbations, and embracing disciplines such as planning, urban geography or, more multidisciplinary, urban studies. Increasingly, these have also included a more outward-looking perspective, as globalisation added a political-economic lens of analysis, such as in the discourse on 'global cities'. These are portrayed as potent actors in the globalising economy, including in trans-border relations (e.g. trans-border regionalism). This view of cities as active players in globalisation contrasts with earlier interpretations of cities (and other localities), especially in the late 1970s/early 1980s, as passive local arenas, at the mercy of an international 'restructuring for capital' (e.g. Massey and Meegan 1978). The underlying concern with the social costs of these changes was later picked up and developed further in work on urban political ecology, with an interest in cities as expressions of local democratic mobilisation (Heynen et al. 2006). But the 'local' largely remained in a passive role vis-à-vis the 'international'. Despite these very different theoretical and ideological starting points, the connections between sub-national and supra-national scales were recognised as gaining considerably in importance vis-à-vis political-economic internationalisation and, ultimately, globalism. Their active engagement, however, challenged established structures and organisational principles of economic rationality, societal structuration and political engagement.

Opposite the urbanism-led interpretations and analyses Fig. 1.1 depicts some of the main approaches to internationality and globalism within IR. Here, the theoretical standpoints range from realist and neo-realist interpretations to those of post-modernism and constructivism. In the former, realist, view, the international is a fixed mosaic of nation states whose policies are solely driven by maximising self-interest, including securing their territorial integrity as defined by borders. They do so through the projection of power and influence in a presumed otherwise anarchic 'outside'. Opportunities are there to be maximised out of self-interest. Understood in this way, there are some interesting parallels to the economic theory of neo-liberal globalism and the pursuit of maximum profit/advantage. Essentially, states, understood as nation states in their nineteenth-century derived rationality, are viewed from the outside as a black box whose internal structures and workings are of little consequence—and thus interest—to the presumed predominant opportunistic, advantage-maximising rationality of state action. This may go so far as depicting the state as protector of its citizens' liberty vis-à-vis the subordinating economic (but, ultimately, also political) forces of economic globalism. This understanding of the state as a homogeneous entity becomes questioned by the critical internationalist and, especially, constructivist and post-modernist theoretical strands in IR theory. They recognise the potential role and impact of state-specific internal factors, such as histories, established political cultures, or place-specific institutional structures and practices. From a more economy-oriented view, this could also include variations in relative comparative advantage—or disadvantage—in relation to a globalised economy.

Seen from a discursive point of view, and taking into account the general direction of some of the work on either 'side' of the diagonal line, there seems to be evidence of potential linkages that could be drawn between the questions raised and interpretations offered by the IR and the urbanism fields. Nevertheless, very few bridges have been built across a seeming 'conceptual gap' between a primarily introspective urban focus, where analysis of cities' international engagement is a minority interest, and on the other side, a mainly 'extra-spective' view, where consideration of what is going on beneath the political 'surface' of a nation state is considered of little relevance and thus also remains a minority concern. One of the few connectors between these two distinct academic traditions and established practices is 'paradiplomacy', seeking to combine the sub-national with concepts of conventional state-based international engagement, diplomacy. Yet, that too remains rather a niche interest within IR. In terms of policy fields, the apparent conflictual priorities and rationalities between a globalism-based competitiveness agenda, and a globally-oriented climate change and sustainability interest, highlight the close interaction between urban agendas and analytical scales, and questions of internationality in terms of necessary effective policy targeting and regulation.

Given the growing fluidity and fuzziness of borders in economic decisions and capital movements as part of globalisation, this book thus postulates an urgent need to bridge the conceptual gap between IR and urbanist approaches to, and understandings of, the role and relevance of cities as international actors. The following chapters set out to examine this complex, yet increasingly important, relationship which so far has remained in the academic 'no-man's land' wedged between disciplinary comfort zones.

1.2   OUTLINE OF CHAPTERS

Following on from this chapter, Chap. 2 discusses the conceptual, analytical and practical challenges posed by a globalised 'internationality' to the notion of a territorially cohesive state which acts as a single entity, when it comes to international engagement. Fundamental change to international settings, especially the end of the Cold War at the end of the 1980s, set in train a growing dynamic that underpinned a 'frozen' geo-political territoriality as part of security arrangements between the two superpowers. A growing perforation of borders in the wake of globalisation, which partially, at least, also contributed to the downfall of communism in Eastern Europe (Herrschel 2007), sought to exploit, and thus highlighted,

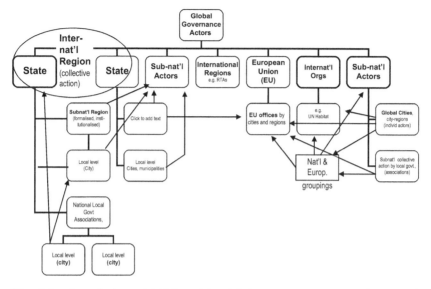

Fig. 1.2 Complexity and 'thickness' in global governance: growing horizontal and vertical engagement by actors

underlying inequalities in scope and opportunity to participate in, and benefit from, a growing openness of borders, at least in economic terms. Yet, political-institutional structures, built on the concept of the bordered territory of the nation state, found themselves increasingly challenged by a growing economic and functional dynamism. Consequently, fixed territories of power and administrative responsibility developed mismatches with the economic spaces that configured around cities and their interconnections. And this, Chap. 2 shows, extends to the international arena. There, a growing number of cities and regions seeks to participate in, and influence, global governance. They try to do so by working around their respective nation states, either as part of agenda-based networks, as individual actors, or through lobbying IOs. The outcome is a multi-layered geography of more or less contiguous entities of political engagement which reach right through the nation state from the global to the local level. Fig. 1.2 illustrates this complexity—or 'thickness'—of actors, and their interdependencies, as they build three clusters of engagement across scales: the sub-national arena of governance, the supra-national arena, and the EU and cities/city-regions as primary interlocutors between these two spheres. Their cross-scalar reach has been addressed to some degree in such concepts as new regionalism which includes trans-border relations between cities and regions, such as city twinning. Across the scale, international-ity, with the two primary traditional players—states and IOs—also reaches 'down' to the sub-national level in the form of IOs opening up to direct lobbying by, and engagement with, sub-national actors. Importantly, the established main analytical lenses—Urban Studies and IR—are located at the opposite ends of this multi-scalar system of international governance, with international urbanism and Global Political Economy at least recog-nising, and engaging with, the interdependency between, and co-working of, the 'urban' and the 'international'.

The implications of these developments for forms and principles of governing are the primary interest of Chap. 3. This includes variations in the analysis and explanation of 'global governance', especially also per-spectives on network governance and its varying scales. Networks serve as an important vehicle for sub-national actors to engage internationally. In this context, the chapter examines the utility of adopting the multi-level governance perspective to capture the 'bracketing' of the nation state by the local and the international scales. The second main point of interest in Chap. 3 is understanding the rationales behind new interna-tional imaginaries of power, opportunity and interdependencies, as well as, importantly for democratic systems, questions of authority and legiti-macy in the emerging new, and increasingly complex, multi-scalar and multi-actor forms of global governance. The relationship between state, IOs and sub-national actors has witnessed a continuous evolution, not least in response to economic success and thus confidence and capacity in being proactive. This impacts on scalar positioning, self-identification both in terms of scope and political rationale and justification, and insti-tutional modus operandi.

External contexts matter here, as evidence from the EU's international-ity compared with that of the global arena beyond, clearly demonstrates. This shows the importance of political and institutional context for the likelihood of cities and regions, especially those outside the 'elite' global cities group, venturing into the arena of global governance. Based on the evident differences in international engagement strategies, the chapter distinguishes between three modes of international urban (sub-national) engagement beyond the borders of the respective nation state: (1) *col-laborative, horizontal networks*, (2) *collaborative vertical engagement* with IOs as established agents of international governance, and (3) *open and direct local engagement*, building and utilising both horizontal and vertical actor relationships. The third approach shows the great number of highly individualised and tailor-made policies attempting to maximise prospects for likely success. This shapes the relationship between state, IOs and sub-national actors, which, as the chapter points out, has witnessed a continuous evolution in terms of modus operandi, scalar positioning and operational confidence of urban actors vis-à-vis the nature and challenge of global governance.

Chapter 4 goes a step further and looks in more detail at city networks as one of the main international engagement strategies adopted by cities and regions, as distinguished in the previous chapter. Those networks claiming a stake in the international realm tend to reflect particular local or regional economic circumstances, either as drivers of, or obstacles to, engagement and relevance in global governance. The chapter points to the variations found between city networks in terms of the topicality of engagement, their geographic reach, and the composition of networks, such as types and range of cities involved. And this, in turn, as the chapter further illustrates, influences the growth and organisation of these networks of sub-national governments, including their global and regionally-based relationships with IOs. They serve, in effect, as 'amplifiers' for local government international policy agendas, to project them up to the global scale of governance, especially in instances with more restricted capacity and confidence by local actors owing to constitutional constraints, economic weakness or limited size. IOs vary in their policy-making efficacy and legitimacy, with the latter often considered taken care of by the results achieved. 'Legitimate' policy outcomes may well be the result of 'structural asymmetry' among participants, with some exercising greater influence than others, to the point of being de facto hegemonic in relation to others. How well new global networks and IOs manage on the world stage depends on their grasp of the opportunities and political capabilities to translate those interests, concerns and ambitions into effective lobbying and policies.

Chapters 5 and 6 examine illustrative examples of individual strategic policy approaches in the EU (Chap. 5) and North America and beyond (Chap. 6). This allows assessment of the importance of the particular circumstances of internationality provided by the EU, in relation to more 'normal' single state conditions of 'national' and 'international' as operating environments for cities and regions, as they pursue their economic interests. Both chapters distinguish between the two principal avenues for international engagement: 'going it alone' through individual, singular action, versus working indirectly through either city or regional actor networks, or through IOs as interlocutors between local and national/international actors of global governance. Chapter 5 clearly shows the role a European internationality plays for cities and regions to venture onto the international stage. This is manifested in the growing number of Brussels offices or grander embassy-style representations, as favoured by confident and latently 'separatist' regions, such as Bavaria in Germany, Catalonia and the Basque region in Spain, or Scotland in the UK (Calzada 2014).

The North American tradition provides much less opportunity—or desire—to engage internationally, not least because of the continent-wide scale of the two states involved, the United States and Canada, and the established traditions in distinguishing between the 'local' and the 'national'. 'Local' is much associated with 'community' and policy issues of day-to-day life. It is the biggest cities that are more likely to possess an inherently larger-scale, outward-looking, perspective. As a result, international engagement is largely limited to individual action by mostly larger metropolitan areas and/or well-known cities. By contrast, city networks, representing all sizes and types of municipalities across the United States and Canada, are much more content with lobbying no further than their respective national governments to act internationally (also) on their behalf. Engaging and participating in global governance thus clearly emerged as a variable, even fluid, combination of elements of urban politics and elements of international diplomacy, as captured by IR. There is no clear-cut dividing line, and promises to be increasingly less so, between the sub-state and supra-state spheres of political-economic engagement and action, serving as as a sign of a trans-scalar 'glocalisation' of global governance. Theoretical explanations in academic disciplines need to follow suit. Chapter 7 elaborates on these conclusions from the discussions and evidence provided in this book.

References

Agnew, J. 2009. *Globalization and Sovereignty*. Lanham MD: Rowan & Littlefield.
Bouteligier, S., 2013. Inequality in new global governance arrangements: the North–South divide in transnational municipal networks. *Innovation: The European Journal of Social Science Research, 26*(3), 251–267.

Brown, M.E., Lynn-Jones, S.M., and Miller, S.E., 1995. *The perils of anarchy: contemporary realism and international security*. MIT Press.

Bulkeley, H., Edwards, G., & Fuller, S., 2014. Contesting climate justice in the city: Examining politics and practice in urban climate change experiments. *Global Environmental Change* 25, 31–40.

Bulkeley, H., Carmin, J, Castán Broto, V, Edwards, G., & Fuller, S., 2013. Climate justice and global cities: Mapping the emerging discourses. *Global Environmental Change 23*(5), 914–925.

Bulkeley, H., 2012. Governance and the geography of authority: modalities of authorisation and the transnational governing of climate change. *Environment and Planning A, 44*(10), 2428–2444.

C40 Cities, ARUP, 2014. *Climate Action in Megacities,* http://issuu.com/c40cities/docs/c40_climate_action_in_megacities, accessed 23 Jan 2016.

Calzada, I., 2014. The Right to Decide in Democracy between Recentralisation and Independence: Scotland, Catalonia and the Basque Country. Regions, no 296, 2014 Issue 4, pp. 7–8.

Cooke, P., 1996. Building a twenty first century regional economy in Emilia Romagna. European Planning Studies, *4*(1), 53–62.

Cooke, P., 1989. Localities: the changing face of urban Britain. London: Unwin Hyman.

Curtis S., 2014. Introduction Empowering Cities in S.Curtis, ed *The Power of Cities in International Relations*. Routledge, pp. 1–15.

Hall P., 1966. *The World Cities*. London: Weidenfeld and Nicholson.

Harrison, J., and Hoyler, M., 2015. Megaregions: foundations, frailties, futures. *Megaregions: Globalization's New Urban Form*, pp. 1–28.

Harvey, D., 1989. From managerialism to entrepreneurialism: the transformation in urban governance in late capitalism. *Geografiska Annaler. Series B. Human Geography*, 3–17.

Herrschel, T., 2007. Regions between imposed structure and internally developed response. Experiences with twin track regionalisation in post-socialist eastern Germany. *Geoforum, 38*(3), 469–484.

Heynen, N.C., Kaika, M., and Swyngedouw, E., 2006. In the nature of cities: urban political ecology and the politics of urban metabolism (Vol. 3). Taylor & Francis.

Jessop, B., 1998. The rise of governance and the risks of failure: the case of economic development. *International social science journal, 50*(155), 29–45.

Massey, D.B. and Meegan, R.A., 1978. Industrial restructuring versus the cities. *Urban Studies, 15*(3), 273–288.

Katz B., and Bradley J., 2013. *The metropolitan revolution how cities and metros are fixing our broken politics and fragile economy*. Washington, DC: Brookings Institution Press.

Krätke S., 2014. Cities in Contemporary Capitalism *International Journal of Urban and Regional Research 38*(5), 1660–1677.

Lee T., 2014. *Global Cities and Climate Change: The Translocal Relations of Environmental Governance*. London: Routledge.

Ljungkvist K., 2016. *The Global City 2.0 From Strategic Site to Global Actor*. London: Routledge.

Lloyd, T.H., 2002. *England and the German Hanse, 1157–1611: a study of their trade and commercial diplomacy*. Cambridge University Press.

McCann, E., Ward K., eds., 2011. *Mobile Urbanism: Cities and Policymaking in the Global Age*. Minneapolis: University of Minnesota Press.

McCarney, P., Segbers K., Amen M., Toly N., 2011. Concluding Remarks, *In* Amen M, Toly N, McCarney, P., Segbers K., eds *Cities and Global Governance*, Ashgate: Farnham.

McCarthy J., 2007. States of nature: Theorizing the state in environmental governance. Review of International Political Economy *14*(1), 176–194.

Moran M., 2010. Policy-making in an interdependent world 25–42 in C Hay ed *New Directions in Political Science. Responding to the Challenges of an Interdependent World*, Basingstoke: Palgrave.

Sassen S 2006 *Territory, Authority and Rights*, Princeton University Press.

Schofield, J., 2012. The medieval port of London: publication and research access. *London Archaeologist*, winter 2012/2013, pp. 181–186.

Scott, A., 2002. *Global city-regions: trends, theory, policy*. Oxford University Press.

Sol, J., Beers, P.J. and Wals, A.E., 2013. Social learning in regional innovation networks: trust, commitment and reframing as emergent properties of interaction. *Journal of Cleaner Production, 49*, 35–43.

Staber, U., 1996. Accounting for Variations in the Performance of Industrial Districts: The Case of Baden-Württemberg. *International Journal of Urban and Regional Research, 20*(2), 299–316.

Swyngedouw, E., 1992. The Mammon quest. 'Glocalisation', interspatial competition and the monetary order: the construction of new scales. In: M Dunford, G Kaukalas (eds): *Cities and regions in the New Europe*, London: Belhaven, pp. 39–67.

CHAPTER 2

Cities and the Global Arena—From Connectors to Actors: The Questions of Space and Territory

2.1 Introduction

A central issue in this chapter is the challenge to the notion of a territorially cohesive state, acting as a single entity when it comes to international engagement. This matters, as the international no longer can be viewed as an ungoverned, anarchic space, within which nation states, as the only relevant and legitimate actors, seek to defend their fixed boundaries around equally fixed territories. And that they do this by projecting power beyond these borders, including through calling alliances, while also protecting their self-interests. This is, put simply, the widespread, conventional view that predominated in the realist discourse in IR during the Cold War years, and continues to command attention. Maintaining the status quo through protecting borders—as part of mutual deterrence and distrust—was seen as states' primary objective. Any change to this was considered a threat to stability—a term that, in itself, implies fixity and continuity, even predictability. By contrast, the post-Cold War period, especially the 1990s, has been one of previously not seen dynamics of continent-wide extent, when communism collapsed, to be replaced by uncertainty and unpredictability. This was despite the attempt to project Western-style neo-liberal democracy as the only show in town, thus making post-communist changes more predictable—at least in theory (Herrschel 2007).

This change in international settings, with a stark political-economic and society-historic underpinning, soon, however, revealed considerable

© The Author(s) 2017
T. Herrschel, P. Newman, *Cities as International Actors*,
DOI 10.1057/978-1-137-39617-4_2

variations in the ways in which 'transition' acted itself out and produced new dynamics and tensions between ideas of nationality and economic functions on the one hand (still in search of clarification and finding themselves), and fixed administrative structures of government, on the other. At the same time, globalisation-driven free trading increased the pressures of competitiveness across borders and all scales—national to local—with impacts in all global regions. The 'international' changed from an apparently frozen, politically and strategically defined mosaic of state territories to an increasingly dynamic, economic opportunity-driven space of flows of communication, capital and opportunity. Borders became an obstacle, rather than a line of defensive protection. The result has been a growing tension between territorial and institutional state power and structure, and opportunity-driven dynamics and agency, especially since the beginning of the new millennium. Although globalisation has begun to increase the dynamics of the underpinnings of the arena of inter-state engagement since the 1970s, it did so only gradually, as security interests during the Cold War prevailed with the emphasis on maintaining the status quo of borders and state territories. Since the early 1990s, however, this rapidly changed. This not only affected the role of territory and borders, but also that of government vis-à-vis other, especially private sector, actors, as the concept of governance began to quickly supersede that of government more generally, even though its origins, too, go back to the 1960s (see, for example, Dahl's: *Who Governs?*, 1961), and some IR theorists began to talk about 'interdependence' between state and private actors and a wider, global 'diffusion' of, especially economic, power.

For the discussion of the international arena, this meant a growing discourse of globalisation and globalism, a new focus on the role of corporate and financial actors, the growing influence of the World Trade Organization (WTO) and the World Bank, and thus the 'market' as agent of international relevance. This also meant a realisation that states no longer simply try to 'go it alone', engaging at best in 'distance relationships', but, instead, collaborate and combine into regional groupings and associations, for which they are prepared to surrender and pool some of their sovereignty. The outcome may be a form of 'hegemonic regionalism' where the global sphere is managed by regional groupings of states (Acharya 2012), rather than individual state hegemons. And, lastly, a growing proliferation of actors, both horizontally and vertically, has become evident through the joining of a range of non-governmental actors, as well as other scales of the state than the nation states and their national governments.

All this is an indication of the growing dynamics in the nature and configuration of the governance of the international realm. The outcome has been a more flexible, variable and dynamic constellation of the international as arena of strategic governance—with a continuous reconfiguration of functional spaces defined by relations between political and economic actors and their interests. These interests may be shared or conflicting—and, as a result, involve correspondingly variable relationships with tensions through possible overlaps between fixed government state territories, and evolving collaborative policy spaces which are based on shared values and interests—be they culturally, historically, economically or governmentally driven. Here, global regions revolve around norms, values and identities held by governmental (political) actors, civil society groups and business interests. Some of this focus on cultural values and histories acts as a glue for (here) state-based international regionalism, such as 'culture blocs' (Meinig 1956), where cultural, rather than economic relations (trading blocs) and interests, are used to circumscribe an international region of collaborating states. In contrast, then, to the dominant theoretical 'realism' of IR, more recent 'constructivism stresses the instrumental uses of regionalism to promote specific political and economic ends. To constructivists, actors create social facts by assigning functions to various spatial units' (Väyrynen 2005, p. 26).

The resulting reality of the international arena is thus much more complex and 'thicker' in both its geographic and institutional layout and design, going well beyond the rather one-dimensional understanding that realist approaches suggest. In response to these changes since the early 1990s, constructivist concepts within IR have tried to capture this variability of the formation and enacting of state behaviour, by allowing for a broader range of actors, their nature and spatial reach, and place-based societal, historic, cultural and political-economic characteristics. It is these that constructivism views as making states predisposed to particular patterns of behaviour vis-à-vis the international realm.

The concept of 'new regionalism' has tried to address this growing complexity and its impact on finding governing answers for an increasingly dynamic international realm. Based in IR theory, regionalism refers to international regions, also referred to as 'macro-regions' (e.g. Hettne 2006) as groupings of states which collaborate on the basis of multi-lateral agreements. This discussion (Hettne et al. 1999) emerged in the 1990s, very much at the time that 'globalisation' established itself as an overwhelming concept in academic as well as public political debate. Thus,

Payne and Gamble (1996) point to underlying dynamics of international macro-regions, as they are agreed by inter-state negotiation. This dynamic they describe as 'regionalism', as it has to do with an agenda and state action: 'regionalism is a state-led or states-led project designed to reorganize a particular regional space along defined economic and political lines' (p. 2). Sub-national regions may, while also following this principal modus operandi, of course, also be shaped through national government fiat as laid down by national constitution and powers. But it does not *per se* affect the issue of sovereignty.

It is in this respect that Hettne (2006) clearly points to the interdisciplinary differences in conceptualising regions: 'in the field of geography, regions are usually seen as subnational entities, either historical provinces (which could have become nation-states) or more recently created units. In IR, regions are often treated as supranational subsystems of the international system. It is of some importance whether regions are seen as subsystems of the international system or as emerging regional formations with their own dynamics' (Hettne 2006, p. 543). This difference matters, as it has important implications for the understanding of the role of the state vis-à-vis notions of political and institutional collaboration—also discussed as integration—between territorial entities: 'Regional integration as a translocal process, simply defined in terms of market factors, has occurred over a long period of time', while 'regional integration is, in contrast, normally taken to imply some change in terms of sovereignty' (ibid, p. 543). And integration is understood as 'matching up' state-administrative structures and territorialities to the growing transnationalisation of markets, both in support of such trends to maximise economic prospects for the respective populations, but also to maintain regulative efficacy. This, as, for instance, Nye (1987) points out, leads to considerable complexity of the concept of 'integration' with associated political and administrative challenges, including conflict and contestation about agendas, distribution of powers, representation, etc.

The issue of state sovereignty is crucial here, as it circumscribes the degree to which a state may feel challenged in this respect by internationally operating regional entities. While at the sub-national level, regional ambitions may be watched carefully by the superior national government, possibly also leading to contestations, especially in federal arrangements, such wariness may lead to a constant hesitation of surrendering sovereign powers to the constructed new macro-regions. And this, in turn, potentially hinders their efficacy as international actors. The EU is a good example of this dilemma. Regional *cooperation* as a less binding form of transnational engagement may thus be preferred by states over 'integration', because it is easier to step back and revert to national agendas, albeit at the price of likely contest through self-interested national manoeuvres.

In the 1990s, at the same time as IR's established interpretations of state and the international faced challenges from emerging constructivist suggestions of a more differentiated, uneven and dynamic element, a different scale of actor entered the stage through contributions from Urban Studies and economic geography: internationally engaging sub-national actors questioned the supreme position of the nation state as established guardian of the international arena. Saskia Sassen's proposal of 'global cities' in the early 1990s, and Manuel Castells' suggestion of globalisation as point-to-point networks of 'flows', opened the view to a level of actors *beneath* the nation state. This also challenged the understanding of the world order as a global mosaic of fixed state entities, and, instead, suggested an arena of less clearly defined relational flows between individual actors, including also cities and, regions next to states. This, in turn, pointed to a very different, much more fragmented and constantly reorganising, international/global 'space of flows', which represents, and reinforces, a growing unevenness in who matters and who does less so. The challenges that fluidity pose for governance is clear, given the likely mismatches between fixed structures of power and responsibility versus fluid spaces as targets of policies. Can they remain relevant and appropriate, and thus effective? This change in the international realm thus challenges both IR and Urban Studies and exposes analytical differences that the different take on, and use of, the term 'new regionalism' illustrates well. 'New regionalism' seeks to capture the conceptual fuzziness (Markusen, 2003) of the very notion of 'region' as a spatial entity, be that as 'arena' or 'actor in its own right', reaching, on the one end, from that of 'global region' as a cluster of states, to, on the other, that of the 'city-region' as cluster of localities, as well as individual (larger) cities, each being owned by either discipline. Fig. 2.1 illustrates this distinction.

Figure 2.1 contrasts the two conceptualisations of regionalism by the two main relevant disciplines—IR/IPE and Urban Studies. Both possess an immediate default understanding of what region means—supranational groups of states versus sub-national entities between the local and national level of government. This distinction illustrates the inherent conceptual gap between the two main lenses through which the nature of the global arena and its governance may be, and are being, viewed. This gap

Characteristic	International (Global) Regions (e.g. RTAs)	Sub-national (City-) Regions, incl Global Cities
scale	Supra-national, state level, joint trading areas, bi-/multi-level collaborative agreements between states	sub-national: local to supra-local (collective, regional), formal regions as sub-divisions of states, informal, collective policy (soft, virtual) regions'
primary actor	Nation state	Cities, regions (especially in federal states), shaped by state structure (central-federal)
territoriality	Fixed, based on whole state entities, brought into collective association	Fixed (if part of state territorial hierarchy, variable, if local collective action (virtual region)
governance	'thin', governed through member states, representative office, few formal powers, possible involvement of IOs	Variable, state defined (federated) and/or locally defined (collective, depending on agreed transfer of local powers, quango possible)

Fig. 2.1   Supra- and sub-national regionalism

involves four main dimensions: (1) geographic scale, i.e. supra-national groupings of states or sub-national groupings of localities, (2) related to that, type of primary governmental actor, i.e. national or sub-national tiers of government, (3) the nature of territory, e.g. the distinction between 'old' or 'hard' territory and 'new' or 'soft' spaces, and (4) type of governing, e.g. 'old' or formal government and 'new' and informal (network) governance.

Over 20 years ago, now, Agnew and Corbridge (1995) introduced the term 'territorial trap' to capture the fixation of social sciences on the state as a cohesive territorial entity when it comes to international matters. They argued that the 'emergence of new *spatial practices* demands that we rethink our representations of space and our prognoses concerning possible "*representational spaces*"' (p. 207). This call becomes all the more urgent as cities and regions are increasingly representing themselves as international actors, effectively bypassing the state and challenging its established prerogative as the by-definition natural international actor.

Another 15 years later, debates within IR include much greater recognition that there is more to the international realm than nation states as actors (see Fig. 2.1). Nevertheless, Agnew (2009) still saw the need to argue that authority of the state was never complete and we should not be surprised to find ourselves focused on a fragmented state, and that these fragments have interests beyond the state's boundaries. But alongside the geographers' discussion of Agnew's 'territorial trap', which, perhaps tellingly, seems to have attracted only limited attention in traditional IR, there is another, separate debate within the political science of IR. As we have been arguing, critics of IR's realist theoretical tradition, which was exclusively focused on sovereign states as international actors, opened new constructivist and post-modern (Campbell 2007) debates about the changing roles of IOs, private (corporate) power, international networks and the challenges facing an emerging global governance (Held and McGrew 2002; Finkelstein 1995; Kearns and Mingst 2004). Yet, there has been limited progress in terms of developing this into a more comprehensive, holistic interpretation and conceptualisation of 'region' as simultaneously both a supra- and sub-national phenomenon, and the relations between them.

2.2   The Dual Meaning of 'Region': Connecting the 'International' and the 'Sub-National'

Scale matters as the most obvious and fundamental distinction between the two main takes on regionalism (Fig. 2.1) as proxy for the conceptual gap about the nature of global governance and its primary actors and their actions. The main connector between the two concepts is globalisation and its universal dynamic, putting continuous pressure on political-administrative systems, forms of governance, definitions of spaces of identity and belonging, and notions of inside and outside of a state border to continuous test. Both understandings of region, at either end of the scale, share their continuously reconfigured context of economic interests and search for opportunities, and the simultaneous attempt by governments to devise effective policy responses with the particular means they possess. In both instances, this could include a choice between collective action to boost the prospect of succeeding with the set goal, or go it alone, if sufficiently confident of one's own capacity and capability to succeed. Global cities, for instance, fall into the latter category. What they share is their growing claim to be actors in their own right (Ljungkvist 2016), rather than merely being arenas for global economic

interests playing themselves out (Hettne 2006). Nevertheless, such external interests in a region as locale for strategic opportunities matter in their
variation for a region's relative bargaining position and scope for agency with
regard to fiscal scope, institutional capacity, and political urgency. Successful
global cities, for instance, hold a much better hand than small, peripheral
towns and regions off the map of global economic interests.

2.2.1   Regions and State-Centric Internationality

International, or macro, regionalisms as state-based constellations, are
generally understood as being a combination of pure economic rationales
about interdependencies and comparative advantage (free trade areas,
regional trade associationss), where connectivity matters—either through
proximity or efficiency of connecting infrastructure—and of political
choices and agendas, such as in the cases of the EU or strategic alliances
such as NATO (Mansfield and Milner 1997). Identities and common cultures have also been used as descriptors and constructors of 'regions' as
collaborative groupings of states. Put generally, 'such macroregions can be
defined in different ways: as continents or as supranational formations of
countries sharing a common political and economic project and having a
certain degree of common identity' (Hettne 2006, p. 543). It is this identity which underpins the degree of regional cohesion, i.e. acceptance by
people and political actors that a region is genuinely one identity in interest, agenda and characteristics. The reality of a region has also been labelled
as 'regionness', described by Hettne (2006, p. 548) as 'the position of a
particular region in terms of regional cohesion', for which he distinguishes
five factors that define the degree—or strength—of regionness: territoriality (i.e. geographic area), social cohesiveness (interdependencies between
localities within a regional entity), degree of internationality (international
connectivity and engagement, collectively shared values (community)),
institutionalisation, and representation (i.e. policy-making capability).

The outcome of recognising the likely effect of such 'regionness' is
the constructivist strand of IR, i.e. the construction of territories, including the notion of internationality, on the basis of political interests and
agendas, senses of cultural and historic commonalities, or economic
shared rationales or geo-strategic (e.g. defence) interests. 'Regionness'
thus draws on the combination of economic (market-based) interests and
rationales, political objectives and strategic interests, and cultural-historic
(societal) factors that circumscribe the nature, composition and purpose

of the international as sum of nation states. In this IR political economy perspective, however, the territoriality of the nation state per se is not in question. International 'regionness' is territorialised as the aggregate of states in different, varying, opportunistic groupings aimed at the pursuit of shared—even if merely temporary—common interests. It is a state-centric perspective that views all actors and actions solely through the nation state lens. Yet, such strategic agendas and dynamics also apply within states, at the sub-national level. Here, too, administrative and state-territorial entities seek strategic advantage in collaboration, face competitive pressures, and hold animosities and distrust towards each other. The increasingly solitary standing—both economically and politically—of large metropolitan areas, especially the capital cities, within a state territory, challenges notions and discourses of a cohesive nation state, as it experiences repeated redefinitions and reallocations of opportunities and senses of belonging and exclusion, which manifest underlying divisions and unevenness.

Depending on the degree of collaboration, i.e. the 'depth' of integration of the different state (economic) spaces into the joint space of a trading area or customs union, etc., a another distinction is being made between 'old' and 'new' regionalism (see below) in terms of the degree to which, in effect, state sovereignty has been surrendered to, or affected by, the agreed pooling of some controlling powers. Thus, a another distinction is being made between 'shallow' and 'deep' integration, with the latter meaning a broader range of combined policy fields and thus surrendered national sovereignty, including its own institutionalisation (Burfisher, Robinson and Thierfelder 2004), while the former is little more than an agreement of coordinating national policies to eliminate trade barriers.

During the 1980s, and thus still in the shadow of Cold War politics and a static global political structure, trade policy was the main arena of adding a more dynamic element, in the form of free trade areas, although they were only few. The main examples are the North America Free Trade Agreement, NAFTA, and ASEAN (the Association of South East Asian Nations) as multi-lateral agreements of sharing economic space. However, the speed and multitude of such arrangements accelerated rapidly under the new de-politicised post-Cold War globalism of the 1990s. Within a few years, there were some 400 such trade agreements (Crawford and Fiorentino 2005; Baldwin and Low 2009), raising questions about their compliance with the idea of global free trade and multi-lateralism as advocated by the WTO (Estevadeordal, et al., 2008). Increasingly, also, the regionalism of the 1990s moved towards 'deep integration', i.e. including a broader range of topics than merely trade as common interest, e.g. sustainability. This, as well as collective responsibilities for the relevant participating states, reached inevitably beyond the respective national borders. The changing nature of regionalism during the 1990s meant a growing complexity of multi-lateral agreements, often coinciding with the installation of a regional trade area as part of a more integrationist agenda. Regionalism and multi-lateralism no longer seemed entirely alternative models of governing the international.

The growing proliferation of macro-regionalism at the end of the Cold War was largely driven by free trade considerations to boost national economic prospects. Multi-lateral trade deals seemed the most promising way forward. In many instances, the EU has remained the gold standard to refer to, as illustrated, for instance, in the renaming of what is now the African Union. Much of this has to do with what is seen as a high degree of institutionalisation to give what began as a collective trading area some teeth in international governance (Söderbaum and Sbragia 2010). Nevertheless, it seems, academic debates, especially those around new regionalism, have considered the EU experience as a special case which can thus offer only limited insights into macro-regionalism elsewhere (Warleigh-Lack and Rosamond 2010). One reason may be the internal variability of the EU's functioning, so that there is no universal EU mode of governance that may be transferred elsewhere as a blueprint. Such internal variation, of course, challenges realist IR's presumption that states and state-based regions act as integral entities based first and foremost on their institutional structures, rather than socio-cultural or historic differences. This, of course, reflects the complexity of such international regionalism with an internal and an external dimension: both are interdependent and affect the way in which regionalism per se interacts with conditions related to globalisation and world order (Katzenstein 2005).

While for IR-based concepts of regionalism this includes the need for a recognition of sub-national conditions and their effects on state action, for EU-based studies, it means a look beyond the external boundaries of the EU to take into account interdependencies with, and effects of, globalisation on the *internal* mechanisms of 'multi-level governance' and its different types and scales of interest and engagement of actors. Such cross-fertilisation between the two spheres of academic work and debate may aid the conceptualisation and interpretation of the growing (awareness of a) 'thickness' of global governance as a rising number and types of actors enter the international arena (Robinson et al. 2010; Laursen

2003). And this, Söderbaum and Sbragia (2010) point out with reference to Polanyi's work *The Great Transformation* (1944), highlights the inherent contradictions between the connecting effect of neo-liberal economic globalisation and the counter-efforts of control and regulation through politics via regionalisation. 'There is thus a transnational struggle over the political content of regionalism/regionalisation, as well as over that of globalisation' (Söderbaum and Sbragia 2010, p. 571). Yet, the scope for, and capacity of, such a 'return of the political' to globalism (Söderbaum and Sbragia 2010; Hettne and Söderbaum 2000) varies considerably between actors by type (governmental versus non-governmental) and scalar position (sub-national versus national and supra-national). It therefore remains to be seen how far governance can be mustered effectively, as 'resistance is localized, regionalized, and globalized at the same time that economic globalization slices across geopolitical borders' (Mittelman 2000, p. 177, quoted in Söderbaum and Sbragia 2010, p. 572).

In political economy, the role of comparative advantage and thus locational specificity matters, including cluster building and thus spatial proximity, but also functional economic relations and thus interdependencies, based on shared interests, rather than mere proximity. Mansfield and Milner (1997) bring some of the different views together, although all of them are clearly of the state-centric, supra-national perspective. The two main understandings of region, as they point out (Mansfield and Milner 1997) revolve around the role of spatial or functional factors: is it mere geographic proximity that decides over the specific make-up of a grouping of countries in a shared economic region, or is it, rather, functional interdependency that pre-determines who goes with whom? This debate coincided with the idea of global cities that gained a foothold in public debates (Sassen 1991).The global city clearly points to the importance of linkages and flows, rather than spatial propinquity. Manuel Castells introduced the distinction between 'place' as 'a locale whose form, function, and meaning are self-contained within the boundaries of physical contiguity' (Castells 1996, p. 423), and linear, relationally-defined 'spaces of flows' as 'organizational outcome of social practices that work through flows' (Castells 1996, p. 412). While the former is about a static mosaic of territorial entities with set characteristics which may be shared across separating borders, the latter includes an inherently dynamic process of changing and reconfiguring linkages and relations on the basis of arising—or waning—perceived opportunities through collaboration. Networks between actors and places thus grow more important, and this is where cities become important gateways or connectors in this relational network of political, economic and socio-cultural relationships (connectivities).

Together with the discussions in globalisation debates, the notion of spaces of flows added to this growing awareness that relationality may be at least as, if not more, important than geographic positionality (Sheppard 2002), when it comes to shaping economic interests and rationalities on a globalised, market-based arena. By the same token, rather than having economic rationales decide on the shaping of the organisation of the international, strategic political and policy choices may seek to build international regions as strategic entities to boost the prospects for achieving set goals. From an economy-centric perspective, region is in effect synonymous with a defined trading area, usually based on a free trade agreement or customs union, which combines national (state) economic spaces into a larger entity to achieve economic (trade-based) advantages. These international relations are being addressed in IPE and IR through the concept of multi-lateralism (Freund 2000; Ethier 1998), usually in relation to reducing trade barriers in the interest of free trade exchanges. States are thus placed in the role of actors, who negotiate on behalf of their whole territories as jurisdictional containers which are brought wholly into the legally merged common trade region. There is no further distinction in terms of intra-national differences, such as between cities and non-urban parts, and no look beneath the surface of a state territory and its government. This produces a vacuum between superficial state architecture and underlying, increasingly dynamic structures and relationships, because, 'whereas physical definitions of regions are usually provided by states in an attempt to reaffirm their boundaries and to organize into territorially exclusive groups, functional conceptualizations of regions emanate from the interplay of subnational and transnational economic, environmental, and cultural processes that the states are only partially able to control. Thus, the control of places and the control of flows require different ideas and instruments depending on which definition of region one employs' (Väyrynen 2005, p. 26).

A considerable new impetus to the theory and practice of regionalism has thus come from understandings of the EU and its integrationist agenda. While the EU is, in essence, also a regional trade agreement, with nation states coming together for collective action in the interest of improved economic prospects and positive political side-effects for each of them, the political agenda of fostering integration has also opened up a sub-national perspective and understanding of region (Morgan and

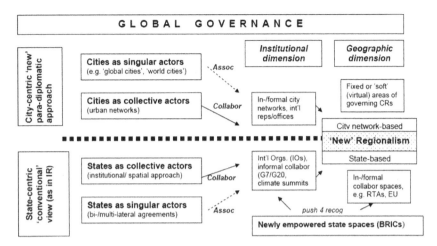

Fig. 2.2 Understanding of regionalism in International Relations and Urban Studies

Cooke 1998). The EU thus combines the established conventional view of the international as an opportunistic multi-lateral agreement between sovereign states in their individual territorial manifestation, as in realist IR, with the implicit acknowledgement that states are not merely uniform black boxes, but, rather, also composites of spatial, societal and economic variations. And this sub-national, intra-state perspective of regionalism adds the geographic and Urban Studies understanding of regions as being a scale down from the nation state. The outcome is a greater thickness of international governance within the EU, as it reaches not just to the borders of the individual nation states, but further down to the local level. Internationality thus includes, and embraces, the local as well as supra-local regional level. In this way, one might argue for Euro exceptionalism (Acharya 2012), as also addressed in the concept of multi-scalar governance, as it adds an important dimension to the notion of region. It is here that new regionalism becomes interesting, as it has become, not entirely intended at first, the connector and 'catch all' for the upward and downward view of 'region', with the state sitting sandwiched in between (Fig. 2.2). In terms of global governance, the 'constructivist turn' in IR has shifted in this direction of seeking to capture both the conventional international realm and outlook of state action when it comes to regionalism, and the internal particularities and processes of political, economic and historic-cultural specificities of each state, which, in turn, influence its actions and priorities and ways of acting.

This deeper look into the underlying factors that shape a state and its actions, including both its institutions and population, brings sub-national structure and agency into the play of international engagement and thus form of governance. It is here that the recognition of a sub-national arena of decision-making and political and economic choices and interests made clear that the EU-inspired concept of multi-level governance not only links the local scale to the international tier of political decisions and action, but also offers a shared arena for the scalar perspectives of spatial science and international relations—here expressed in their approaches to regionalism as respectively sub-national and supra-national phenomena. In IR, 'constructivists see ideas, norms and identity as playing a crucial role in regionalism. These elements shape expectations and facilitate cooperation through shared understandings of goals and outcomes. They act as cognitive factors that condition how new approaches to economic, political and security management are received. They also provide a yardstick for measuring the outcome of regionalism' (Acharya 2012, p. 8). In spatially-oriented interpretations, such as in Urban Studies, meanwhile, regionalism is considered a fuzzy concept (Markusen, 2003) because of its unclear scalar position between the local and national level of organising a state. This makes it difficult to grasp and govern, possibly varying between a state-centric top-down approach, where regions are no more than a formalised geographic subdivision of a state territory, and a locally-driven self-organising space of collaborating local governments that bring their territories into such marriages of convenience to achieve a common agenda. In principle, this bottom-up, self-organising approach matches that of international regionalism, whereas the top-down organising principle, which presumes a superior power, does not exist in the international realm. It is also here that the much bigger conceptual gap between the realist strand of IR and spatial science perspectives becomes evident, more so than it does for the constructivist interpretations of IR, which share the recognition with spatial sciences of the importance of sub-national patterns and dynamics in framing governance mechanisms that work.

New regionalism, although at first borne out of a more conventional, state centric, one-dimensional IR view of the international and its governance, has increasingly opened up to a broader and deeper perspective of state action and its driving forces and descriptive parameters. And this has introduced the recognition that there are more than just nation states and their agreed IOs that shape international governance. Other, new actors are joining the international arena, at first in the shape of a few global cities, branching out increasingly to also include other sub-national actors—city networks, national and international associations of local government, and a growing range of individual cities and regions as solitary actors on the international parquet. This growing diversity of actors, and the associated dynamics in agendas and collaborative arrangements and rationales, has moved things on from defining regionalism in realist fashion as 'largely in terms of formal intergovernmental organisations with a charter and a bureaucracy' (Acharya 2012, p. 12), to a more dynamic and differentiated, multi-scalar and multi-purpose construct. Instead, regionalisation is conceptualised as 'market-driven and less political, although not entirely apolitical'. Constructivist analyses thus argue 'that regions are not a geographic given, but are socially constructed, made and remade through interactions' (Acharya 2012, p. 12). So, does that mean, then, that we are moving towards a new governance of the international realm, characterised by an 'absence of formal rules, mandates, and government control', where stakeholders opt instead to use networks and 'cooperate, irrespective of their power or status, to resolve public problems in a socially optimal and equitable manner' (Alexander 2011, p. 634)?

2.2.2 The Sub-National Use of 'Region'

Over ten years ago, against the background of intensive globalisation and thus competitive economic pressures, both actual and imagined, the main focus of attempts at raising national (and EU) competitiveness was on regions as dominant geographic scale of regulative intervention to counteract a growing market-driven unevenness in opportunity. At that time, while there was talk about a 'Europe of the Regions' in public debates, discussions about new forms of regionalism took hold (Siegel 1999; MacLeod and Goodwin 1999; Keating 1998). As part of that discussion, regions, for once, came to be recognised as actors in their own right, rather than as mere spatial platforms for dispensing (perhaps no more than incidentally) national and EU policies. The attribute 'new' meant that they were projected as variable relational spaces, rather than, as conventional images go, fixed territorial containers (Agnew 1994) for the application of area-based policies within the scalar, nested organisation of the state. As such, regions were presumed to be clearly bounded territories (Leitner and Sheppard 2002; Paasi 2002). Yet, equipped with the attribute 'new' (Söderbaum and Shaw 2003; MacLeod 2001) they have increasingly become associated with more dynamic elements, favouring less formalised alliances around actor networks (Whittle et al. 2008; Murdoch 1998) built around shared policy objectives at a particular time (Herrschel 2014), but also less clearly manifested geographically. In particular, boundaries—whether territorial, institutional or by type of actors—have become less clear.

'To many, regionalism entails traditional prescriptions for metropolitan areas such as centralization and consolidation of governments and functions, or the creation of regional organizations' (Feiock 2007, p. 4). For this particular nature of regions, with their strong functional interdependencies, the straddling of the scale of the 'local' and the 'regional' adds potential for conflict between different jurisdictions within such a city-region, because such is inherently difficult to define and geographically pinpoint. Following Coe et al. (2004), it is the *interactive effects* that contribute to regional development' (p. 469), and not mere structure or innate regional qualities per se. So it is the ability to connect local qualities with supra-local, even global, corporate and other actors'—including other cities'—strategic interests that ultimately decides on the success or failure of regional policy and development (Fig. 2.2). This echoes David Harvey's argument that space *in itself* needs to be understood as a 'system of relations' (Harvey 1989, p. 191), while, 30 years later, in the face of growing globalisation of linkages, Keating (1998) emphasises the importance of cross-scalar reaches of connections and relations between actors located on different scales.

This, now, raises questions about the nature and operating systems of the interrelationships between these two principles of geographic organisation—structure and fluidity. Put differently, it is about (1) the link between the formal geographic organisation and distribution of state-territorial power, resources and legitimacy for action across predefined territorial entities, and (2) the more differentiated, even fragmented, informal spaces loosely and temporarily circumscribed by individual functional networks. The external reach of such networks vaguely describes the boundaries of such variable, virtual space (Herrschel 2012, 2013) or discursive 'soft space' (Walsh 2014) of strategic purpose and ambition.

The outcome is a complex, continuously revised and rearranged self-organising web of opportunity-seeking interrelations and connections, as embodied in the concept of governance. This involves differing explanations, such as political-administrative (Rhodes 2007; Davies 2011) perspective, or multi-level governance (Bache and Flinders 2004; Hooghe and Marks 2009) with its traditional, clearly organised state-hierarchical perspective. The respective geographic expressions of these concepts include (1) 'network' as skeleton underpinning a projected virtual (or 'soft') space, and (2) 'multi-level' as backbone of a conventional, hierarchical, nested organisation of territoriality. Scale is the main connector between these two forms of geography, tying relations to structure to permit government (Brenner 1998). It is at this point that cities may expand their spatial operation—and thus presence—right up to the global level, as has been argued to be the case for global cities (Sassen 1991) and their pivotal role in the new network society as imagined by Castells (2011). Both have shaped the growing urban focus in discussions on globalisation. As a city reaches further, its links become more selective and exclusive, as fewer will be able to work at that level effectively and be recognised as actors that matter on the evolving stage of global governance.

Scope for such a role varies, however, depending on both the sub-national and supra-national distribution of power and policy-making capacity at the international/global level. Within the EU, the situation is particularly interesting, as its multi-level system allows for a wider range of actors across different tiers of government to engage internationally. Although state structures vary between more centralised and more devolved, federalised models, regions, and, increasingly, cities, have gained a higher profile as international actors in their own right. The Committee of the Regions (CoR), for instance, while being primarily a consultative, rather than executive body, gives intra-state (sub-national) entities scope for raising their visibility, learning from each other, and forging possible collective lobbying at both national and EU-level institutions. 'Its very existence, however, does help define what a "region" is within the EU—i.e. it is an intra-state rather than crossborder enterprise' (Söderbaum and Sbragia 2010, p. 575). Regions in an EU context are thus immediately understood as sub-national units that may also act across internal EU borders (and thus be international and use para-diplomatic modes of operation), although such does not automatically involve reaching further, to a global level.

But such a proactive role is not universally available. For instance, as our discussions with the Brussels Capital City Region (8 July 2015) highlighted, the degree of de-centralisation and devolution of powers to sub-national actors (e.g. cities) produces greater awareness of urban scope for, and capacity of, as well as experience with, proactively shaping policies and agendas. In centralised states that seems to be less frequent than in devolved (federalised) state arrangements, with functional specialisms, historic urban traditions and national cultures of governing also having an impact. Such projection of urban power and ambition certainly involves the immediate context at the sub-national level, such as within a city-region. And it is this form of regionalisation that has attracted much attention from Urban Studies and geography as a matter of course (Harrison 2012; Herrschel 2014). International regionalism, and the role of cities within that, however, has done much less so—both in Urban Studies and IR, despite the implications for nation states. Thus, for instance, the City of London has made it quite clear that its leading global position as a finance centre makes its interests superior to those of the rest of the country and thus the British state as a whole—claiming that they ultimately would benefit from the City's success. Yet, not all places/players will be able to avail themselves of such positions of bargaining strength and play a relevant role at the international level and thus act as bridgehead for connecting the intra-national to the global.

The outcome of such selective, nucleated connectivity between state territory and global processes and governance is, in effect, a strengthening of previously underlying, yet not quite as clearly exposed, inequalities in the engagement with, and participation in, new regionalism. Localised, especially urban, interests become expected to act as the primary, perhaps even sole, drivers of a territory's economic development with all its implicit differential opportunities for the population. This raises questions about the scope for less well connected and less opportune and attractive localities and actors to avail themselves of the same opportunities as the more experienced, globally recognised and engaged, and institutionally capable larger cities and city-regions. The political justification for such an urban-centric approach has been that of creating new geographies of opportunities by allowing some self-organising bundling of interests around a shared agenda. And this includes seeking to push horizons in scalar operation, with global networks seemingly promising the widest opportunities and highest status.

The changes in favour of a relationally-defined, agenda-based, produced spatiality have been debated for a few years now under the conceptual umbrella of new regionalism, which some authors see as part of a shift towards 'post-positivist' (Hajer and Wagenaar 2003) or 'postmodern' forms of governance (Ward and Williams 1997). Justifications for this may vary, but what they share is a much more flexible, broader understanding of process, actors and agenda of governing sub-national regions, especially the more complex city-regions. Adopting a more explicit urban focus, the *new* governance embraces two key new qualities: (1) virtual spatiality as the *new manifestation of, and challenge to*, conventional administrative territoriality, and (2) governance as the *new* version of conventional government. This may be part of a new spatial logic of global flows of capital (Castells 1989) as spatial connectors, transcending—and organising—local entities, to meet the spatial logic of capitalism (Sassen 1991). And the resulting organisation of space suggests a different order than one where the nation state sits at the top supremely as primary actor of relevance in global governance. The mechanisms for defining and operationalising these relationally linked, yet distinctly locally-shaped, modes of operation in city-regionalism vary in response to the combined effects of local circumstances, including policy-making 'milieu' and its degree of innovativeness (Camagni 1995), and national institutional, statutory and political frameworks. Effectively, therefore, new city-regional governance involves a threefold fuzziness in terms of geography, governance and legitimation.

Just as at the sub-national level of regionalisation, opportunity-seeking entrepreneurialism (Greve and Salaff 2003) is also a primary driver of collaborative action at the international level between individual actors across institutional and territorial boundaries and scales, be they nation states, international regions, or city networks or single cities. In collaborative networks, perceived individual benefits for each of the network members resulting from engaging in such a collaborative arrangement, are the primary drivers of relations, rather than, necessarily, that of the collective. Actors may leave or regroup in pursuit of their changing interests and circumstances, thus producing shifting 'geographies of centrality and marginality' (Paasi 2006, p. 194). This shift, however, also means uncertainty and unpredictability, something disliked by private sector investors. Thus, while Amin and Graham (1999), for instance, see progressive aspects of 'reflexive' networks which consciously adapt to external challenges, such adaptation may be possible to some, but not to others. More influential and powerful, as well as politically apt, players may benefit from ceasing proactivity, while others may find themselves in a passive role, waiting for opportunities to come along. And the expanding forces and pressures of economic opportunity-seeking under globalisation increase the challenge to structures of political regulation. It is this that questions the underlying rationale and perspective of the realist IR perspective of the international sphere as essentially being ungoverned anarchy beyond national borders as fixed lines of separation and defence between, on the one hand, an orderly, familiar inside of a nation state and, on the other, a disorderly international outside which is subject to, and shaped by, inter-state competition and grappling for self-interested power and advantage. Political economy- and constructivism-based understandings, by contrast, require no such presumed anarchy as the playing field of nation state interests. Instead, they seek to take on board the growing role of a globalising economic and functional rationality which shapes political agendas, as they seek to maximise identified functional (competitive) opportunities. Collaborative regional trade associations (RTAs) agreed between two or more states, based on identified shared interests and expected advantages, are one such example of politics following the lead of economic reality. Likewise, the sheer scale of the tasks, such as global warming, may require a pragmatic-collaborative approach on the basis of collective success benefiting all individuals.

2.3   Summarising Comments

This chapter explored the twin nature of regionalism and, related to that, regionalisation between, on the one hand, an IR-based default conceptualisation as international space, shaped through collective agreement between nation states, and, on the other, an Urban Studies-based understanding as sub-national unit of administration and governing between the local and national level. In both instances, there is a realisation of the growing importance of underlying dynamics driven by globalisation, and thus the pressure of political agency. The conceptual construct of new regionalism tries to capture the subsequent tensions between fixed formal state structures and rather more variable, often just temporary, 'soft' spaces (Haughton and Allmendinger, 2008) of policy agendas with 'fuzzied' boundaries and forms of institutionalisation (Brenner and Theodore 2002; Jouve 2003; Kearns and Paddison 2000).

A good match between these two organising principles of political-economic geography ultimately determines the degree of policy efficacy by identifying, constructing and utilising interlinkages and interdependencies between them. Yet, in the resulting new (virtual) 'spheres of authority' (Rosenau 1997), boundaries of responsibility and legitimacy are inherently in flux, being more shaped by leadership and the appraisal of political opportunities, at a particular time and for individual actors, than by institutionalised and territorially-defined policy objectives. As a result, policy-makers need to make judgements about balancing agendas and the political utility of different alternatives in the geometries of possible collaborative network relations within and across a region—be that at the sub-national or supra-national level—and the role of cities as political actors and economic bodies within that. And this may vary between a more self-centred, nationalist/localist agenda, as against a more outward-looking, international perspective. This balance in policy focus and perspective, in turn, is shaped by the composition of actors—multi-purpose or single-purpose representations, public or private sector, national versus inter-national priorities, etc. as part of intra-/extra-national governance (Heinelt and Kübler 2005). And cities, especially those acting globally or, at least, aspiring to do so, take a pivotal position in this cross-scalar reach of regionalism. The disciplinary foci need to recognise just that and to try to complement their respective perspectives to gain a more holistic understanding of the interdependency between what is going on sub-nationally, and how that relates to international processes and developments. And it is the large cities that are at the forefront of bridging the conceptual gap between sub- and supra-national lenses of interpretation of global governance.

Such growing governmental fragmentation and differentiation (Parks and Oakerson 2000) need not necessarily mean a continued conceptual gap between the two main scales of regional agendas—sub- and international—as long as the individual benefits of such engagement are clear for all actors. And here political capability—and also risk taking, and political courage and innovative capacity—are required from political actors at different levels, as there is no clearly established system of political 'reward' for cross-scalar action by, in this instance, urban actors. Much depends on the ability of leading actors to establish trust and a working rapport in favour of collaboration. Internal resources will matter particularly strongly in such instances, as external variables—such as institutional structures and flows of legitimation processes—are not designed for cooperation—not only at the sub-national level in many instances, but also, and in particular, the supra-national scale, where national interests and policy outcomes continue to be of primary importance. In some instances, endogenous capacity and political capability need to *overcome* a disadvantageous context. And this needs to be recognised in the analysis of political agency and its outcomes. Regionalism here thus becomes a conceptual, disciplinary bridge across a major scalar divide between the local and the global.

If advantages are unclear, collaborative engagement may be avoided or, where it exists, abandoned in exchange for some less binding forms of agreement, such as 'coordination' (Kantor 2008). Their main feature is an absence of 'formalized alliances and programs' (Kantor 2008, p. 114). Given the selectivity and, increasingly, individuality, of competitive policies by cities, be that at sub-national or international level, there can be no participation by mere association as conventionally associated with state action. 'Relational complexity' (Healey 2013) means that no longer is there a general, inclusive safety net of contiguous state territory and associated notions of sovereignty and exclusivity in shaping global governance.

Instead, as the previous discussions in this chapter highlighted, there is pressure on at least the major cities to seek opportunities individually, rather than relying on the agency and cohesiveness of the region/state as primary actor. And so, governing arrangements need to be more imaginative and variable, perhaps even smart, so as to be able to capture such differentiation and individuality in shaping city-regional governance 'regimes' (Mossberger and Stoker 2001), at whatever scale of operation—inside or outside a nation state. Arrangements need to do so while continuing to use existing state structures and institutional arrangements as providers of scope, capacity and capability to do something independently and even unorthodox. While globalisation may have changed the imagination, reproduction and utilisation of space, 'it has by no means undermined the significance of location, of *place*' (Martin 1999, p. 16), not just as a locale for economic activity and competitive search for opportunity, but also the source of policy-making agency right up to the global level. Successful metropolitan areas thus may well shape not just sub-national, but also supra-national, global space *by being* 'nodes' of decision-making and capitalist interest.

The potentially conflictual relationship between the different geographies needs to be turned into a mutually dependent symbiosis, even if it may lead to seemingly contradictory policy agendas and narratives: constructed 'space' of agency encourages and reflects strategic visions and plans, together with opportunity-driven innovative policy-making, while a more realist view of states adds the certainty of fixed territory, and clear political-institutional, fiscal and legal authority. The EU's continued propagation of cohesion of opportunities across all its territory, while concurrently advocating a lead role for cities in driving regional, national and European global competitiveness, reflects this inherent contradiction which is also manifested in the conceptual gap between the Urban Studies- and an IR-based understanding of regionalism. While the explicit urban focus implies inherent inequality in opportunity, tied to cities and their functional and physical interconnectivity, cohesion adopts a conventional holistic view of territory as an integral entity from an administrative-governmental perspective, as it is *government* that is to administer relevant policies to foster cohesiveness across defined territorial entities on behalf of the electorate as basis of its democratic legitimacy. The following chapter will take a closer look at the structures and mechanisms of global governance vis-à-vis a growing role of cities as international actors.

REFERENCES

Acharya, A., 2012. Comparative Regionalism: A Field Whose Time has Come?, *The International Spectator: Italian Journal of International Affairs, 47*(1), 3–15.

Agnew J., 2009. *Globalization and Sovereignty*. Lanham MD: Rowan & Littlefield.

Agnew, J., 1994. The territorial trap: the geographical assumptions of international relations theory. *Review of International Political Economy, 1*(1), 53–80.

Agnew, J. and Corbridge, S., 1995. *Mastering Space: Hegemony, Territory, and International Political Economy*. London: Routledge.

Alexander , L., 2011. The Promise and Perils of "New Regionalist" Approaches to Sustainable Communities Legal Studies Research Paper Series Paper No. 1160, *38 Fordham Urban Law Journal*, available under: http://ssrn.com/abstract=1818030.

Amin, A. and Graham, S., 1999. Cities of connection and disconnection. In: J. Allen, D. Massey and M. Pryke (eds.): *Unsettling Cities*, pp. 7–38.

Bache, I. and Flinders, M., 2004. Multi-level governance and the study of the British state. *Public Policy and Administration, 19*(1), 31–51.

Baldwin, R. and Low, P. eds., 2009. *Multilateralizing regionalism: challenges for the Global Trading System*. Cambridge University Press.

Brenner, N., 1998. Global cities, glocal states: global city formation and state territorial restructuring in contemporary Europe. *Review of International Political Economy, 5*(1), 1–37.

Brenner, N. and Theodore, N., 2002. Cities and the geographies of 'actually existing neoliberalism', In: N. Brenner and N. Theodore (eds.): *Spaces of Neoliberalism: Urban Restructuring in North America and Western Europe*. Blackwell, pp. 32–48.

Burfisher, M.E., Robinson, S. and Thierfelder, K., 2004. Regionalism: Old and new, theory and practice. *Agricultural Policy Reform and the WTO: Where Are We Heading*, 593–622.

Camagni, R., 1995. Global network and local milieu: towards a theory of economic space, In: S. Conti, E. Malecki and P. Oinas (eds.): *The Industrial Enterprise and its Environment: Spatial Perspectives*. Avebury: Palgrave Macmillan, pp. 195–214.

Campbell, D., 2007. Poststructuralism. *International relations theories: Discipline and diversity*. In: T. Dunne, M. Kurki, S. Smith (eds.): *International Relations Theories. Discipline and Diversity*, Oxford: Oxford University Press, pp. 203–228.

Castells, M., 1989. Flows, networks and identities: a critical theory of the informational society, In: M. Castells, R. Flecha, P. Freire, H.A. Giroux, D. Macedo and P. Willis (eds.): *Critical Education in the Information Age*. Rowman and Littlefield, pp. 37–64.

Castells, M., 1996. *The network society* (Vol. 469). Oxford: Blackwell.

Castells, M., 2011. *The rise of the network society: The information age: Economy, society, and culture* (Vol. 1). Oxford: Wiley-Blackwell.

Coe, N. , Hess, M., Yeung, H., Dicken, P. and Henderson, J., 2004. 'Globalizing' regional development: a global production networks perspective. *Transactions of the Institute of British Geographers, 29*(4), 468–484.

Crawford, J.A. and Fiorentino, R.V., 2005. The changing landscape of regional trade agreements. Geneva: World Trade Organization.

Dahl, R., 1961. *Who Governs?: Democracy and Power in an American City*. Yale University Press.

Davies, J., 2011. *Challenging Governance Theory: From Networks to Hegemony*. Bristol: Policy Press.

Estevadeordal, A., Freund, C. and Ornelas, E., 2008. Does regionalism affect trade liberalization toward nonmembers?. *The Quarterly Journal of Economics*, 1531–1575.

Ethier, W., 1998. The New Regionalism. *The Economic journal 108*(449), July.

Feiock, R.C., 2007. Rational choice and regional governance. *Journal of Urban Affairs, 29*(1), 47–63.

Finkelstein, L., 1995. What is global governance? *Global governance*, 367–372.

Freund, C., 2000. Multilateralism and the endogenous formation of preferential trade agreements. *Journal of International Economics, 52*(2), 359–376.

Greve, A. and Salaff, J., 2003. Social networks and entrepreneurship. *Entrepreneurship theory and practice, 28*(1), 1–22.

Hajer, M. and Wagenaar, H., 2003. *Deliberative policy analysis: understanding governance in the network society*. Cambridge University Press.

Harrison, J., 2012. Life after regions? The evolution of city-regionalism in England. *Regional Studies, 46*(9), 1243–1259.

Harvey, D., 1989. From managerialism to entrepreneurialism: the transformation in urban governance in late capitalism. *Geografiska Annaler. Series B. Human Geography*, 3–17.

Haughton, G. and Allmendinger, P., 2008. The soft spaces of local economic development. *Local Economy, 23*(2), 138–148.

Healey, P., 2013. *Local Plans in British Land Use Planning: Urban and Regional Planning Series* (Vol. 31). Elsevier.

Heinelt, H. and Kübler, D., 2005. Metropolitan governance, democracy and the dynamics of place. In: H. Heinelt and D. Kübler, (eds.): *Metropolitan*

Governance: Capacity, Democracy and the Dynamics of Place. London: Routledge, pp. 8–28.

Held, D. and McGrew, A. G. eds., 2002. *Governing globalization: power, authority and global governance.* Cambridge: Polity Press.

Herrschel, T., 2013. *Cities, State and Globalization:* London: Routledge.

Herrschel, T., 2007. Regions between imposed structure and internally developed response. Experiences with twin track regionalisation in post-socialist eastern Germany. *Geoforum, 38*(3), 469–484.

Herrschel, T., 2012. Network Regionalism, Development Agencies and Peripheralisation Through 'Loss of Voice'—Moving towards post-Regionalism? In: A. Bellini, M. Danson and H. Halkier (eds.): *Regional Development Agencies: The Next Generation. Network, Knowledge and Regional Change.* Routledge *'Regions and Cities'* series. London: Routledge.

Herrschel, T., 2014. *Cities, state and globalisation: City-regional governance in Europe and North America.* London: Routledge.

Hettne, B. and Söderbaum, F., 2000. Theorising the Rise of Regionness. *New Political Economy, 5*(3), 457–472.

Hettne, B., 2006. Beyond the 'new' regionalism, *New Political Economy, 10*(4), 543–571.

Hettne, B., Inotai, A. and Sunkel, O. eds., 1999. *Studies in the New Regionalism,* Vols I – V. Houndsmill. Basingstoke: Macmillan.

Hooghe, L. and Marks, G., 2009. A postfunctionalist theory of European integration: from permissive consensus to constraining dissensus. *British Journal of Political Science, 39*(1), 1–23.

Jouve, B., 2003. *La gouvernance urbaine en questions.* Paris: Elsevier.

Kantor, P., 2008. Varieties of city regionalism and the quest for political cooperation: a comparative perspective. *Urban Research & Practice, 1*(2), 111–129.

Katzenstein, P., 2005. *A world of regions: Asia and Europe in the American imperium.* Ithaca, NY: Cornell University Press.

Kearns, A. and Paddison, R., 2000. New challenges for urban governance. *Urban Studies, 37*(5–6), 845–850.

Kearns, M. and Mingst, K., 2004. *International organizations: the politics and processes of global governance.* London: Lynne Rienner Publishers. P. 4.

Keating, M., 1998. *The new regionalism in Western Europe: territorial restructuring and political change.* Cheltenham: Edward Elgar.

Laursen, F., ed., 2003. *Comparative regional integration. Theoretical perspectives.* Aldershot: Ashgate.

Leitner, H. and Sheppard, E., 2002. "The city is dead, long live the net": harnessing European interurban networks for a neoliberal agenda. *Antipode, 34*(3), 495–518.

Ljungkvist K., 2016. *The Global City 2.0. From Strategic Site to Global Actor.* London: Routledge.

MacLeod, G., 2001. New regionalism reconsidered: globalization and the remaking of political economic space. *International Journal of Urban and Regional Research, 25*(4), 804–829.

Macleod, G. and Goodwin, M., 1999. Space, scale and state strategy: rethinking urban and regional governance, *Progress in Human Geography, 23*(4), 503–527

Mansfield, E. and Milner, H., 1997. The Political Economy of Regionalism: An Overview. In: E. Mansfield and H. Milner (eds.): *The Political Economy of Regionalism* . NYC: Columbia University Press.

Meinig, D.W., 1956. Culture blocs and political blocs: emergent patterns in world affairs. *Western Humanities Review*, 10, 203–222.

Markusen, A., 2003. Fuzzy concepts, scanty evidence, policy distance: the case for rigour and policy relevance in critical regional studies. *Regional studies, 37* (6–7), 701–717.

Martin, R., 1999. *Money and the space economy.* London: Wiley.

Morgan, K. and Cooke, P., 1998. The associational economy: firms, regions, and innovation. *University of Illinois at Urbana-Champaign's Academy for Entrepreneurial Leadership Historical Research Reference in Entrepreneurship.*

Mossberger, K. and Stoker, G., 2001. The evolution of urban regime theory. The challenge of conceptualization. *Urban Affairs Review, 36*(6), 810–835.

Murdoch, J., 1998. The spaces of actor-network theory. *Geoforum, 29*(4), 357–374.

Nye, J., 1987. Peace in Parts: Integration and Conflict in Regional Organization. Little, Brown & Co.,1971, reprint: University Press of America.

Ornelas, E., 2005. Trade creating free trade areas and the undermining of multilateralism. *European Economic Review, 49*(7), 1717–1735.

Paasi, A., 2002. Place and region: regional worlds and words, *Progress in Human Geography, 26*(6), 802–11.

Paasi, A., 2006. Texts and contexts in the globalizing academic marketplace: comments on the debate on geopolitical remote sensing. *Eurasian Geography and Economics, 47*(2), 216–220.

Parks, R.B. and Oakerson, R.J., 2000. Regionalism, localism, and metropolitan governance: Suggestions from the research program on local public economies. *State & Local Government Review*, 169–179.

Payne, A. and Gamble, A., 1996. Introduction: the political economy of regionalism and world order, In: A. Gamble and A. Payne (eds.): *Regionalism and World Order*. Houndsmill, Basingstoke: Macmillan, p. 2.

Polanyi K., 1944, reprinted 2001. *The Great Transformation: The Political and Economic Origins of Our Time.* Boston: Beacon Press.

Rhodes, R., 2007. Understanding governance: ten years on. *Organization studies, 28*(8), 1243–1264.

Robinson, N., Rosamond, B. and Warleigh-Lack, A. eds., 2010. New Regionalism and the European Union. Dialogues, Comparisons and New Research Directions. London: Routledge.

Rosenau, J., 1997. Along the Domestic-Foreign Frontier: Exploring Governance in a Turbulent World. Oxford: Blackwell.

Sassen, S., 1991. *The global city: New York, London, Tokyo. New York*: Princeton University Press (also later editions, 2001, 2013).

Sheppard, E., 2002. The spaces and times of globalization: place, scale, networks, and positionality. *Economic geography, 78*(3), 307–330.

Siegel, F. 1999. Is regional government the answer?, *Urban Illusions (II), The Public Interest*, No. 137, 85–98.

Söderbaum, F. and Sbragia, A., 2010. EU Studies and the 'New Regionalism': What can be Gained from Dialogue?, *Journal of European Integration, 32*(6), 563–582.

Söderbaum, F. and Shaw, T. M., 2003. *Conclusion: what futures for new regionalism?* Basingstoke: Palgrave Macmillan.

Väyrynen, R., 2005. Regionalism: Old and New. In: *International Studies Review* 5, pp. 25–51.

Walsh, C., 2014. Rethinking the Spatiality of Spatial Planning: Methodological Territorialism and Metageographies, *European Planning Studies, 22*(2), 306–322.

Ward, S. and Williams, R., 1997. From hierarchy to networks? Sub-central government and EU urban environmental policy. *Journal of Common Market Studies* 35, 439–464.

Warleigh-Lack, A., and Rosamond, B., 2010. Across the EU studies–new regionalism frontier: invitation to a dialogue. *Journal of Common Market Studies, 48*(4), 993–1013.

Whittle, A. and Spicer, A., 2008. Is actor network theory critique?, *Organization Studies, 29*(4), 611–629.

CHAPTER 3

Cities and the Changing Nature of International Governance

3.1 Introduction

This chapter examines the various types of international engagement by cities and city-regions, and the impact that has had on the constellation, operation and explanation of global governance. This involves identifying the key issues in emerging understandings of, and theoretical perspectives on, new international relationships. Particular attention will be given to the variations that emerge in the analysis and explanation of global governance, as well as different perspectives on network governance and its varying scales. In addition, the utility of the multi-level governance perspective will be examined, and ideas about regime formation through international networking as the increasingly more widespread mode of governing. From this discussion we move on to a second set of questions about understanding the rationales behind new international imaginaries of power, opportunity and interdependencies, as well as, importantly for the democratic systems examined here, questions of authority and legitimacy in the emerging new, and increasingly complex, multi-scalar and multi-actor forms of global governance.

In this chapter we explore the differing ways in which sub-national actors have expanded into the international political-economic realm either as individual actors, or as part of one or more collaborative networks with a local, regional or global reach. As argued in Chap. 2, this type of collective action may be of lesser importance for established global cities like London with the desire and resources to act independently, but it is vital

© The Author(s) 2017
T. Herrschel, P. Newman, *Cities as International Actors*,
DOI 10.1057/978-1-137-39617-4_3

for cities further down the hierarchy as a means of seeking influence and/or gaining credibility as locations of economic activity and opportunity, and as credible actors at that level of engagement. We are also interested here in how nation states and IOs have responded differently to these changes, opportunistically collaborating with, and/or supporting endeavours by, sub-national actors as a way of finding new ways of gaining for themselves a better stake in international development matters. The result will thus be different forms of engagement, reaching from challenge and containment, or even obstruction, to protect individual interests, to collaborative engagement in the pursuit of mutual advantages. Collaborative action may thus take on different forms with correspondingly varying policy-making capacities and agendas. In particular, the relationship between state, IOs and sub-national actors has witnessed a continuous evolution, affecting modus operandi and scalar positioning, as well as self-identification both in terms of scope and political rationale and justification.

Figure 3.1 shows three main, overlapping modes of international engagement by cities, with a suggested underlying growing degree of

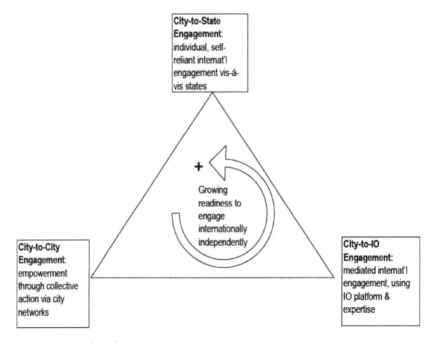

Fig. 3.1   Modes of international engagement by cities

individuality and independence in engaging as singular actors. First, the diagram shows the growth of city-to-city engagement through city networks (Allen 2010). These are likely to be preferred by cities with lesser confidence, experience or capacity to step out individually into the international arena as actors in their own right. These networks may operate at a range of scales, stretching from national to global involvement. The former includes those with a spatially relatively contained reach, such as international collaboration across an international border between neighbouring countries. Examples in Europe include Euro-regions as EU-supported, cross-border local and/or regional collaboration, or common bilateral agreements and engagement between neighbouring Canadian and US cities. Detroit and Windsor in Ontario are such a pair, based on a closely integrated car manufacturing system (Brunet-Jailly 2000, 2006; Nelles 2011). The latter, i.e. farther-reaching international collaboration, involves such multi-national city networks as Eurocities, the United States Conference of Mayors, CityNet in Asia, and UCLG.

Then, as the second mode of internationalisation, there are engagements by sub-national actors with IOs. Such include the EU which offers very much a special scenario and opportunity for relationships of cities with regional IOs, such as Eurocities, but also with the EU itself as an international governing body. This includes office representations in Brussels for direct lobbying of EU policy-makers, as well as engagement via the self-organising Committee of the Regions. IOs may sit next to the EU, such as the European Economic Area, or within it, such as Eurocities or the Nordic Council. They differ in scale, thematic focus and thus policy agendas, but all serve as platforms and access points for cities to lobby for their interests as a group. This will be discussed in more detail in Chap. 5. Beyond the EU, European cities and cities elsewhere have developed much closer direct relationships with the UN, especially under the Habitat umbrella, including such programmes as the 'Safer Cities Programme', which was set up in 1999 in response to lobbying by African mayors (http://unhabitat.org/urban-initiatives/initiatives-programmes/safer-cities/, accessed 25 Jan 16), or the Cities and Climate Initiative, aimed at climate change mitigation especially in cities of developing countries (http://unhabitat.org/urban-initiatives/initiatives-programmes/cities-and-climate-change-initiative/, accessed 25 Jan 16). Other bodies which affect cities and are targets of lobbying include the World Trade Organization (WTO), the International Monetary Fund (IMF) and the World Bank. How far these new relationships open up opportunities to access resources and expertise, or, rather, act to constrain and direct local initiative, is an important theme running through the book.

The third point of our triangle of engagement modes refers to city-to-state relations as the modus of greatest operational independence and degree of separateness from the state. Here, the conventional notion is challenged, which views most (or all) cities being inherently an integral part of a state territory, because the state is viewed as the natural care-taker of urban matters and relations. It is here that cities are most likely to step out of their national territorial and institutional embeddedness and become actors in their own right. This may go so far, as in the case of the largest global cities, that the city dominates its state in terms of eco-nomic relevance. Since the 1980s, many states have actively encouraged their major urban assets to engage in international economic competition, and many now find it difficult to rein them back in. The state becomes dependent on, and de facto controlled by, the city's policy preferences. Such a step out into the international realm, away from the traditional state framework, may also be the result of feeling held back by the state context. This may thus act as de facto push-factor, as an act of liberation to maximise perceived opportunities without the constraints imposed by the national environment. The three points of the triangle thus identify different ways in which sub-national, national and international actors are all adjusting to, and selecting or creating, new relationships and new forms of more or less effective global governance, within which they play varying roles in equally varying relationships of influence to each other.

The view emerging from our discussion here is that we need to recog-nise the growing presence and roles of sub-national actors in the interna-tional arena of political-economic relations, and the resulting overlapping, at times competing, even conflicting, relationships between, on the one hand, well-established actors, such as states and international organisations created by them, and, on the other, a range of sub-nationally defined types of internationally engaging actors. These include both state and non-state organisations and bodies. The next sections of this chapter review these shifts and their implications for established perspectives on the interna-tional, national and sub-national arenas of internationally-oriented forms of governing. These embrace, as shown in Fig. 3.1:

1. International organisations—established traditionally by nation states as a way to promote international order (e.g. IMF, World Bank, G7, G20, UN Habitat), and equipped with varying degrees

of institutional powers and resources. Increasingly, however, they are lobbied and also formed by cities and city-regions as international platforms and agents to further their (local/regional) interests by claiming the roles as cross-national governance actors.

2. International networks as a bottom-up movement to connect representative actors of cities and regions and thus allow them to expand into, and claim, governance scope at the international level. Such networks based on shared agendas may be built by states (e.g. RTAs) just as well as by groups of cities (e.g. Eurocities, Metropolis, Sister Cities International), in the pursuit of particular political/policy goals (e.g. Mayors for Peace).

3. Individual lead cities (or regions) acting unilaterally and independently on the basis of their existing international economic relevance and status, such as exemplified by the so-called world or global cities. They possess sufficient economic capacity and connectivity and thus recognition as a place, that they enjoy enough credibility to act independently of their respective nation states which they may de facto leave behind if national policy is perceived to be economically unhelpful.

Before looking in more detail at these three modes of international engagement by sub-national government, especially cities, we need to discuss the notion of the international in its varying disciplinary and discursive, as well as practical, manifestations.

3.2   Understanding the 'International' in Global Governance—Some Conceptual Views and Debates across the Disciplines

Some of the major issues this book explores are understandings of network governance and, in particular, their scales of operation, vis-à-vis what may be seen as an emerging new mode of global governance. From examining first the utility of the multi-level governance perspective and ideas about regime formation through international networking, this discussion then moves on to questions about understanding the rationales behind new international imaginaries of likely arenas, opportunities and challenges, and associated questions of authority and legitimacy in emerging forms of global governance. As Fig. 3.1 illustrates, the sub-national is pushing the understanding of global governance in three directions, with varying degrees of independent, singular action by individual cities: (1) engaging in, and working through, networks; (2) engaging with, and lobbying, international organisations as agents of more visible and potentially effective international/global governance; and (3) acting individually on the basis of existing economic and functional strength, and competing with, perhaps even challenging, their nation states. As the diagram further indicates, cities may pass through, and shift between, these three modes. They may do so in response to changing political and economic stature, changing public discourse and policy-making capability, and the courage of the political and/or business leadership. Local engagement internationally is thus not merely a static situation based on administrative structures and hierarchical organisations of power, but a dynamic, changing arrangement in response to shifting circumstances both locally and beyond.

Running through our review of the international and regional contexts for sub-national actors are ideas about an emerging global or transnational governance that goes beyond a well-established focus on nation states as primary actors, with a few IOs added. Debate about global governance has grown since the 1990s (Sinclair 2012), marked by the first edition of the academic journal *Global Governance* in 1993. New ways of seeing the international, beyond nation states and IOs, are needed to account for new, and changing, relationships between public and private sector interests, NGOs and IOs, regional trade groups, regional configurations at different scales and new roles for sub-national actors. As will become evident, global governance may not necessarily mean that it is indeed global and therefore inclusive of all potential actors, as initially presumed and understood by the notion of the global. Nation states remain reluctant to transfer sovereignty to higher-level institutions and thus seek to retain and defend their traditional dominance in governing the global. In relation to the governance of taxation, for instance (Dietsch and Rixen 2016), attempts at finding globally accepted and applied mechanisms and ways of working may, at least at present, 'at best be the art of muddling through' (Lane 2013, p. 253). The debates about tax avoidance by multi-national companies that move profits between jurisdictions, illustrate this point (Brundsen 2016).

Nonetheless, the idea of global governance has played a part in shifting IR's theoretical realism about the role of relative state advantage which underpinned the discipline in the Cold War years (see Chap. 2). As the Cold War imaginary of sovereign states dominating the international gives ground to recognition of a more complex, varied and continuously changing interdependence between state and non-state actors, and to a global diffusion of power and interests (Guzzini and Neumann 2012) across scales and institutional boundaries, the need for new understandings of global governance assume greater importance. Keohane (1982) identified the importance of understanding 'international regimes' through their norms, principles, rules and procedures, regimes with if not global, then at least an international dimension. Such regimes may develop on the back of cross-border interactions or involve a wider spatial reach. At the same time, emergent global governance may, as the notion of international regime suggests, add some structure to emerging policy and politics that go beyond the nation state, either involving it or seeking to circumnavigate it. More recently constructivist and post-modern theoretical strands of IR (Hopf 1998; Zehfuss 2002; Guzzini 2000; Jarvis 2002; Ruggie 1993) open up such state-centric views of the international sphere to consider non-state actors and with a preparedness to see cities more generally as contributors to societal structures and political milieux. They do so, in particular, in debates about the changing roles of international organisations, private (corporate) power, international networks and the challenges facing an emerging global governance (Held and McGrew 2002; Finkelstein 1995; Kearns and Mingst 2004). Such a 'pluralist global governance' (see Cerny 2010), then, involves many more actors than merely national governments as the primary agents of international politics. Global governance, then, is understood through a number of concepts including fragmentation (Biermann et al. 2009), polycentricity (McGinnis 1999) and international regimes with actors located at multiple scales (Hasenclever et al. 2000; Keohane 1982). And this understanding is not just about existing scales of organisation and authority, but increasingly includes diffuse, new sets of relationships in multiple networks. In the arena of emissions trading, for example, Paterson et al. (2014) favour the idea of 'polycentric diffusion' paying attention to the interaction of local and national forces with parts of transnational networks.

A basic lesson from IR refers to the complexity of intergovernmental—usually understood as international—cooperation, multi-lateral agencies, multi-national corporations (MNCs) and other private and civil society transnational actors. Where authority is diffused, questions need to be raised about the kinds of diffusion that different policy areas (Neumann 2012) produce. Some policy arenas attract more transnational actors than others (Jönsson and Tallberg 2010), as the examples of climate change and economic development illustrate (Tol 2009). The governance of climate change is characterised by a complex world of transnational actors, and highlights specific authority issues, based on a realisation of the interdependent nature of the problem, which requires collaboration. Economic development, by contrast, focuses on competitiveness and its inherently more individualised agendas, thus creating a potential conundrum for policy-makers seeking to reconcile both (Herrschel 2014).

Global governance can be imagined as part of a 'global public domain' of increasingly institutionalised action by a range of interests (Ruggie 2004, p. 504). Some non-state, market-oriented actors, as Bernstein and Cashore (2007) suggest, may have more flexibility than state actors in responding to changing norms and demands in a global marketplace. While states with formal authority in such arenas may have less flexibility, they possess legitimacy to act and enforce structures and ways of working, and thus circumscribe the scope for responsiveness by sub-national actors, as well as costs imposed on them as actors. Their scope and capacity to embrace international action may be shaped in these ways. The world stage that cities and regions are seeking is not a blank sheet, but already reflects the complex ways in which the national and extra-national 'blend' in unfolding institutional structures (Kuus 2015). Adding sub-national players makes an ever more complex blend. In this complexity and interdependency, analysis of non-state actors suggests conclusions about city and regional actors, which show growing intergovernmental connections and increasing transnational mobilisation, all of which emphasise that participation depends on both the increasing opportunities offered and domestic resources available to social movements and private actors (Hanegraaff et al. 2015). And the same may be expected to also apply to sub-national governments. Scope to do so, however, is also circumscribed by capacity to act, leadership and competence, and so may face greater or fewer constraints.

We return to the concern with authority and legitimacy effected by the emerging norms, principles, rules and practices of pluralist global governance. Before that, the multi-scalar nature of this new governance modus operandi will be considered, as the cross-scalar, multi-level relationships and interactions mark an important characteristic of the growing 'thickness' of global governance, well beyond the rather 'flat', single-level perspective of conventional IR with its fixation on the state as the only relevant actor. While in this understanding the legitimation to act clearly rests in the sovereignty of the nation state as primary international actor, the situation is less clear in a more complex, multi-level arrangement (Marks et al. 1996), where collaborative action in both the vertical and horizontal direction cuts across the territorial boundaries of institutionalised responsibilities and empowerment. The result is a fuzzier picture of the sources and mechanisms of the legitimacy to take such 'expanded' action. It is for that reason that a closer look needs to be given to the growing, scalar 'thickness' of global governance, as it 'sets the scene' for discussion of legitimacy and power.

3.2.1 Growing Complexity in Scale and Multi-Level Governance

The complexity of state, international, sub-national and non-state actors is the subject of major debates about scales or levels of governance. Changing urban priorities in the design of policies and framing of political agendas may be interpreted as part of a long-term restructuring of the state territory for capital (Scott 2012), a rescaling (Brenner 1999) of governance arrangements in response to an equally rescaled economy, and as 'bound up with a neo-liberal project to decentre political authority and rescale the national polity' (Curtis 2014, p. 29). Here, the 'global cities' have come in for much attention (see Acuto and Steele 2013; Curtis 2014; Ljungkvist 2015). More geographically oriented perspectives prefer to see new institutional relationships through the idea of scales. One of the challenges in conceptualising new governance relationships is finding an understanding of the institutional connections between different levels or scales. Lee (2014) suggests that the term 'translocal' may better encompass the range of formal and informal actors involved in linking the local level to other scales of governing. Scholte (2014), meanwhile, favours the notion of 'trans-scalarity', arguing against the statism of the past and ideas about the global spread of Western values in the structuring of new governmental relationships. For Scholte, 'trans-scalarity' better reflects the relational links from sub-national to international governments than the idea of different levels, which implies more fixed positions. Furthermore, he continues, the term captures the 'trans-scalar' nature of democratic qualities without privileging any particular scale. In 'global democracy', the qualities of cities and regions may have equal weighting as sub-national actors vis-à-vis those at the national level.

The complexity of interacting scales, reordering of hierarchy and transformation of territorial, scalar and network relationships is at the heart of much recent work in political geography (see Jessop 2016) with an emphasis on the particular effects of that complexity at different scales on the scope and role of local, national and international bodies. Related debate, and especially in the EU institutional and discursive context, has focused on the notion and practice of multi-level governance with its intergovernmentalism (I. Bache 1998) in relationships and policy-making.

This multi-level governance (MLG) approach developed on the basis of the EU's combination of supra- and sub-national government tiers, with the national states 'in between', acknowledges three main spheres of governing—international, national and sub-national (Hooghe and Marks 2001; Bache and Flinders 2004). In contrast to a conventional hierarchical understanding of state government, MLG suggests that powers and competencies reach *across* these three tiers 'upwards' *and* 'downwards', much in the mould of the 'principle of counterflow' of federal Germany's governmental system (Herrschel and Newman 2002). This provides scope for regions to use the trans-scalar governance possibilities of MLG and define their own policies as part of the European integration agenda (Marks et al. 1994; Magone 2003). In this context, Europeanisation may thus be regarded as 'co-evolution between the domestic and the European [i.e. international] level' (Radaelli 2006, p. 59). And this process includes a shift to governance, as other, non-state actors are recognised as part of the governing actors. Consequently, the location of powers and responsibilities no longer is neatly located in distinct spaces/territories at different spatial scales, with compartmentalised, clearly defined powers and responsibilities, but rather follows varying directions of interests and relations, including from the (urban) local right across to the international, with or without involvement of the state level 'in between'. As a consequence, boundaries between territories and spaces of responsibilities and institutional competencies are becoming fuzzy, reflecting the growing complexity and dynamic (variability, flexibility), as well as entrepreneurialism, of territorial governance. And the cross-scalar actions by cities are extending formal, hierarchically organised powers by building new, and using existing, relations to project influence and aspirations, without the underpinning of corresponding formal structures.

The literature discusses issues such as incentives, strategies and the effectiveness of the mobilisation of actors at different levels in a multi-level context. Sub-national actors have to take account of, and need adjust to, other scales. And equally, states and international organisations find themselves in new relationships on the world stage both with each other and with new sub-national actors. MLG can thus be seen as a 'system of continuous negotiation among nested [hierarchically organised] governments at several territorial tiers' (Marks 1993, p. 392) in which 'supranational, national, regional, and local governments are enmeshed in territorially overarching policy networks' (Marks 1993, p. 403). The concept of MLG has become a 'palatable, easily digestible paradigm for grasping how the European Union (EU) works in practice' (Stephenson 2013, p. 817), that is widely cited by academics and policy-makers to describe (and promote) a policy-making system based on vertical and horizontal interactions and interdependencies across levels of government and sectoral divisions. Cities in Europe thus possess a firmly established dual role as originators, as well as recipients, of external effects, developments and influences. Cities matter in European policy discourse as functional, political, social and economic entities. And the understanding is that its core ideas are transferable to other global regions as a readily available model for governance that is hierarchical in locating powers and responsibilities, but not in the ways in which these are exercised. Yet, that need not be the case. In North America, for instance, cities, except a few special cases of established international renown, are much less obviously presumed to act across spatial scales (see also Chap. 6),and exercise central roles as automatic and natural aspects of governance. The strong and growing roles of suburbs, often separate entities with their own agendas and potentially in direct competition to those of the old central city (Herrschel 2014), add to a more diffuse picture of what the position and scope of a city is. The rather inflated use of city as descriptor of essentially suburban settlements with few, if any, signs of urbanity in a European understanding, instead of being based solely on meeting statistical criteria alone, adds to an understanding of cities as less prominent and special within the state hierarchy, compared with other municipal or regional governmental actors. Many are firmly rooted in, and tied to, the local level.

To move beyond a European context, authors make links between the EU system, other forms of federal, intergovernmental systems, and other instances of public and/or private multi-level politics (see Alcantara et al. 2015; Piattoni 2010; Stephenson 2013).There is, however, a substantial challenge in moving MLG from, in essence, a mere descriptor of governing arrangements, to the development of theoretical propositions (Piattoni 2009). Yet the notion of a tiered allocation of responsibilities and policy-making continues to work as a norm of good governance with its favouring of devolution of powers and responsibilities to the lowest suitable level of governing, and the building and using of network relations to support that (Curry 2015). As we will see in Chaps. 5 and 6, practice and forces working on multi-level governance in Europe vary. For example, the case of sub-national mobilisation in Greece emphasises the importance of domestic context, i.e. in that case, relatively weak and state-dependent sub-national units unable to respond to the EU's incentives (Oikonomou 2016) and devise effective, tailor-made policy answers. And whilst the European multi-level model has entered policy discourse in Africa (Sinclair-Smith 2015), actual relationships across rapidly growing 'urban' areas and through scales of government resist any simple conceptual transfer. Intergovernmental relationships in China also have their own distinctive character (Wu 2015).

3.2.2   *International Organisations and Regimes in Multi-Level Arrangements*

As pointed out above, the politics of scale and multi-level governance leads on to questions about how sub-national governments with their growing penchant for agency orient themselves in relation to the 'international' as a policy-making and political arena. How do they interact and engage, and operationalise strategic agendas? In this context, (Bartelson 2000) distinguishes between three forms of urban engagement on the international arena:

1. A balanced relationship, i.e. city-regions and their policy agendas influence each other in a reciprocal way, so that local action exercises as much influence on the world outside, as that has on shaping their own local action, in return.
2. A pro-active urban policy reaching from the local outward by projecting local agendas onto an international arena next to states and other established such actors.
3. A relatively more passive, weaker position for the city, being shaped in its development and policies by external context.

Typical examples of the second, locally pro-active scenario, are internationalisation strategies and associated linkages between local and regional actors. They seek to extend their political-economic reach through active engagement with businesses or other levels of government, employing lobbying and political pressures, be that through individual international relations departments/units, representational offices (such as in Brussels), or joint initiatives through collaborative action in networks. Such an inside-out agency thus clearly puts the emphasis on local political pro-activism and policy innovation to boost local prospects in an increasingly more fluid competitive world of global interdependencies, relations and interests.

This scenario differs fundamentally from an emphasis on global neo-liberal economic forces (Curtis 2014) that puts sub-national—and national actors—in a purely responsive role. Urban geography has given some attention to this relationship between 'real' governmental territori-ality, i.e. 'geo-politics' (Dierwechter 2008; Harrison 2013) and virtual, imagineered and function-defined spatiality, i.e. 'geo-economics' (Ward and Jonas 2004; Herrschel 2009, 2014). The inherently selective nature of self-organising, opportunity-driven policy networks contradicts the notion of the democratically egalitarian and territorially contiguous state. Tensions between the two rationales and modus operandi are inevitable. Both draw on very different concepts of framing and implementing eco-nomic policies, and the role of the state within that. A growing trans-scalar reach by sub-national actors produces a much more differentiated, even fragmented and uneven picture of the political economic geography of a state, with cities as the new prime foci of competitiveness (Amin and Thrift 2002), challenging, fixed, hierarchically scaled state structures and territorial hegemonies. At play are interacting relationships between poli-tics, policy and territory (see Jones 2016), as well as the effectiveness and legitimacy of both national and international institutions. These are, of course, the major themes of the literature on global governance.

Particularly important to our understanding of the international ori-entation of sub-national governments, is the engagement between cities and regions and international organisation, which undergoes changes in response to the pressures and opportunities attached to globalisation (see Fig. 3.1). There is considerable debate about how such relationships are organised, and the extent to which new governance 'regimes' are emerg-ing. What are the consequences and how is authority in global gover-nance created and projected? These are important questions that require attention to gain a better understanding of the changing nature and work-ings of global governance. De Burca et al. (2013) distinguish different types of governance regimes: some may be largely state-centric, 'integrated international regimes', such as the WTO, for example, where governing the global economy is clearly understood as first and foremost a matter for nation states. The governance of financial globalisation still seems to focus on such arrangements, with relatively few global elites and state authorities presumed—and expected—to lead (see Baker et al. 2011) on the basis of a confirmed—state-based—ideology. Such 'integrated regimes', also dominant in IR concepts of internationality, may be distinguished from the emergence of more 'diverse forms and sites of cross-national decision making by multiple actors, public and private as well as local, regional and global, forming governance networks and "regime complexes" as part of orchestrating new forms of authority by international actors and organisations' (De Burca et al. 2013, p. 2).

'Orchestration' is 'a mode of governance widely used by international organisations (IGOs) and other governance actors (Blauberger and Rittberger 2015), but rarely identified or analyzed. IGOs engage in orchestration when they enlist intermediary actors on a voluntary basis, by providing them with ideational and material support, to address target actors in pursuit of IGO governance goals' (Abbott et al. 2015, p. 3). Orchestration, just as implied by its name, is about directing and facilitating. This may be effected both indirectly through intermediaries as facilitators, and through soft power, as the international organisations lack power and direct control to enforce their agendas, as their competencies and capacities to act are defined through collective agreements between states. Orchestration is one of four modes of operation in exercising the powers in international governance as distinguished by Abbot et al. (2015), whereby the first is rarely available to international organisations. They are: hierarchisation, delegation (see also Hawkins et al. 2006) collaboration (see also Barnett and Duval 2005), and orchestration.

Orchestration is distinguished from traditional hierarchical governance with its clear flows of powers and executive capacities by less evident power relationships and ways of taking influence, such as found in informal and interpersonal relationships. The adoption of such a modus operandi results from the limited governmental capacities of international organisations in a state-centric international arena, so that scope for implementing policy preferences and enforcement is limited so as not to infringe national sovereignty. As a result, IOs have had to devise alternative, more implicit and indirect modes of pursuing their objectives, such as through incentivising or lobbying established players, including governmental, private sector and civil society actors, rather than *enforcing* compliance (Abbot et al. 2015).

Rooted in both New Public Management theory and New Domestic Governance theories, the concept of orchestration focuses on the idea of 'facilitation', rather than direct engagement and/or intervention in a more centralised, top-down tradition. Instead, this new approach favours non-traditional, often private regulatory instruments as ways of delivering on the underlying goals. Accordingly, orchestration implies a different role for states and IOs in global governance than that envisaged in the neo-liberal tradition of New Public Management (Schleifer 2013) with its emphasis on competitive market forces and drive for efficient (cost-effective) service delivery. So, in contrast to traditional global governance through state governments and international organisations—directly or indirectly constructed through national action—the 'key to orchestration is to bring third parties into the governance arrangement' (Abbott et al. 2010, p. 1) and thus guide them towards the set goals. The focus, therefore, is on capacity building among a wider range of actors, including, especially, from the private sector, and on encouragement of their—coordinated—international action (Abbott 2012). And it is in achieving this coordination—and collective operation—where the main task—and challenge—lies for the orchestration of effective collaborative action between public and private sector actors with their different, particular interests and established ways of doing things (Schleifer 2013). As with public–private partnership generally, the question of democratic legitimacy and ownership of policies becomes important in this context, as exercising pressures and orchestrating—which may also be seen as little more than backseat driving—desired responses by policy-makers, and may imply some overstepping, or, at least, pushing to the limit, established formal powers and exerting influence. So, as orchestration may work through a range of 'directive' or, less interventionist—'facilitative'—measures (Abbott and Snidal 2009), the notion is never far away that created and utilised relationships, and the flow of power and control, may push the limits of transparency of decision-making and exercising power, and raise questions about sources of legitimacy, as discussed later on. Cities moving on to the international stage may benefit from networking and engaging with IOs, but may also be constrained through these interactions.

These ideas of networks, regimes and, in particular, the notion of the orchestration of authority as the contextual forms that may constrain or open opportunities for sub-national actors on the world stage, are of interest here. In particular they highlight the—in practice—fuzzy gap between the respective views of what makes up international governance by IR and Urban Studies practitioners. New and evolving forms of global governance, which challenge the sovereignty of nation states, demand attention as they make novel claims to authority and attempts at the orchestration of authority. IR has become less concerned with hegemonic world politics to focus more on 'horizontal' relationships and claims to authority, including sub-state and non-state actors, while attempting to distinguish different forms of engagement on the international arena. As a result, there are emerging attempts to categorise such new forms and modes of operation of international governance. For example, Hale and Roger (2014) label groupings of sub-state actors as 'transnational governance', whereas the leadership of non-state actors can be seen as 'entrepreneurial governance' (Green 2014), and cross-sector networks can be distinguished as 'part-nered governance'. But states and IOs can also be involved with horizon-tally connected actors and, indeed, be drivers of transnational governance, whereby IOs, or particular states, use their capacities and resources to take a strong role in orchestrating such governance. For instance, in the policy field particularly favourable to multi-level collaboration, such as climate change, Hale and Roger suggest that the World Bank and the UK govern-ment are two of the 'most active orchestrators' (2014, p. 59).

For private authority, the potential benefits of collective action may include reduced transaction costs, enhanced credibility and improved reputation (Green 2014). It is here, in offering win-win scenarios, that incentives, and thus orchestration, may become effective. Sub-national governments may draw down authority from engagement in interna-tional collective action on climate change to influence local reputation (Bulkeley 2012, p. 2428). Formal legitimacy may be available through para-diplomacy as some cities and regions make representation to higher level governments, either nationally or, in the EU, also internationally (see Chaps. 5 and 6). Para-diplomacy combines elements of the conventional understanding of diplomatic activity as international engagement by sov-ereign nation states and applies this principle of engagement with the sub-autonomous nature of sub-national actors. The EU experience, with its explicit multi-level arrangement of governing activity, has taken the prac-tices of para-diplomacy (see e.g. Rowe 2011) beyond studies of those sub-national regions which hold a strong national identity, such as Québec, Catalonia (Duchacek et al. 1990) or the Basque Country (Calzada 2015), with their quests for independence, or commercial para-diplomacy (export promotion and foreign direct investment [FDI] prospecting) (Rioux Ouimet 2015), to include the implications of regional representations in Brussels. This Brussels presence provides an international arena which allows sub-national actors to 'scale-jump' to the international realm, even if situated in something akin to a miniature world. In this context, the

EU case has generated work on the capacities of sub-national units to engage internationally (see Tatham and Thau 2014), types of sub-national networks, the transferability of network lessons (Niederhafner 2013), and the impacts of international networks on sub-national participants (e.g. Payre 2010).

IOs are perceived as significant sources of 'cognitive authority' (Broome and Seabrooke 2012, p. 13) through setting governance norms and circulating policy ideas. The analytical work of IOs can be 'the driving force behind efforts to change state behaviour by changing how national actors think about their domestic populations and how they conceive the appropriate role of the state in international policy' (Broome and Seabrooke 2012, p. 13), and, the benefits arising for the domestic political arena. The International Political Economy strand of IR acknowledges the role of such 'strategically situated agents' in IOs as policy entrepreneurs that 'play a critical brokerage role at the intersection of organisations involved in networked governance, linking technical analysis to policy problems' (Eccleston et al. 2013, p. 9). The secretariats of some IOs or networks may have more influence than others (Jinnah 2014), reflecting the range of actors involved, the political stature of the organisation, and capacities and capabilities in shaping governance. 'Cognitive regimes' (Haggard and Simmons, in Lipson and Cohen 1999) and 'cognitive authority' (Broome and Seabrooke 2012, p. 13) set governance norms and circulate policy ideas. The analytical work of IOs can be, 'the driving force behind efforts to change state behaviour by changing how national actors think about their domestic populations and how they conceive the appropriate role of the state in international policy' (Broome and Seabrooke 2012, p. 13), and, we can add, sub-national actors. Cities and regions may find themselves internalising norms, from UN Habitat, for example, about the unavoidable connectivity of global competitiveness and thence governance forms, including the importance of international cooperation and lesson learning. Such analyses of the interactions of states and IOs have relevance for the scope, opportunities and expected possibilities and likely rewards for cities and regions to enter, and operate on, the world stage. IOs and states, and their interdependencies, can have a constraining effect on sub-national actors. By the same token, cities and regions can also draw benefits from IOs and their role as nodes in an international system of network relations, where states still dominate as actors.

De Burca et al. (2013) see the increasing importance of 'diverse forms and sites of cross-national decision making by multiple actors, public and private as well as local, regional and global, forming governance networks and "regime complexes", including the orchestration of new forms of authority by international actors and organisations' (p. 2). The 'orchestration of authority', the co-option of EU 'partners' for example, may circumscribe the scope and capacity of city-regional networks, as well as the national and international norms they form and work within. Yet, while potentially good for policy efficacy, the developments in, and debates about, governance and networked regimes raise fundamental questions about the authority and legitimacy of forming new relationships outside formal governmental structures and organisational principles. These network regimes contrast with the territorially contained, and thus clearly defined and identifiable, traditional authority and sovereignty of nation states, as they are more difficult to detect, follow and monitor. Network regimes make it much more difficult to uncover and identify sources of legitimacy of action and exercise of power. This will now be examined further.

3.2.3   Questions of Authority and Legitimacy of International Urban Action

The Urban Studies literature has much to say about the authority of urban leaders. An important aspect of understanding the drivers and motivations of city and regional actors is thus a debate about the authority of leaders (Jouve 2007), and of the particular authorisations (see Bulkeley 2012b) for them that may derive from international engagement. Representing the values of a societal base may create moral authority and delivering economic gains may create performance-based authority. The legitimacy derived from performance takes us back to debate in political science about regime politics (e.g. Peters and Pierre 2010), around the observation that as social change leads to a waning of traditional electoral support, local governments seek the investment, enhanced profile and prestige to be gained from international development projects. From this perspective, grounded in urban theory, questions arise about how such new economic or moral authority is achieved through such international action, and about the resources, activities and mechanisms needed, as the local state retreats in some policy competences (social housing, for example), while advancing in others that demand new forms of imagination (Blanco et al. 2014, p. 3134). Obviously, the relatively favourable competitive position of some cities makes it easier for them to secure and reinforce performance-based authority through 'success stories', but such 'soft' resources need to be fostered and promoted, and 'hard' institutional resources may be crucial for allowing such work to come to fruition.

The European example (see Chap. 5) points to the great variations in national contexts in the circumstances for intergovernmental cooperation, reflecting governmental traditions, histories and state structures. Thus, those regional governments with more national autonomy and control of resources, as well as more politically able leaders, may enjoy 'unmediated access' to the EU (Swenden and Bolleyer 2014; Brusis 2014) and its power structures, in order to promote their interests (Tatham 2008; Tatham and Thau 2014). The variations in size and representational appearance of the different Brussels offices of cities and regions, stretching from a shared small office suite to embassy-style mini chateaux (see Chap. 5), physically reflect ambitions and claimed status by different sub-national actors. In some cases 'fragile' states and competitive regions may be in conflict (see Marciacq 2015), with the latter taking on a more state-like form of international engagement, such as in the case of Belgium and the international role of its three regions (see Chap. 5). Para-diplomacy addresses this multi-level approach to international relations, and challenges the primacy attributed to the nation state in IR. New cross-border alliances blur the territorial definition of the state, as they produce 'perforated sovereignties' (Duchacek 1990) for nation states, as sub-state entities negotiate their own 'lower key' relationships across the border (Herrschel 2011). There may be benefits for cities and regions, but also for states and for IOs, such as the EU, in supporting sub-national actors, especially cities, in such para-diplomatic engagement, as the best national horses in the competitive race for success are 'recruited as "partners" into various EU policy fields' (Perkmann 2003, p. 156). The cognitive authority exercised through setting governance norms and circulating policy ideas, and the offering of selective incentives to collective action, may be seen as features of the 'operating system' (Stone 2013). It is this that makes informal governance across scales and sectors possible, coherent and potentially effective.

Across policy sectors, representing the city may have consequences for practical governance at city level, such as changes in cities' organisational structures, including the recruitment of project leaders, or encouragement to attend international workshops and participate in working groups as a means of exchanging 'good practice' at an international level, while identifying shared objectives and likely partners, and designing joint policy initiatives (Payre 2010). The most productive engagement across the range of disciplines engaged in understanding global governance stresses the active role of cities and international institutions in developing and deploying the resources and capacities to work beyond traditional boundaries. For example, Princen and Kerremans (2008) draw on the European experience to focus on novel 'international political opportunity structures' where perceived opportunities beyond the status quo arrangements entice cities and regions to engage more actively and imaginatively on the international arena. It is the expectation of rewards for individual cities and regions and individual political actors that drives the willingness for such entrepreneurial policies. Opportunities may be perceived to allow, for example, 'venue shopping', as sub-national actors choose where to represent their interests, or 'scale-jumping' to what may be more appropriate forums for pursuing new local political aspirations—for the city as a whole, or individual policy-makers and their political clienteles.

It ought to be pointed out, however, that such relationships are not a given for cities, but reflect the work of numerous actors and practices (Allen 2013), pushing into this international realm. The capacity to perceive opportunities is crucial. Here, work in IR offers insight into understanding new ways of imagining the global. Cerny (2010) analyses a fundamental shift in ways of thinking from the *raison d'état* that built the modern world of states, to a *raison du monde* that is rooted in globalisation and transnationalism. This shift of thinking, he argues, affects state actors 'whatever the playing field actors are operating on' (2010, p. 20). The focus is on actors and their interpretation of international opportunities and constraints, as it is those that push for action. Interpretive approaches in political science, that are applied to the government of nation states (see Bevir and Rhodes 2003), offer potential for being applied to the global, while relating well to the constructivist strand of IR and those approaches that emphasise qualities such as leadership alliance building, policy innovation, and agile engagement with international frameworks (see Acuto 2013).

Engaging with, or creating, new networks, and managing network effects, both need new attitudes, skills and competencies (Dawes et al. 2009). IR identifies the importance of significant actors in these processes. For example, 'Neither international agreements nor international regimes are created spontaneously. Political entrepreneurs must exist, who see a potential profit in organizing collaboration' (Keohane 1983, p. 155). And in their work on 'global governors', Avant et al. (2010) take a constructivist approach, focused on actors and their societal embeddedness. Some networks may be high profile, symbolic politics, while others demand more depth of cooperation (Giest and Howlett 2013) and collective action among institutional actors (Feiock 2004). Across policy sectors, representing the city may have consequences for practical governance at city level, such as change in organisational structures (Payre 2010). They may demand new practices, skills and resources both in political leaders and professional staff, and also may start from very different bases of resources and powers (Johnson et al. 2015).

The concept of 'political opportunity structure' suggests that networks or other international connections may offer both opportunity and constraint. 'Regime complexes' (see Gehring and Faude 2013) may impose structural constraints. It may be that some 'first movers', in the C40 group, for example, can push their city-focused agenda based on their perceived status (Ljungkvist 2015), but laggards and weaker members in coalitions may have less scope to do likewise. As a result, regime complexes may create competition between institutions, and even generate conflicts about defining and prioritising agendas and modes of operation. Or, they may settle on a division of labour both within and between member institutions (Gehring and Faude 2013) to the exclusion of others. This is visible in the organisational arrangements of UCLG, for example, or the separation of the United States Conference of Mayors as an elite group (based on population size) within the broader church of the National League of Cities, or, in Canada, the Big Cities Mayors within the Federation of Canadian Municipalities (FCM). Power in such regimes is unlikely to be concentrated but, rather, dispersed within networks that engage co-joining state and non-state organisations (see, for example, Nordberg 2012 on the G20). In such arrangements, however, competition may develop between formal authority and the informal practices of network-based relations and, as Kuus argues, require decision-making that blends the national and extra-national. Yet this, in turn, raises 'serious questions about transparency and accountability' (Kuus 2015, p. 436). There is the fundamental issue of how authority is claimed and achieved on an international stage which is moving beyond the authority of sovereign nation states.

Yet, there are challenging conceptual issues in developing such conclusions from analysis of the range of international work being undertaken by cities and regions. Legitimacy and authority generate fundamental debate in political science. Here, the distinction between input and output legitimacy is helpful in contrasting the formal legitimacy of democratic states with the economic and other—less formally democratic—outputs that cities may deliver as a result of their international orientation. There is resonance both with the longstanding focus on performance-based authority of local regimes, claimed from perceived competence and effectiveness in policy delivery—following the old adage that the end justifies the means—and the idea of 'capacity-based authority' associated with 'global governors' (Avant et al. 2010a, b). This also embraces notions of 'entrepreneurial authority' of some leading actors in global environmental politics (Green 2014), gained from the success of their political action. Potentially useful here is the work of Rousselin (2015, pp. 3–4), distinguishing between, on the one hand, legitimacy as a property of the rules and processes of governance arrangements, and, on the other, the legitimacy of solutions derived from debate and interaction of a variety of actors. 'Legitimate' policy outcomes may well be the result of 'structural asymmetry' (Rousselin 2015, p. 13) among participants, where some participants are more influential than others. And this may change over time or between agendas and policy fields. Here, the transparency and accountability of the decision process may help legitimate outcomes. We noted earlier Bulkeley's (2012b) discussion of the specific 'authorisations' of policy, which city actors bring back from international work. In considering 'inputs' we might see the formal legitimacy available through para-diplomacy, alongside the international treaty-based authority of IOs. But bargaining and uneven resources—not least in cognitive authority—may serve to emphasise the focus on process and outputs, rather than the structure of administrative-governmental responsibilities, as para-diplomatic work is more likely to win support if seen to deliver results.

3.3   THE GROWING INTERNATIONAL SPHERE OF GOVERNANCE

Ever since the experiences of the First World War, which resulted in the first attempt at establishing international governance through dedicated IOs, here the League of Nations, the international sphere has become more than an anarchic wilderness against which states need to position themselves (Deudney and Ikenberry 1999). The difficulties of transferring 'real' power from the many nation states carefully guarding their sovereignty (Barkin and Cronin 1994), to the international level became evident in the inability to prevent the Second World War. This, and a rapidly growing internationalisation of national economies, produced new attempts at political and economic global governance (on the United Nations and the Bretton Woods Agreement respectively, see e.g. Paolini et al. 1998). Economic globalisation means that states, even if reluctantly, have to negotiate with MNCs to secure investment and politically important economic growth. Consequently, states have collectively transferred authority to organisations such as the WTO, World Bank and IMF to provide some regulation of a globalising economy in the interest of more predictable developments. In addition to such 'global solutions', various levels of free trade agreements in different parts of the world are changing international economic governance rules, effectively creating sub-units of preferential agreements within a 'borderless' neo-liberal global economic sphere (Cooper et al. 2007). They create spaces of collective economic interest with little in terms of institutional representation. Studies of financial globalisation emphasise this interdependence of private power, international authorities and nation states (see Baker et al. 2011). For some analysts, this interdependence contributes to the new context for cities, which, as it promotes and enforces neo-liberal rules (see Curtis 2014), thereby also encourages urban policies and styles of city building that accommodate free–moving business and economic elites, and seek to define responses that allow them to influence these developments (Porter 2005).

Such interdependence around financial globalisation has therefore implications for sub-national governments. Perhaps more clearly visible has been the growth of direct engagement between IOs and national governments, and policy at sub-national scale through the UN's range of interests and programmes (e.g. UN Habitat 1996, 2010). Through a series of international conferences starting in Vancouver in 1976, states and other actors became involved with UN Habitat and a range of policy interests and with the UN's mechanisms for engaging with sub-national actors. The Rio Conference in 1992 established specific mechanisms for addressing environmental issues, including the Agenda 21 programme, specifically targeted at local actions as recognised key arenas for implementing relevant policy measures. Through its Climate Change Summits, the UN aimed to use sub-national units to strengthen and expand national government pledges to reduce emissions. The 2014 UN Climate Summit published a specific 'Action Area' for cities (www.un.org/climatechange/summit/action-areas) that includes both working with other levels and doing more at sub-national scale through existing local government networks. Alger (2011, p. 1) notes the 'escalating participation in the UN system' of governments other than states, and this has meant defined roles for associations of sub-national governments at conferences as internationally promoted and visible arenas of political ambition to be counted internationally, and the further development of international/sub-national programmes. We will return to this international/sub-national reciprocity in the later parts of this chapter.

In addition to the issues of environment and climate change, the UN has a long history of programmes focused on international development. As these have expanded they have also shifted from engagement with national governments to incorporation of sub-national governments. The UN's Millennium Development Goals for example gave the UN specific interest in the policy and governance of cities in developing countries, moving the UN's interest beyond states and into the sub-national realm. The post-2015 agenda continues sub-national involvement through extensive publications, conferences and a joint 'World Urban Campaign' with participating 'City Partners' promoting UN objectives.

As a lobbying group coordinated by UN Habitat, the World Urban Campaign (WUC) is a platform for raising awareness globally about possible urban change to bring about greener, healthier and safer and less divided cities. This, so the campaign claims, requires a move of urban agendas to the top of development agendas. The WUC has currently 136 'partners' from different parts of the world, who participate in, and contribute to the achieving of, the campaign agenda. The WUC builds on the outcome of the Habitat II Conference in Istanbul in 1996, which highlighted the need to broaden traditional government towards governance by including civil society and its organisations,as well as the private sector in the interest of a shift towards sustainable urban development. This notion of partnership led to a number of global campaigns: the first two were in 1999 on Secure Tenure and Good Urban Governance, leading in 2009 to the WUC (http://www.worldurbancampaign.org/about).

Broadening out in objectives beyond the initial focus on development issues, the UN Habitat World Urban Forum now brings sub-national actors together around issues of equity, building links between private actors, civil society and sub-national governments. There are thus distinct elements of fostering democratisation and democratic ownership of such developments. Other international partners have joined some of the initiatives in these fields, for example the UN Habitat/World Bank Cities Alliance: Cities without Slums. Developed by the Cities Alliance in 1999, this action plan was given high international visibility through a launch event in Berlin involving Nelson Mandela (http://www.citiesalliance.org/cws-action-plan).

The Cities Alliance is a cross-scalar and horizontal collaborative partnership involving local and multi-national governmental and NGOs, including the UN as an international policy platform (http://www.citiesalliance. org/our-members). This city-driven initiative—in the form of city alliances (UCLG, Metropolis, for example—see Chap. 4), has now moved onto the UN's official policy agenda and thus the conventional delivery channels of international policy, as reflected in the UN's Millennium Declaration on 'development and poverty eradication'. Across different policy fields, the 'escalating participation' of governments other than states, especially cities, thus becomes evident.

Sub-national governments relate to the UN in various ways. Just prior to the Habitat II (United Nations Conference on Human Settlements) conference in Istanbul in 1996, which constituted the beginning of the various thematic global campaigns, local governments set up a World Assembly of Cities and Local Authorities in a formal declaration to engage with the Habitat agenda (http://www.uclg.org/sites/default/files/ wacla_i_eng.pdf). This declaration clearly points out that 'the world is becoming increasingly urbanised' and that therefore strengthened 'direct cooperation' between municipalities is required, as the need 'to develop a constructive dialogue with the States, the international community and all partners about activities and practices at the local level' (http://www. uclg.org/sites/default/files/wacla_i_eng.pdf). There is thus clear reference to international horizontal cooperation at the local level, as well as vertical engagement—and effective influence-taking—with nation states and IOs and businesses.

The UN set up an Advisory Committee of Local Authorities (UNACLA) in 2000 and increased direct links with local government networks and international groupings. This legacy of 1996 Habitat II had a clear international mandate for local authorities by pointing to its task of 'strengthening the international dialogue with local authorities involved in the implementation of the Habitat Agenda' (Governing Council Resolution 17/18 of 1999, http://unhabitat.org/advisory-groups/unacla/). The UN's Best Practice and Local Leadership Programme, which includes the World Urban Forum and Sustainable Cities Programmes, was created in 1997 as a follow-up to Habitat II 'in order to identify and showcase innovative, exemplary projects of sustainable development, especially in urban areas', and had an explicit international dimension and ambition by seeking to build a 'global network' of a broad range of locally relevant actors from governmental and non-governmental background (http://i2ud.org/2013/08/un-habitats-best-practices-and-local-leadership-program/). As we shall see in Chap. 4, sub-national governments increasingly engage with the UN through their own global networks and through lobbying at, and collaborating with, regional and national scales of government, and do so across the UN's policy fields.

In Europe, sub-national engagement with the international institutions of the EU is formalised through the consultative Committee of the Regions (CoR). 'The role of the Committee of the Regions (CoR) is to put forward local and regional points of view on EU legislation. It does so by issuing reports ("opinions") on Commission proposals' (http://europa.eu/about-eu/institutions-bodies/cor/index_en.htm). The consultation process is 'activated' at specific moments in policy-making processes and offers collective opinions from the (in terms of powers and resources, highly variable) sub-national scales. Since the Lisbon Treaty of 2007, such consultation processes have been a compulsory requirement for the European Commission to engage with local and regional public authorities early on in the pre-legislative phase, so that the Committee of the Regions can act as 'the voice of local and regional authorities' (ibid.). This is clearly an effort to broaden—and deepen—the democratic legitimation of decisions at the supra-national level. Such includes a required second stage of consultations for the Commission to call after a proposed legislation. At least formally, there is thus a much closer connection between the sub-national level and supra-national EU governance. The result has been 'a new dynamic in the relationship between the Committee of the Regions and the European Commission' (CoR, no year, p. 4: 'A new treaty: a new role for regions and local authorities', http://cor.europa.eu/en/documentation/brochures/Documents/84fa6e84-0373-42a2-a801-c8ea83a24a72.pdf). Panke et al. (2015) point out how the EU's consultative committees exchange information for (limited) influence, and offer a legitimacy boost to the EU's formal decision-making institutions that, through such institutions as CoR, may appear closer to European citizens.

3.4   CITIES, REGIONS AND THE INTERNATIONALISATION THROUGH NETWORKS

As pointed out above and in Fig. 3.1, IOs are not merely the result of inter-state agreement and collaboration, but themselves develop ways and mechanisms for encouraging the direct participation of sub-national units.

This, they mostly do by engaging sub-national governments through their collaborative networks aimed at the international realm to address particular challenges—or opportunities—for their local/regional populations, which they identified at that level. Different forms of networks develop, with differing agendas and 'reach', as well as international visibility and relevance. This section looks at the growth in numbers, activity and ambition of these networks.

The last thirty or so years have seen a proliferation of informal international regions as part of a changing global political-economic setting. Whether Regional Trade Agreements (RTAs) or Free Trade Areas (FTAs), such inter-state collaborations are about creating an open market by removing borders as trade barriers (even if not necessarily also as barriers to people movements Crawford and Fiorentino, 2005, as e.g. in the case of the United States and Mexico, both part of the North American Free Trade Agreement (NAFTA)). The result is represented on maps as a spatial entity, even if the member states retain all control of their territories and do not give up any sovereign powers. In most cases, although there are some variations, these trade associations are rather thinly institutionalised, often little more than an office, a secretary and a website (Herrschel 2014).

More recently, over the last decade or so, however, RTAs have gained in complexity and stature as vehicles for international (inter-state) governance and drivers of integration beyond their mostly primary 'free trade' agendas. They are international networks and organisations by *inter-state* agreement, and create new international spaces within which cities may operate as locales of economic activity as well as pro-active agents in promoting economic opportunities for 'their' respective economies. Such spaces, or 'new regions', include global regions as the EU, NAFTA, the Organization of American States (OAS), Asia-Pacific Economic Cooperation (APEC), ASEAN, Mercosur, Economic Community of West African States (ECOWAS) and the Southern African development Community (SADC). Such collaborative state action may include mergers of RTAs into continent-embracing trading blocs (Fiorentino et al. 2005). At the same time, there has been a proliferation of RTAs, although with varying economic capacity and relevance in terms of trade volume. They also differ in their projected lifetime and depth, with a growing number of preferential partnerships as safe options—as they can be annulled at any time—rather than more formal and comprehensive regional integration agendas which are more difficult to walk away from, if so desired. These are partnerships that may be joined or left with a minimum of administrative complications (even if with some potential political fall-out), as opportunities and likely advantage from such engagement change. In 2006, there were more than 350 active RTAs worldwide, grown from less than half that number a decade earlier (Fiorentino et al. 2005).

The end of the Cold War, and with that the certainties of a bipolar world, may well have contributed to this accelerating search for new alliances and expected opportunities. The collapse of the former Soviet Union and the end of the COMECON, the communist economic alliance Council for Mutual Economic Assistance, facilitated new groupings among the newly independent states of the former Soviet Union, and also with and between the other countries of the former communist bloc. Agreements with Western Europe, especially the EU (but also the European Free Trade Association (EFTA)), have been a particular goal on both sides: for the former communist countries as a route to economic betterment, and for the EU as a vehicle to fashion the new states in its own mould as liberal market democracies. As part of that, the EU has been a major propagator of RTAs (Stephenson and Robert 2011) as a means for 'reaching out' to neighbouring countries, be they immediately adjacent geographically, or in relative functional proximity, such as North Africa or the Middle East and Asia beyond the Caucasus. The EU has impacts beyond its boundaries, having for example direct impact in sub-Saharan Africa, through its influence on the SADC.

With such developments, the term 'regionalism' gained a distinct international connotation in the sense of 'international regions'. In the tradition of conventional realist IR, this focused on sovereign nation states voluntarily engaging in collective action to pursue their respective individual opportunistic objectives. Out of this, the term and concept of 'new regionalism' emerged (see our discussion in Chap. 2) as an informal inter-national grouping of two or more states, policy specific and non- (or merely weakly) institutionalised, so as not to infringe on national sovereignty.

In the first, international, instance, much of the argumentation is rooted in trade theory (Burfisher et al. 2004), where the 'new' is seen to encompass deeper integration, mainly through policy coordination, between participating national governments (Panagariya 1999). Ultimately, at least in theory, such integration may lead to some form of institutionalisation of the respective economic region (Hettne and Söderbaum 2003), with its own governing capacity (see Chap. 2). The EU serves as a special example of such a scenario, although the EU's origins draw on a strong idealistic and history-driven rationale. National interests continue to be close to the surface, as, for instance, the ongoing discussions about the Greek financial crisis, and who is to blame, show. The effects of the 2008 financial crash point to a possible growing warming to national protectionist agendas as an attempt to regain national control of national economic matters. The debates about the Greek state's looming bankruptcy highlight the continued relevance of national borders as reference points for defensive notions of 'them and us', despite, maybe even because of, de facto open borders in Schengen Europe.

Elsewhere, Mercosur, for instance, formed in 1991 by Brazil, Argentina, Uruguay and Paraguay, represents a more mixed approach of reconciling tariff protection with strategic liberalisation, than found in US-led NAFTA, for example. The resulting variety of outcomes from this balancing has encouraged a reference to *multiple* regionalisms (see Marchand et al. 1999), with differences reflecting varying balances of powers between institutional interests, and state organisations and traditions. Mercosur entails a market of some two billion people and 'has gained increasingly in political presence as a "strategic and political platform" for the larger countries within it' (Phillips 2003, p. 221). Mercosur thus shows signs of evolving as a 'new regionalist project', with some of the integrationist political agendas found in the EU. With this, it is going beyond a mere opportunistic free trade area and morphing into a strategic development platform by bringing together national strategies and promoting them at a newly emerging international regional governance level. Yet, in contrast to the EU, states are in the driving seat of these selective relations and spaces, suggesting a new, albeit state-centric globalism with rising global relevance and ambition of nation states, rather than sub-national actors (see BRIC countries, i.e. Brazil, Russia, India, China).

This development outside the 'West', and also the discussions above, suggest that the nation state is clearly an important actor in 'nationalising' or 'regionalising' competitive conflicts (Hameiri and Jayasuriya 2011) either directly through bilateral or multi-lateral agreements, or via constructed international organisations, This applies to the Asia-Pacific region with its aspiring, rapidly growing newly industrialising economies, contrasting with developments in the European setting with its 'denationalising' and 'transnationalising' characteristics (see Kauppi 2013). The nation state has not disappeared as a powerful actor, but its international operating environment is changing. To capture this, new ways of understanding such networks of relationships are required. They need to move beyond an imaginary global politics composed first and foremost of inter-state relationships. Other actors and relationships join the stage and disturb established patterns and relationships.

Cities moving onto the world stage face shifting relationships between states. As shown above, the WTO framework and negotiated FTAs between states and between global regions (Trans-Pacific or Trans-Atlantic) set the economic context. The WTO and international trade are no longer dominated by the United States, as rising economic powers, such as the BRIC countries, vie for influence and a voice, and, as a result, for many commentators change should be seen as a 'succession of hegemonies' (see Clark 2011) between states and chiefly focused on the economic rise of China. Changing global governance may be seen in terms of the relative power and influence of states—directly in international agreements and economic relevance, but also indirectly in the ways of influencing international organisations. Much attention has been given to the influence of newly imagined groups of states in the form of economic relations-based free trade-style 'new regions'. Conceived as a purely analytical notion, the BRIC countries held their first summit meeting in 2009, and were joined by South Africa in 2010. The group lobbies on behalf of its member states, thus adopting an entirely nation state-focused perspective. The BRIC (also: BRICS) organisational structure has no place for sub-national actors and is not representing, for example, the countries' main cities, such as São Paolo, Johannesburg or Shanghai, in global forums. This is clearly different to the EU, where cities and regions are provided with a discursive and institutional platform to act more independently, and suggests a more conventional understanding of international governance as a matter for nation states.

The relative influence of states, therefore, continues to be important for setting the global regional context for cities, which may be conducive to urban forays into the international sphere, or rather less so. China, for example, has increased its involvement in the Asian region, working through ASEAN, ASEAN+3 and the East Asia Summit (Goh 2011). Lansong (2009, p. 82 cited in: CCIEE and UNDP, 2013, p. 32) argues that China finds such regional organisations 'better calibrated to confront and navigate globalisation and thus, more deftly suited to advance cooperation in global governance. 'Global governance' in this perspective means inter-state relationships as a one-dimensional, horizontal arrangement of collaboration. China is also active in regions further afield, such as in Africa, where it maintains considerable economic interests in securing natural resources through mutual investment deals (Brautigam 2009; Alden et al. 2008).

The Forum on China–Africa Cooperation (FOCAC) has been meeting at an intergovernmental scale since 2000. Contributing to regional groups is perceived as serving self-interest, as it is expected to aid national economic objectives. Collaborative regional groups represent states and their interests, but, as part of that, provide a relatively new and evolving context for cities on the world stage. This may offer new opportunities, as well as necessities, to become more internationally pro-active and 'step out' of their national contexts to be recognised globally as places—and economic players—in their own right. New development models, for example relationships between the BRIC countries, which bring increased mobility in investment and trade, and migration by people, can be seen as replacing an older, state-based North–South model with more differentiated and uneven economic impacts on cities and regions within the BRIC countries. Some cities may be singled out for new, higher profile, economic roles, while others continue to remain marginalised and invisible from an international vantage point. Johannesburg, for example, is seen as a 'gateway' city into sub-Saharan Africa (Cobbett 2014) and thus attracts attention and interest by international actors, especially investors. Subnational actors may thus be expected to be actively seeking new partners within new regional groupings, and new sources of shared experience, as the context changes.

3.5 INTERNATIONAL NETWORKS AND ORGANISATIONS BY SUB-NATIONAL ACTORS

As pointed out earlier (see also Fig. 3.1), networks between political and economic actors have gained in importance as vehicles to boost the individual participants' opportunities and scope for action. For cities and regions, as illustrated in Fig. 3.2, joining networks may be the first step to a relatively easy—or, indeed, the only realistic—route to becoming more independent actors from state policy and administrative state structure, by collaborating with like-interested actors on an international platform. International networks per se have traditionally been considered an interstate affair, as pointed out above, while sub-national actors build networks at the sub-national level within the borders a state territory. This simple distinction, much followed by IR and urban studies perspectives respectively, however, no longer reflects reality. Sub-national actor networks may well reach vertically across scales, embracing other actors than states, while also expanding horizontally to link up shared interests at one scalar level.

C40 Cities Climate Leadership Group	Founded in 2005 by former London Mayor Ken Livingstone, it creates a forum for cities to collaborate and take action on climate change. Today, C40 includes 58 member cities
The City Mayors Foundation	The City Mayors Foundation is an international think-tank dedicated to developing sustainable solutions to urban governance, education and planning, etc.
The Covenant of Mayors	Launched in 2008, The Covenant of Mayors connects local and regional authorities in Europe, aimed at supporting the implementation of local energy policies in cities of all sizes, which committed to meeting the European Union 20% CO2 reduction goal by 2020.
World Mayors Council on Climate Change	The World Mayors Council on Climate Change advocates the engagement of local governments in efforts to address climate change and global sustainability. Its more than 80 members include mayors, former mayors, and other public leading local officials . It is supported by ICLEI
United States Conference of Mayors	UCSM) is "the official non-partisan organization of cities with populations of 30,000 or more" in the US. Today, there are 1,398 such cities, each represented in the Conference by its mayor.
United Cities and Local Governments	Headquartered in Barcelona, brings local governments from around the world together to encourage cooperation and bring their influence to a global scale. The organization is structured through multiple governing bodies, sections, committees and working groups. UCLG's membership consists of cities and national associations of local governments
Local Governments for Sustainability (ICLEI)	ICLEI is an international association of local governments and national and regional local government organisations that have made a commitment to sustainable development. More than 500 cities, towns, counties, and their associations comprise ICLEI's growing internationalmembership.
Global Metro City The Glocal Forum	Global Metro City – The Glocal Forum is a non-profit organisation working to build a new relationship between the city and the global village with the aim of contributing to peace and development.
EUROCITIES	EUROCITIES is the network of major European cities. Founded in 1986, membership of more than 120 large cities in over 30 European countries. EUROCITIES provides a platform to share knowledge and ideas, and gives cities a voice in Europe with the institutions.
Energie-Cités	With over 110 members in 21 countries and representing close to 300 towns and cities, Energie-Cités is the association of European local authorities for promotion of local sustainable energy policies. Because 75% of all energy consumption in Europe occurs in urban areas, local authorities more than ever have a pivotal role to play.
Federation of Canadian Municipalities (FCM)	In 1987, Canadian municipalities gave the Federation of Canadian Municipalities (FCM) the mandate to be their representative internationally.
The National League of Cities (NLC)	Representing more than 18,000 US municipalities, NLC is the oldest and largest organisation representing municipal governments throughout the United States. Its mission is to strengthen and promote cities as 'centres of opportunity, leadership, and governance'

Fig. 3.2   International municipal networks in Europe and North America. *Source*: Based on information from Poole (2014) and http://www.citymayors.com

For instance, sub-national actors may now collaborate and build networks in order to explicitly reach out to the world, an arena viewed as the natural prerogative of the nation state (see Chap. 2), and to use that to challenge national policy agendas. This may go so far as getting involved in issues of national security, nuclear disarmament and global warming. It is thus a growing multi-scalar crowdedness, and layered 'thickness', of networks that characterise the new governance (Rhodes 1996) of the international sphere.

As IOs take an interest in sub-national partners—and the latter also in the former as a means of gaining a voice and policy-making capacity—so have the networks of sub-national governments expanded with a view to also engage at the international level. In the past, most international links between local governments were organised through national associations, albeit with limited ambitions, 'naturally' confined to individual state territories, as we shall see in Chap. 4. National networking continues to be important for many cities (Gordon 2016), yet many networks have outgrown their national geographic entities. Instead, they build new alliances and form concerted action groups and agendas around shared political concerns (e.g. peace, the defence of human rights, cultural diversity and solidarity) across national borders. More recently, an added impetus for such expanded engagement by sub-national governments has emanated from benefits obtained from sharing experiences and engaging in collective action around defined (and shared) urban economic and environmental agendas. 'And it is here, in this governance vacuum, that cities have found the motivation and capability to act in ways in which states either cannot or will not' (Curtis 2014, p. 4). The Lord Mayor of Melbourne, Robert Doyle, for instance, boasts in this context: 'nations talk, cities act' (Curtis 2014, p. 4), while the former president of the World Bank, which closely collaborates with the global city network C40, claimed at the 2011 São Paulo summit of the C40 that 'when the world's largest cities pledge to work together ... they can be a powerful force for change' (Curtis 2014, p. 4). The UN, World Bank and others are supporting partners in the C40 network. The main effect of such networks, and thus their attraction for cities to (qualify and) join, is the increase in power and capacity to influence decisions at national and international level (see Bouteglier 2014). This involves access to extra resources, including sharing experiences and 'good practices' that aid policy-making capacity. Such may help to make the formal fiscal and constitutional powers and capacities—controlled by the central state (which may be national government, but also a different tier of the administrative state)—go that much further.

The European experience possibly shows the highest density and longevity of international networking between sub-national governments (see also Chap. 5). Regional and environmental policy have encouraged and fostered multiple networks, and European studies has focused on the types of sub-national network, the transferability of network lessons, the impacts of international networks on sub-national participants and the capacities of sub-national units to engage internationally (Okereke et al. 2009). European networks tend to focus on two goals: the representation of their interests in EU institutions, and the exchange of experience and transnational learning (see Giest and Howlett 2013. Both approaches seek to boost local/regional development prospects and opportunities. Commentators (e.g. Kern and Bulkeley 2009; Happaerts 2011) note the change in organisational structures, including recruitment of policy-specific teams, and encouragement of all departments to participate in numerous working groups (see Payre 2010). Building networks and relations across institutional and territorial dividing lines is thus an important objective. For some time now the larger cities, and many regions, have dedicated staff to representative offices in Brussels. The Eurocities network, for instance, was set up in 1986 by just six cities, but lists now some 130 members (plus forty partner cities) and an explicit mission to achieve formal roles in the EU's 'multi-level' policy processes (http://www.eurocities.eu/eurocities/about_us). As part of this more EU-focused mission, its headquarter was moved to Brussels in 1992 (Heinelt and Niederhafner 2008) to improve the scope for lobbying EU institutions. Now, Eurocities wants to become the primary address for the EU when urban matters are concerned: 'we want to be the go-to network for European institutions on urban affairs' (http://www.eurocities.eu/eurocities/about_us/history). Strong city mayors, as rotating leaders of the network, have been instrumental in boosting its political capacity and recognition.

Direct cooperation between cities in Europe has a long tradition. Local foreign policy is by no means restricted to membership of local authority associations and transnational networks like the Council of European Municipalities and Regions (CEMR), Eurocities, or the Union of the Baltic Cities (UBC). There are thus also direct relations between municipalities, typically in the form of twinning. The idea of twin city partnerships developed after the First World War but only really came to fruition after the Second World War. It was initiated by, among other organisations, the International Mayors' Union (IBU) which primarily promoted Franco-German twinnings (Grunert 1981, p. 56). As they are seen as a tool for reconciliation it does not come as a surprise that most city twinnings were established between Germany and France.

The two leading municipal network organisations lobbying in Brussels on behalf of municipalities are the CEMR and Eurocities. They differ in nature and membership, with the former being more generally 'sub-national', whereas the latter is more specifically urban. Both opened their offices in Brussels many years ago, but it has been only more recently that their agendas are more in line with the EU's growing focus on cities as drivers of regional development (Harding 1997; Parkinson et al. 2004; Fischer et al. 2013). The CEMR is a municipal 'roof organisation' which represents the national associations of local authorities at EU level. Having opened its first office in Brussels in 1969 (with its headquarters in Paris) as essentially a study centre and 'eyes and ears' for the municipalities in EU policies, this has since morphed into the main political centre for municipal–EU negotiations and political lobbying as a short-cut to the traditional route for such links via the national governments. Eurocities is a transnational city network of more than 130 large cities with populations in excess of 250,000 in about thirty European countries, which thus goes beyond the immediate EU member states (http://www.eurocities.eu/eurocities/about_us). Exploring the effect of 'Europeanisation' on local politics and policies under the CIVITAS programme in France, Pflieger (2014) observes that such engagement is not merely about chasing funding. It is also about visibility as a relevant political and economic place and actor. Thus, despite a lack of funding under some European programmes, such as CIVITAS, for instance, local authorities mobilise strongly at a European level in order to distinguish themselves and to promote their policy agendas more visibly. And an international presence helps there.

This drive for international visibility as a way of attracting attention and gaining recognition among potential investors and visitors has also gained in importance in the EU's initiative European Capital of Culture (ECoC, initially European City of Culture). This is an interesting programme, as it combines, and links, the internal aspects of urban development and policy—as the traditionally assumed prerogative of 'urban studies' and urbanism—with the external arena of international networks and EU institutions and policies—conventionally the primary field of interest for IR. The nature and implicit focus of ECoC has moved from showcasing 'the best of' European culture in established centres of culture and arts, such as Florence, Amsterdam or Paris, some of the early ECoCs (Santinelli 2015; Griffiths 2006), to driving urban economic development and re-invention, such as spearheaded by Glasgow in 1991, to a national and, increasingly, international, audience. Increasingly, also, the ECoC programme has become a vehicle for engaging public debate and linking citizens to their cities and their images and meanings for them. This has been the explicit and central theme and agenda of Siena's bid for ECoC status in 2019 (interview with ECoC office, Siena, 12 June 2014). The city wanted to move away from the threat, as it was seen, of becoming a second Venice—a lifeless pastiche of itself, merely an exhibit and 'stage' for tourists to pass through and 'consume' the city's image. As various reports and own research have revealed in Umeå, Siena and Riga in 2014, preparation of a bid for ECoC selection and designation has become a major vehicle for reconnecting, and thus legitimising, local politics and governance to people's interests and sense of being part of the debate and (local) story. This matters, as ECoC status is about perception, representation and the marketing of a particular urban image to the outside world, with hopes/expectations attached that this will yield economic returns—and not just in the cultural industries (Herrero et al. 2006)—for the local population. Imagined relations, and business and cultural (i.e. professional-managerial and ideational-professional) linkages are thus important elements in the emanating strategies. They are effectively to be the sum of the various individual local businesses and cultural artists/businesses and their external linkages. Fostering a sense of togetherness among the population is thus an important part of the ECoC programme. This may, as in the case of Siena's candidature, mean a re-examination of the meaning of the city for its residents, and their relationships with the city in comparison to that of the (passing) tourists who want to see the image projected in the tourist guides. Another important vehicle for internationality has become shared agendas, such as 'smart cities' or 'green cities' (Campbell 2012; Beatley 2012). And this growing role of cities requires reflection in national and European competitiveness agendas in a global context, as the Mayor of Sala (Sweden) and CEMR representative, Carola Gunnarsson pointed out at a CEMR council meeting in Riga in June 2015: 'An EU urban agenda recognising the role of cities, providing a framework for better integration of their needs in EU policies' (http://www.ccre.org/en/actualites/view/3062).

Whilst national trade deals are now seen in many global regions, the EU again is a special case, as it combines such inter-national regionalism and collaboration with other global regions as a whole, such as NAFTA (see also the current—within the EU much-contested—discussions around the TTIP negotiations (http://ec.europa.eu/trade/policy/in-focus/ttip/about-ttip/impact/index_en.htm), with sub-national regionalism, and thus does more to encourage the internationalisation of sub-national entities. The EU identified various super-regional 'arcs' as virtual spaces for the purpose of strategic development debates (Gänzle et al. 2015, Stefan et al. 2015), which resulted in the recognition of a variety of 'inter-regionalisms', linking formal sub-national regions across international borders through joint projects and trans-border initiatives. The *international* framework provides the main parameters circumscribing scope for, and perceived requirement of, regional responses; the *sub-national* dimension revolves around inter-local relationships as the expression of regionalisation, shaped by particular combinations of legacies and histories, and also identities (Paasi 2001). These may circumscribe a sense of belonging and thus the perceived relevance and reality of a region (see also MacLeod and Goodwin 1999). But that is not a prerequisite. Sub-national new regionalism is essentially pragmatic and topic-driven, and as such subject to continuous review and reassessment.

But it is here that the responses at an intra-national, general inter-national, or EU-specific inter-national level seem to vary in their understanding and expectation of what cross-border collaboration and engagement involve. Accordingly, the nature of borders and boundaries, actual and imagined, varies too in its relevance to policy objectives and perceived opportunities by sub-national actors. It is these sorts of variable, 'soft' or 'virtual' spaces that make up much of the Baltic Sea Region (BSR) (Herrschel 2011a), seeking to overcome borders, while creating new, albeit virtual, ones by defining who is part of such a policy-defined space, and who is not. Each such space revolves around a specific set of policy agendas and includes an equally specific set of participating actors who share an interest in those policies. Because of this, the boundaries are contested and can be moved and overlap in various ways. By the same token, they may change quickly, and repeatedly, in response to shifting policy agendas and actor groupings and policy priorities. There is much less predictability and continuity and thus scope for scrutiny and participation in decision-making, therefore also raising questions of legitimacy.

Increasingly, however, individual cities have begun to set up their own offices for more effective pursuance of local interests with the EU as part of internationalisation strategies. The first such city was Malmö (interview City of Malmö, Department of Strategic Development, 10 December 2014), an, at first sight, unlikely candidate for such ground-breaking moves, rather than the obvious candidates like London or Paris. Its growing international outlook as part of the Danish–Swedish Øresund region, created in 2000 as a virtual (international) economic/marketing region around the new reality of the Øresund Bridge linking Denmark (Copenhagen) and Sweden (Malmö), has developed from the courage and political vision of local policy-makers, especially the long-term Mayor of Malmö (Herrschel 2011b, in Herrschel and Tallberg, eds).The City of Malmö's website (http://malmo.se/English/EU-and-International-Cooperation-.html) makes explicit and detailed reference to its international outlook and engagement, including the running of an international office in Brussels: The City of Malmö's representation in Brussels is a service-provision body for the City of Malmö's departments. The duties of the Brussels office are to:

- monitor programmes and funds,
- make and develop contacts,
- assist with project applications,
- develop project concepts in collaboration with the departments and
- practise lobbying activities"

(http://malmo.se/English/EU-and-International-Cooperation-.html). Lobbying internationally (here the EU) as a form of building relations and networks is thus an explicit goal. Indeed, every city government department needs to demonstrate awareness and consideration of international dimensions in their work and strategies (interview Malmö Office in Brussels, 14 June 2015). As a multi-level policy network, the BSR offers a fascinating example of local-to-international multi-level regional policy-making, involving different degrees of institutionalisation and policy-making remits, as well as forms of spatial manifestation—'virtual' and 'formalised actual'. The BSR thus brings together the two main scalar references of new regionalism, inter-national and inter-local, as well as various modes of operation—self-organising collaboration versus formal hierarchisation. The result is an intersection between types of regionalism—virtual (new) and geographically real (old)—and scalar variability. This, then, offers a number of combinations between those two variables. In addition, the BSR straddles different legacies of Europe's post-war divisions, including Nordic, Western, Central and Eastern (post-Soviet) political cultures and values (Herrschel 2011a). The end of communism and the removal of bloc discipline has brought over the years a plethora of organisations, reaching across a region with no clear and fixed external boundaries, and, instead, many overlapping and intersecting policy spaces with their own, specific agendas and collaborative rationales, membership-based virtual territorialisation and forms of administration. In so doing, actors—that is both institutions and places—seek to overcome past divisions and pursue collective engagement as a way of boosting policy efficacy and likely success. This may have to do with the nature of objectives, such as environmental issues that transcend boundaries, or attempts at boosting cross-border tourism (e.g. Tallinn (Estonia)–Helsinki (Finland)), or raising awareness among international investors about pooled economic resources and opportunities. The Øresund region is one such space, involving local and regional actors, albeit with the blessing of the respective national governments. There are signs, however, that the concept of a transnational polycentric, metropolitan region, with Copenhagen the largest and internationally traditionally most visible city, could become 'conventionalised' by returning it to the two largest traditional entities—Greater Copenhagen as a mono-centric Danish city-region, and Skåne as a large, traditional territorial entity of the Swedish state—where cities are merely an integral part (interview Skåne international office, Brussels, 17 June 2015).

The international most explicitly urban network within that Baltic space is the Union of Baltic Cities (UBC). The UBC is an interesting example of cities collaborating to set an international political agenda in the aftermath of the end of the Cold War, and thus clearly stepping into a realm of international relations traditionally reserved for nation states. Seeking to continue the tradition of the Hanseatic League with its city-based domination of Baltic trade in the late Middle Ages/early modern period, the UBC has sought to establish itself as an explicitly transnational, cross-border network of inter-city relations, to overcome the stark Cold War divisions between the 'East' and 'West' that dominated the BSR until 1991. So it has been a project of bridging these divisions and thus de facto European integration—outside the Brussels EU bureaucracy. Effectively, this followed, the rationale of the first Franco-German sister city exchanges of the 1950s. The UBC's other objective has been to boost the Baltic cities' international visibility on the geographic edge of Europe. Having its seat in Gdansk, Poland, is intended to highlight the Hanseatic tradition of city networking, as well as the transcendence of the Iron Curtain borders, by emphasising the historic urban commonalities in economic and cultural matters, going well beyond the era of the Westphalian nation state (see also Baldersheim and Stahlberg 1999). Currently, the UBC has about 100 member cities in the BSR, including many smaller ones, for whom such international collaboration is an important vehicle to demonstrate connectedness and relevance in a globalised world, and thus avoid the impression of peripherality and irrelevance. By the same token, some of the large players, especially Stockholm or Malmö, have left the organisation, as its initial drive has been considered fading, especially with regard to influencing/lobbying EU decision-making processes (interview UBC, 5 March 2012).

Thus, the ongoing discussion in the UBC about international engagement resulted in 2006 in an office in Brussels—called UBC Antenna Office—as an international access point and connector for/to the UBC member cities, as well as for continuous lobbying activities at the EU. However, that lasted only a few years, and now has given way to internationalisation efforts by individual cities (see Fig. 3.3). The strategies here are quite varied, with many of the UBC member cities, which vary widely in size and international profile, choosing to be represented by their respective (state-defined) regions. The slow, and ultimately failed, attempt by the UBC to reach out to the EU and its policy-making processes has been one of the reasons for its loss of membership among the large Baltic cities. Neither Stockholm nor Malmö are members, for instance, as the UBC is considered to have stood still in its development and to be much too unimaginative in terms of EU engagement to offer sufficient advantages to justify membership. Other organisations, such as Eurocities or CEMR are considered to offer better connections and access to EU policy-making (interview Malmö Brussels office, 14 June 2015). The UBC seems to have responded by streamlining its organisational structure—halving the number of Commissions so as to achieve 'more targeted and efficient' policy responses to better match members' expectations (Baltic Cities Bulletin, June 2015, statement by UBC chair). There is explicit commitment to effective EU work to benefit members' interests. But delivering on that, and convincing members of the effectiveness of doing so, does seem to require more effort.

Country	City	Brussels office (representation)
Denmark	Åalborg	North Denmark EU Office
	Åarhus	Central Denmark EU Office
	Kolding	South Denmark European Office
	Guldborgsund, Vordingborg, Køge, Naestved	Zealand Denmark EU Office
Estonia	Elva, Haapsalu, Hiiu, Jogeva, Johvi, Keila, Kuressaare, Maardu, Narva, Rakvere, Sillamae, Tartu, Viljandi, Voru	No individual/specific office, represented by The Brussels Office of the Association of Municipalities of Estonia and the Association of Estonian Cities
	Parnu	No own office, and no membership of the Assoc of Municipalities of Estonia Indirect access to Brussels: One the member of City Council belongs to the national delegation at Committee of the Regions.
	Tallinn	Represented at EU through own office: Tallinn European Office,
Finland	Jyvaskyla, Vaasa, Pori	West Finland European Office
	Kemi	East and North Finland EU-office
	Kotka	City of Kotka , represented via Regional Council of Kymenlaakso at Helsinki EU Office.
	Helsinki, Porvoo, Espoo, Lahti	Helsinki EU office
	Mariehamn	vice chairman in the Town Government represents Finland (the Åland Islands) in the EU Committee of Regions.
	Tampere	Tampere Region EU Office. The House of Cities
	Turku	TURKU-Southwest Finland European Office, Baltic Sea House
Germany	Greifswald	Hanseatic City of Greifswald has no office in Brussels, represented through a Member of the European Parliament
	Kiel, Lübeck	No city offices, represented through Schleswig-Holstein, Hanse-Office
	Rostock, Greifswald	No city office, represented through state (Information Office of the State of Mecklenburg-Vorpommern) in Brussels
Latvia	Jurmala, Liepaja	Represented through: Latvian Association of Local and Regional Governments
	Riga	No Office in Brussels

Fig. 3.3   UBC cities—representation in Brussels.
Source: Based on information from UBC

	Panevezys	EU Office of Association of Local Authorities of Lithuania
Lithuania	Siauliai	Permanent Representation of Lithuania to the European Union
	Vilnius	No office, represented through: The Association of Local Authorities in
Norway	Bergen	West-Norway Brussel office
	Kristiansand	South Norway European Office
Poland	Elbląg	Represented through: Regional Office of the Warmińsko-Mazurskie Voivodeship in Brussels
	Gdańsk, Gdynia	Represented through: Pomorskie Regional EU Office
	Szczecin	Represented through westpomerania regional office
Sweden	Kalmar	Represented through Småland Blekinge South Sweden regional office
	Karlstad	Represented through West Sweden regional office in Brussels
	Malmo	City of Malmö EU office
	Örebro	Represented through: Central Sweden European Office
	Östhammar, Visby	Stockholm Region EU Office
	Trelleborg	No office
	Umeå	Represented through: North Sweden European Office

Fig. 3.3   (continued)

3.6   LEADING CITIES: MONO-LATERAL INTERNATIONAL ENGAGEMENT

Cities' international engagement and participation in global governance is not restricted to acting collectively within and/or through networks, as shown in Figure 3.1. Individual cities with strong economic capacity, image and institutional capacity may well go it alone (see also Fig. 3.3). Some of the largest cities are at least as big as many smaller to medium-sized states in terms of population and also economic capacity. In 2007, half of global GDP was generated by 380 cities in developed regions, and over 20% of global GDP came from 190 North American cities alone (Dobbs et al. 2011). It is not surprising that some mayors have been identified as likely major global players. Thus, to illustrate the potential of city mayors in global governance, Barber (2013) profiles twelve leaders, including those from New York, London, Delhi, Seoul and Moscow. Some cities are seen to be taking the lead where national governments are falling short in tackling global challenges, especially in the field of climate change (see above). Some cities appear to be also, at times even more so, active in inter-city networks, giving impetus to networking, such as in the case of Paris and the Metropolis network in the 1980s, Glasgow and Lyon with Eurocities in the 1990s, and London and New York in the C40 network in the 2000s. A group of 'world cities' (Friedmann 1986) and a group of three 'global cities' (Sassen 1991) were argued to have dominant positions in a globalising economy, acting as part of a tripartite elite group. This academic work, plus the subsequent popularity of city ranking schemes according to 'success' or 'opportunity' (see inter alia *The Guardian*, 16 April 2015), and the active lobbying on the part of large cities (see Clark, G and Moonen, T, 2013), all play a part in encouraging competitiveness between cities and the desire to learn economic and policy lessons from other, seemingly more successful, cities in terms of their identified higher competitive ranking—however questionable the indicators actually may be. This includes, for instance, the measurement of a city's degree of globalisation (Caselli 2013).

Some analysts see the claims to world city status and associated networking as evidence of the fundamental weakening of nation states by the neo-liberal orthodoxy in world trade (for example, Curtis 2014). Others, on the other hand, challenge this perspective, and argue that 'the 2008 global financial crisis has firmly proven that nation-states, but not cities, wield power' (Fujita 2013, p. 30). This view points to the notion that even global cities remain rooted in nationally and regionally shaped cultures and political-institutional structures, practices and values, turning them into multi-scalar locations—or junctures—where all scales get interconnected, local to global, and interact (Herrschel and Newman 2002; Herrschel 2014). Nevertheless, what is clear is that some cities see themselves as (natural) economic leaders and have adapted their urban policies to prioritise competition (Newman and Thornley 2011). As a result, such cities tend to invest more in inter-city links to boost both trade and reputation as an enhancement to their political capital and influence in international affairs and their governance. Despite the focus on networks and inter-city relations, territoriality continues to matter as an expression and manifestation of state power, governmental responsibility and democratic accountability (Kersbergen and Waarden 2004; Esmark 2007). But it takes on many more forms and expressions than imagined by conventional realist concentration on the national state as solely relevant international actor. While fixed boundaries matter to define legal territorial entities, so do imagined and projected virtual spaces described as 'backcloth' to linear connection and relations between urban nodes (Herrschel 2011b). Consequently, it is not just the state that matters as an international actor in shaping globalisation and its governance, but also large cities and metropolitan areas—either individually, or as part of a collective network—as places that matter for economic, cultural and political globalism.

3.7   Conclusion: 'Thickness' of Internationality and Modes of Sub-National Engagement

This chapter examined the growing complexity and 'thickness' in the understanding and modus operandi of internationality as a policy-making and political arena. This is owing to a growing number of sub-national governmental actors stepping out into this realm to find regulative answers to globalisation and the growing interconnectedness of economic, environmental and other challenges. This thickening of international governance through a deeper—layered—vertical engagement of institutional actors, challenges the established notion that the international sphere is, in essence, a one-dimensional flat space of only one type of (relevant) actor—the nation state. Instead, a multi-tier, vertical network of collaborating institutional-territorial actors emerges, which invites another look at the concept of multi-level governance as a stepping stone to a broader theory of global governance. The chapter distinguished between three modes of international engagement by sub-national actors, especially cities, with increasing local immediacy and singularity of engagement: (1) *collaborative, horizontal networks*, (2) *collaborative vertical engagement* with international organisations as established agents of international governance, and (3) open and *direct local engagement*, building and utilising both horizontal and vertical actor relationships. The latter, third mode of international engagement (see Fig. 3.4) offers the broadest range of the most individualised, tailor-made and thus likely effective, opportunities to assemble alliances and networks through specific, and varying—over time and between policy agendas—combinations of vertical and horizontal collaborative engagement.

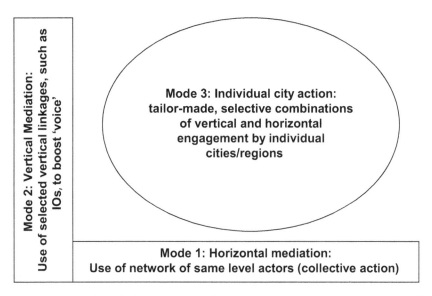

Fig. 3.4 Modes of city internationalisation between horizontal and vertical collaboration

In exploring the international engagement by cities and city-regions, we have identified the key issues in emerging understandings of, and theoretical perspectives on, new international relationships. We gave particular attention to the variations that emerge in the analysis and explanation of global governance, as well as different perspectives on network governance and their varying scales. International engagement by cities and regions was shown as taking on different forms of collaborative action, based on their own views of existing policy-making capacities and agendas, or relying on individual cities' own, singular, action. This affects in particular the relationship between state, international organisations and sub-national actors, which has witnessed a continuous evolution, affecting modes of operation, scalar positioning and confidence in being able to muster successful policies independently. This includes both scope and capacity, to engage more or less directly in global governance in pursuit of an expected own advantage. Economically weaker and/or less confident and experienced actors seem likely to engage with national or international networks of local government (cities), seeking collective and thus more powerful voice vis-à-vis lobbying partners. They also seek to draw down advantages indirectly through the networks' activities, such as knowledge transfer about 'best practices' in policy-making. The second, more directly and independently followed mode of engagement, was found to work through engagements by sub-national actors with IOs. The EU, with its explicit and broad platform for local and regional engagement with the European institutions and modes of governance, offers here a very specific framework of internationality. IOs may serve as amplifiers of individual cities' interests and policies, to project them up to the global scale, and thus give them more influence on global governance. The third, most direct, form of engagement involves larger cities and/or metropolitan areas or city-regions with sufficient confidence and political and economic stature and policy-making capacity to pursue their interests independently. Here, the conventional notion of a flat, state-based practice of internationality and its governance is challenged the most. This may go so far, as in the case of the largest global cities, that the city dominates its state in terms of economic relevance and thus political options. This, as the chapter elaborates, raises important questions about the utility of the multi-level governance perspective, ideas about regime formation through international networking, and the rationales behind new international imaginaries of power, opportunity and interdependencies, and the implications of that for the democratic systems examined. This, as the chapter pointed out, mirrors the manifestation of authority and legitimacy in the emerging new, and increasingly complex, i.e. multi-scalar and multi-actor, forms of global governance.

References

Abbott, K., Genschel, Ph., Snidal, D. and Zangl, B. 2015. Orchestration: Global Governance through Intermediaries. In: K. Abbott, Ph. Genschel, D. Snidal and B. Zangl (eds.): International Organizations as Orchestrators. Cambridge: Cambridge University Press, pp. 3–36.

Abbott, K., Genschel, P., Snidal D. and Zangl, B., 2015b. Two Logics of Indirect Governance: Delegation and *Orchestration British Journal of Political Science*, FirstViewArticle / July 2015, 1–11.

Abbott, K., Snidal D., 2009. Strengthening International Regulation Through Transnational New Governance: Overcoming the Orchestration Deficit. *Vanderbilt Journal of Transnational Law, 42*(2), 501–578.

Abbott, K., 2012. Engaging the Public and the Private in Global Sustainability Governance. *International Affairs, 88*, 543–564.

Acuto, M., 2013. Global cities, governance and diplomacy: The urban link. London: Routledge.

Acuto, M., Steele, W., eds., 2013. Global City Challenges: Debating a Concept, Improving the Practice. New York: Palgrave Macmillan.

Alcantara, C., Broschek J. and Nelles, J., 2015. RethinkingMultilevel Governance as an Instance of Multilevel Politics: A Conceptual Strategy, *Territory, Politics, Governance.*

Alden, C., Large, D. and Soares de Oliveira, R., 2008. *China returns to Africa: A rising power and a continent embrace.* Columbia University Press.

Alger, C., 2011. Searching for Democratic Potential in Emerging Global Governance:What Are the Implications of Regional and Global Involvements of Local Governments? *International Journal of Peace Studies, Volume 16, Number, 2,* 1–24.

Allen, J., 2010. Powerful City Networks: More than Connections, Less than Domination and Control *Urban Studies, 47*(3), 2895–2911.

Amin, A., Thrift, N., 2002. Cities: Reimagining the Urban. London: Wiley.

Avant, D., Finnemore M., Sell S., 2010a. Who governs the globe? In: Avant D., Finnemore M., Sell S. (eds): *Who Governs the Globe?* Cambridge: Cambridge University Press, pp. 1–34.

Avant, D., Finnemore, M. and Sell, S. eds., 2010b. *Who governs the globe?* (Vol. 114). Cambridge University Press.

Bache, I., 1998. The Politics of European Union Regional Policy. Multi-Level Governance or Flexible Gatekeeping? Sheffield: UACES and Sheffield Academic Press.

Bache, I. and Flinders, M., 2004. Multi-level governance and the study of the British state. *Public Policy and Administration, 19*(1), 31–51.

Baker, A., Hudson, D., & Woodward, R., 2011. Conclusions: Financial globalization, multilevel governance and IPE, in: A. Baker, D. Hudson, & R Woodward (eds.) *Governing Financial Globalization,* pp. 213–222. London: Routledge.

Baldersheim, H. and Stahlberg, K., eds, 1999. Nordic Region- Building in a European Perspective, ed. Aldershot: Ashgate.

Barber, B., 2013. *If Mayors Ruled the World. Dysfunctional Nations, Rising Cities.* New Haven: Yale University Press.

Barkin, J.S. and Cronin, B., 1994. The state and the nation: changing norms and the rules of sovereignty in international relations. *International Organization, 48,* 107–107.

Barnett, M. and Duval, R., 2005. Power in Global Governace. In: Barnett, M. and R. Duval (eds.) Power in Global Governance. Cambridge: Cambridge University Press, pp. 1–32.

Bartelson, J., 2000. 'Three Concepts of Globalization', *International Sociology, 15*(2), 180–96.

Beatley, T., 2012. Green Cities of Europe: Global Lessons on Green Urbanism. Island Press.

Bevir, M., Rhodes, R., 2003. *Interpreting British governance*. London: Routledge.

Bernstein, S., Cashore, B., 2007. Can non-state global governance be legitimate? An analytical framework. *Regulation& Governance*, *1*, 347–371.

Biermann, F., Pattberg, P., Van Asselt, H. and Zelli, F. 2009. The fragmentation of global governance architectures: A framework for analysis. *Global Environmental Politics*, *9*(4), 14–40.

Blanco, I, Griggs S. and Sullivan H., 2014. Situating the local in the neoliberalisation and transformation of urban governance *Urban Studies 51*(15), 3129–3146.

Blauberger, M. and Rittberger, B., 2015. Orchestrating Policy Implementation: EU Governance through Regulatory Networks. *International Organizations as Orchestrators*, 39–64.

Bouteglier, S., 2014. A Networked Urban World: Empowering Cities to Tackle Environmental Challenges. In: S. Curtis, (ed.) *The Power of Cities in International Relations*. London: Routledge. pp. 57–68.

Brautigam, D., 2009. *The dragon's gift: the real story of China in Africa*. OUP Oxford.

Brenner, N., 1999. Beyond state-centrism? Space, territoriality, and geographical scale in globalization studies, *Theory and Society*, *28*, 39–78.

Broome, A. and Seabrooke L., 2012. Seeing like an International Organisation, *New Political Economy*, *17*(1), 1–16.

Brundsen, J., 2016. Multinational companies face tax avoidance EU crackdown, *Financial Times*, 8 Feb.

Brunet-Jailly, E., 2000. Globalization, integration, and cross-border relations in the metropolitan area of Detroit (USA) and Windsor (Canada). *International Journal of Economic Development*, *2*(3), 379–401.

Brunet-Jailly, E., 2006. NAFTA and cross border relations in Niagara, Detroit, and vancouver. Journal of Borderlands Studies, *21*(2), 1–19.

Brusis M., 2014. Paths and Constraints of Subnational Government Mobilization in East-Central Europe, *Regional & Federal Studies*, *24*(3), 301–319.

Bulkeley, H., 2012a. Governance and the geography of authority: modalities of authorisation and the transnational governing of climate change. *Environment and Planning A*, *44*(10), 2428–2444.

Bulkeley, H., 2012b. Guest editorial *Environment and Planning C: Government and Policy*, *30*, 556–570.

Burfisher, M.E., Robinson, S. and Thierfelder, K., 2004. Regionalism: Old and new, theory and practice. *Conference proceedings Agricultural Policy Reform and the WTO: Where Are We Heading*, pp. 593–622. https://www.researchgate.net/profile/Sherman_Robinson/publication/2937301_Regionalism_ Old_and_New_Theory_and_Practice/links/02bfe5139063471f8e000000.pdf

Campbell, T., 2012. *Beyond smart cities: how cities network, learn and innovate*. Abingdon: Earthscan.

Caselli, M., 2013. Nation States, Cities, and People: Alternative Ways to Measure Globalization. In: SAGE Open, October-December 2013, 1–8.

Calzada, I., 2015. Benchmarking future city-regions beyond nation-states. *Regional Studies, Regional Science*, 2(1), 351–362.

CCIEE (China Centre for International Economic Exchanges) and UNDP, 2013. Configuring Global Governance – Effectiveness, Inclusiveness, and China's Global Role. Conference Report, available under: http://www.academia. edu/11283114/Reconfiguring_Global_Governance, accessed 10 Dec 16.

Clark, I., 2011. China and the United States: a succession of hegemonies? *International Affairs, 87*:(1), 13–28.

Clark, G. and Moonen, T., 2013. Global Cities: Introducing the 10 Traits of Globally Fluent Metro Areas. Brookings Institution.

Cerny P., 2010. *Rethinking World Politics.* Oxford: Oxford University Press.

Cobbett, E., 2014. Johannesburg: Reinventing financial space in *The Power of Cities in International Relations,* Ed Simon Curtis. Routledge.

Cooper, A.F., Hughes, C.W. and De Lombaerde, P. eds., 2007. *Regionalisation and global governance: The taming of globalisation?* Routledge.

Crawford, J. and Fiorentino, R., 2005. The changing landscape of regional trade agreements. Geneva: World Trade Organization.

Curry, D., 2015. Network Approaches to Multi-Level Governance: Structures, Relations and Understanding Power between Levels. Palgrave Macmillan.

Curtis, S., 2014. Introduction Empowering Cities in S.Curtis, ed *The Power of Cities in International Relations.* Routledge pp. 1–15.

Dawes, S., Cresswell, A. and Pardo, T., 2009. From "need to know" to "need to share": Tangled problems, information boundaries, and the building of public sector knowledge networks. *Public Administration Review*, 69(3), 392–402.

De Burca, G., Keohane, R. and Sabel, C., 2013. New Modes of Pluralist Global Governance, *NYU Journal of International Law and Politics, 7*23, Spring.

Deudney, D. and Ikenberry, G.J., 1999. The nature and sources of liberal international order. *Review of International Studies*, 25(2), 179–196.

Dierwechter, Y., 2008. *Urban Growth Management and Its Discontents. Promises, Practices, and Geopolitics in U.S. City-Regions.* Palgrave Macmillan, pp. 274–296.

Dietsch, P., Rixen, T., 2016. Global Tax Governance: What It is and Why It Matters. In P. Dietsch and T. Rixen (eds.) *Global Tax Governance What is wrong with it and how to fix it* , ECPR Press, Colchester, pp. 1–24.

Dobbs, R., Smit, S., Remes, J., Manyika, J., Roxburgh, Ch. and A. Restrepo., 2011. Urban world: Mapping the economic power of cities. McKinsey Global Institute, March. Available under: http://www.mckinsey.com/global-themes/ urbanization/urban-world-mapping-the-economic-power-of-cities.

Duchacek, I., 1990. Perforated Sovereignties: Towards a Typology of New Actors in International Relation. In: Michelmann, H. and Soldatos, P. (eds.).

Federalism and international relations: the role of subnational units. Oxford: Oxford University Press, pp. 1–33.

Eccleston, R., Kellow, A. and Carroll, P., 2013a. G20 Endorsement in Post Crisis Global Governance: More than a Toothless Talking Shop? *British Journal of Politics and International Relations,* 1–20.

Esmark, A., 2007. Democratic accountability and network governance—problems and potentials. In *Theories of democratic network governance,* Palgrave Macmillan.

Feiock, R., ed., 2004. *Metropolitan Governance: Conflict, Competition, and Cooperation.* (Washington, DC: Georgetown University Press).

Finkelstein, L.S., 1995. What is global governance? *Global governance,* 367–372.

Fischer, M.M., Diez, J.R. and Snickars, F., 2013. *Metropolitan innovation systems: theory and evidence from three metropolitan regions in Europe.* Springer Science & Business Media.

Friedmann J., 1986. The World City Hypothesis, *Development and Change, 17*(1), 69–83.

Fujita, K., 2013. Introduction: Cities and Crisis: New Critical Urban Theory in Kuniko Fujita ed *Cities and Crisis: New Critical Urban Theory,* Sage: LA, pp. 1–50.

Gehring, T., Faude, B., 2013. The Dynamics of Regime Complexes: Microfoundations and Systemic Effects *Global Governance, 19,* 119–130.

Giest, S., Howlett, M., 2013. Comparative Climate Change Governance: Lessons from European Transnational Municipal Network Management Efforts Environmental Policy and Governance, *23,* 341–353.

Goh, E., 2011. Institutions and the great power bargain in East Asia: ASEAN's limited 'brokerage' role. In: *International Relations of the Asia-Pacific, 3,* 373–401.

Gordon, D., 2016. 'Lament for a network? Cities and networked climate governance in Canada', *Environment and Planning C: Government and Policy, 34,* 529–545.

Green, J., 2014. *Rethinking Private Authority: Agents and Entrepreneurs in Global Environmental Governance.* Princeton: Princeton University Press.

Griffiths, R., 2006. City/Culture Discourses: Evidence from the Competition to Select the European Capital of Culture 2008. In: *European Planning Studies, 14*(4), 415–430.

Grunert, T., 1981. Langzeitwirkungen von Städte-Partnerschaften. Ein Beitrag zur europäischen Integration. Kehl am Rhein and Straßburg: N.P. Engel Verlag.

Guzzini, S., 2000. A reconstruction of constructivism in international relations. *European Journal of International Relations, 6*(2), 147–182.

Guzzini, S., Neumann, I., eds, 2012. *The Diffusion of Power in Global Governance: International Political Economy meets Foucault. Palgrave Studies in International Relations.* Basingstoke: Palgrave Macmillan.

Habitat, U.N., 1996. An urbanizing world, global report on human settlements. Nairobi: UN Human Settlements Programme.

Habitat, U.N., 2010. The state of African cities. Nairobi: The United Nations Settlements Programme.

Hale, T. & Roger, C., 2014. Orchestration and transnational climate governance *Review of International Organisations, 9*, 59–82.

Hanegraaff, M., Braun, C., De Bièvre, D. and Beyers, J., 2015. The Domestic and Global Origins of Transnational Advocacy: Explaining Lobbying Presence During WTO Ministerial Conferences. *Comparative Political Studies, 48*(12), 1591–1621.

Hameiri, S. and Jayasuriya, K., 2011. Regulatory regionalism and the dynamics of territorial politics: The case of the Asia-Pacific region. *Political Studies, 59*(1), 20–37.

Happaerts, S., Van den Brande, K. and Bruyninckx, H., 2011. Subnational governments in transnational networks for sustainable development. *International Environmental Agreements: Politics, Law and Economics, 11*(4), 321–339.

Harding, A., 1997. Urban Regimes in a Europe of the Cities?. *European urban and regional studies, 4*(4), 291–314.

Harrison, J., 2013. Rethinking City-regionalism as the Production of New Non-State Spatial Strategies: The Case of Peel Holdings Atlantic Gateway Strategy. Urban Studies, *51*(11), 2315–2335.

Hasenclever, A., Mayer, P., & Rittberger, V., 2000. Integrating theories of international regimes. *Review of International Studies, 26*(1), 3–33.

Hawkins, D., Lake, D., Nielson, D. and Tierney, M., 2006. Delegation under Anarchy: States, International Organizations and Principal-Agent Theory. In: D. Hawkins, D. Lake, D. Nielson and M. Tierney (eds): *Delegation and Agency in International Organizations.* Cambridge, Cambridge University Press, pp. 3–38.

Heinelt, H and Niederhafner, S (2008): Cities and Organized Interest Intermediation in the EU Multi-Level System. *European Urban and Regional Studies* 2008 15, 173. doi: 10.1177/0969776408090023.

Held, D. and McGrew, A.G., eds., 2002. *Governing globalization: power, authority and global governance.* Cambridge: Polity Press.

Herrero, L.C., Sanz, J.Á., Devesa, M., Bedate, A. and Del Barrio, M.J., 2006. The Economic Impact of Cultural Events A Case-Study of Salamanca 2002, European Capital of Culture. *European urban and Regional Studies, 13*(1), 41–57.

Herrschel, T., 2009. City Regions, Polycentricity and the Construction of Peripheralities Through Governance. In: *Urban Research and Practice, 2*(3), 240–250. Special Issue on 'City Regions and Polycentric Territorial Development: Concepts and Practice'.

Herrschel, T., 2011. *Borders in Post-Socialist Europe: Territory, Scale, Society.* Farnham: Ashgate.

Herrschel, T., 2014. *Cities, State and Globalisation: City-Regional Governance in Europe and North America*. London: Routledge.

Herrschel, T., Newman P., 2002. *Governance of Europe's City Regions*, London: Routledge.

Hettne, B. and Söderbaum, F., 2003. Theorising the rise of regionness. *New regionalism in the global political economy: Theories and cases, 3*, 33.

Hooghe, L., Marks G., 2001. *Multi-level Governance and European Integration*. Boulder: Rowman and Littlefield.

Hopf, T., 1998. The promise of constructivism in international relations theory. *International security, 23*(1), 171–200.

Jarvis, D., 2002. *International relations and the challenge of postmodernism: Defending the discipline*. Columbia: University of South Carolina Press.

Jessop, B., 2016. Territory, Politics, Governance and Multispatial Metagovernance, *Territory, Politics, Governance, 4*(1), 8–32.

Jinnah, S., 2014. *Post-treaty politics: secretariat influence in global environmental governance*. Cambridge, MA: MIT Press.

Johnson, C., Schroeder, H., Toly N., 2015. Conclusion. Governing the Urban Climate Challenge. In Johnson C., Toly N., Schroeder H. (eds.). *The Urban Climate Challenge*. London: Routledge, pp. 227–243.

Jones, M., 2016. Polymorphic Political Geographies, *Territory, Politics Governance, 4*(1), 1–7.

Jönsson, C. and Tallberg, J., 2010. *Transnational Actors in Global Governance Patterns, Explanations and Implications*. Palgrave Macmillan.

Jouve, B., 2007. Urban societies and dominant political coalitions in the internationalization of cities *Environment and Planning C: Government and Policy, 25*, 374–390.

Katz, B. and Bradley, J. 2013. *The Metropolitan Revolution: How Cities and Metros Are Fixing Our Broken Politics and Fragile Economy*. Washington, DC: Brookings Institution press.

Kauppi, N. (2013). *A Political Sociology of Transnational Europe*. Colchester: ECPR Press.

Kearns, M.P. and Mingst, K.A., 2004. *International organizations: the politics and processes of global governance* (p. 4). London: Lynne Rienner Publishers.

Keohane, R.O., 1982. The Demand for International Regimes *International Organization, 36*(2), 325–355.

Keohane, R., 1983. The Demand for International Regimes, in S. Krasner (ed.) *International Regimes*. Ithaca: Cornell University Press, pp. 141–171.

Kern, K. and Bulkeley, H., 2009. Cities, Europeanization and Multi-level Governance:Tackling Climate Change through Transnational Municipal Networks. JCMS: Journal of Common Market Studies, *47*(2), 309–332.

Kersbergen, K.V. and Waarden, F.V., 2004. 'Governance'as a bridge between disciplines: Cross-disciplinary inspiration regarding shifts in governance and problems of governability, accountability and legitimacy. *European Journal of Political Research*, 43(2), 143–171.

Kuus, M., 2015. Transnational Bureaucracies: How do we know what they know? *Progress in Human Geography*, 39(4), 432–448.

Lane, J-E., 2013. Review of C. Bradford and W Lim (eds.) Global Leadership in Transition: Making the G20 More Effective and Responsive *Political Studies Review*, 11(2), 252–253.

Lipson, C., Cohen, B., eds, 1999. *Theory and Structure in International Political Economy: An International Organization Reader*. Boston, MA: MIT Press.

Ljungkvist, K., (2015). Global City 2.0: From Strategic Site to Global Actor. New York: Routledge.

Lee, T., 2014. *Global Cities and Climate Change: The Translocal Relations of Environmental Governance*. London: Routledge.

Macleod, G., Goodwin, M., 1999. Space, scale and state strategy: rethinking urban and regional governance *Progress in Human Geography*, 23(4), 503–527.

Magone, J., 2003. *Regional Institutions and Governance in the European Union*. Westport: Praege.

Marchand, M., Boas, M. and Shaw, T., 1999. The political economy of new regionalisms. *Third World Quarterly*, 20(5), 897–910.

Marciacq, F., 2015. Sub-State Diplomacy in Malfunctioning States: The Case of the RepublikaSrpska, Bosnia and Herzegovina, *Regional & Federal Studies*, DOI:10.1080/13597566.2015.1083980. first published online 14 Sept 2015.

Marks , G. 1993. Structural policy and multi-level governance in the EC". In: A. Cafruny and G. Rosenthal, eds, The state of the European community. Vol. 2, The Maastricht debates and beyond, pp. 391–410. Boulder, CO: Lynne Rienner.

Marks, G., Blank, L., Hooghe, L., 1996. European Integration from the 1980s: State-Centric v. Multi-level Governance - *Journal of Common Market Studies*, 34(3), 341–378.

McGinnis, M.D., 1999. Polycentric governance and development: Readings from the workshop in political theory and policy analysis. University of Michigan Press.

Nelles, J., 2011. Cooperation in Crisis? An Analysis of Cross-Border Intermunicipal Relations in the Detroit-Windsor Region. *Articulo-Journal of Urban Research*, (no 6).

Newman, P. and Thornley, A., 2011. *Planning World Cities (2nd Edition)*. Basingstoke: Palgrave Macmillan.

Neumann, I., 2012. Conclusion: an emerging global polity. In S Guzzini and I Neumann (eds): *The Diffusion of Power in Global Governance*. Houndsmill, Basingstoke: Palgrave Macmillan, pp. 256–263.

Niederhafner, S., 2013. Comparing functions of transnational city networks in Europe and Asia, *Asia Europe Journal*, 11(4), 377–396.

Nordberg, D., 2012. Return of the state? The G20, the financial crisis and power in the world economy. *Review of Political Economy*, 24(2), 289–302.

Oikonomou, G., 2016. Bypassing a Centralized State: The Case of the Greek Subnational Mobilization in the European Union, Regional & Federal Studies, online version.

Okereke, C., Bulkeley, H. and Schroeder, H., 2009. Conceptualizing climate governance beyond the international regime. *Global environmental politics*, 9(1), 58–78.

Paasi, A., 2001. Europe as a social process and discourse considerations of place, boundaries and identity. *European urban and regional studies*, 8(1), 7–28.

Panagariya, A., 1999. The regionalism debate: an overview. *The World Economy*, 22(4), 455–476.

Panke, D., Hönnige C., Gollub. J., 2015. *Consultative Committees in the European Union No Vote – No Influence?* Colchester: ECPR Press.

Paolini, A.J., Jarvis, A.P. and Reus-Smit, C., 1998. Between sovereignty and global governance: the United Nations, the state, and civil society. Macmillan Press.

Parkinson, M., Clark, G., Hutchins, M., Simmie, J. and Verdonk, H., 2004. *Competitive European cities: where do the core cities stand?*. London: Office of the Deputy Prime Minister.

Paterson, M., Hoffmann, M., Betsill, M., Bernstein, S., 2014. The Micro Foundationsof Policy DiffusionToward Complex Global Governance: An Analysis of the Transnational Carbon Emission Trading Network, *Comparative Political Studies*, 47(3), 420–449.

Payre, R., 2010. The Importance of Being Connected. City Networks and Urban Government: Lyon and Eurocities (1990–2005) *International Journal of Urban and Regional Research*, 34(2), 260–80.

Perkmann, M., 2003. Cross-border regions in Europe: Significance and drivers of regional cross-border co-operation. *European Urban and Regional Studies*, 10(2), 153–171.

Peters, G., & Pierre, J., 2010. Public Private Partnerships and the Democratic Deficit: Is Performance Based Legitimacy the Answer? In M. Bexell and U. Mörth(eds.), *Democracy and Public Private Partnerships in Global Governance* (pp. 41–54). Basingstoke: Palgrave Macmillan.

Poole, R., 2014. 6 Organisations that Bring Mayors Together. Blog of 12 Jan 2014, available under: http://www.shareable.net/blog/6-organizations-that-bring-mayors-together. Accessed 10 Mar 2016.

Pflieger, G., 2014. The local politics of Europeanization: A study of French cities' approaches to participation in the CIVITAS programme. *European Urban and Regional Studies*, 21(3), 331–344.

Phillips, N., 2003. The rise and fall of open regionalism? Comparative reflections on regional governance in the Southern Cone of Latin America. *Third World Quarterly, 24*(2), 217–234.

Piattoni, S., 2009. Multi-level Governance: a Historical and Conceptual Analysis, *Journal of European Integration, 31*(2), 163–180.

Piattoni, S., 2010. *The theory of multi-level governance: conceptual, empirical, and normative challenges.* Oxford University Press.

Porter, T., 2005. *Globalization and Finance.* London: Polity Press.

Princen, S. and Kerremans, B., 2008. Opportunity Structures in the EU multi-level system. In: *West European Politics, 31*(6), 1129–1146.

Radaelli, C., 2006. Diffusion without convergence: how political context shapes the adoption of regulatory impact assessment, *Journal of European Public Policy, 12*(5), 924–943.

Rhodes, R.A.W., 1996. The new governance: governing without government1. *Political studies, 44*(4), 652–667.

Rioux Ouimet, H., 2015. From Sub-state Nationalism to Subnational Competition States: The Development and Institutionalization of Commercial Paradiplomacy in Scotland and Quebec, *Regional & Federal Studies.*

Rousselin, M., 2015. The Power of Legitimation: The Role of Expert Networks in Global Environmental Governance. *Journal of Environmental Policy & Planning,* 1–17.

Rowe, C., 2011. *Regional Representations in the European Union: Between Diplomacy and Interest Representation.* Basingstoke: Palgrave Macmillan.

Ruggie, J.G., 1993. Territoriality and beyond: problematizing modernity in international relations. *International organization, 47*(1), 139–174.

Ruggie, J., 2004. Reconstituting the Global Public Domain – Issues, Actors, and Practices. *European Journal of International Relations, 10*, 499–531.

Santinelli, S. C., 2015. The History of the European Capital of Culture Programme. One Europe. Available under: http://one-europe.info/the-history-of-the-european-capital-of-culture-program. Accessed 2 Mar 16.

Sassen, S., 1991. *The global city: New York, London, Tokyo. New York*: Princeton University Press (also later editions, 2001, 2013).

Schleifer, Ph., 2013. Orchestrating sustainability: The case of European Union biofuel governance. *Regulation & Governance, 7*, 533–546.

Scholte, J., 2014. Reinventing global democracy. *European Journal of International Relations, 20*(1), 3–28, originally published online 29 May 2012.

Scott, A., 2012. A World in Emergence: Cities and Regions in the 21st Century. London: Edward Elgar.

Sinclair, T., 2012. *Global Governance.* Cambridge: Polity Press.

Sinclair-Smith, K., 2015. Polycentric development in the Cape Town cityregion, *Development Southern Africa, 32*(2), 131–150.

Stefan, G., Kristine, K., Antony, P., 2015. A 'Macro-regional' Europe in the Making: Theoretical Approaches and Empirical Evidence. Palgrave Macmillan.

Stephenson, P., 2013. Twenty years of multi-level governance: 'Where does it Come from? What is it? Where is it going?, *Journal of European Public Policy*, *20*, 817–837.

Stephenson, S. and Robert, M., 2011. Evaluating the Contributions of Regional Trade Agreements to Governance of Services Trade (August 30, 2011). ADBI Working Paper 307. Available at SSRN: http://ssrn.com/abstract=1920012 or http://dx.doi.org/10.2139/ssrn.1920012

Stone, R., 2013. Informal governance in international organizations: Introduction to the special issue, *Review of International Organisations*, *8*, 121–136.

Swenden, W and Bolleyer N., 2014. Regional Mobilization in the New Europe: Old Wine in a New Bottle?, *Regional & Federal Studies*, *24*(3), 383–399.

Tatham, M., Thau, M., 2014. The more the merrier: Accounting for regional paradiplomats in Brussels, *European Union Politics*, *15*(2), 255–276.

Tatham, M., 2008. Going solo: Direct regional representation in the European Union. *Regional and Federal Studies*, *18*(5), 493–515.

Tol, N., 2009. The Economic Effects of Climate Change. *The Journal of Economic Perspectives*, *23*(2), 29–51.

Ward, K. and Jonas, A.E., 2004. Competitive city-regionalism as a politics of space: a critical reinterpretation of the new regionalism. *Environment and Planning A*, *36*(12), 2119–2139.

Wu, F., 2015. *Planning for Growth*. London: Routledge.

Zehfuss, M., 2002. *Constructivism in international relations: the politics of reality* (Vol. 83). Cambridge University Press.

CHAPTER 4

Expansion and Activities of Networks of Sub-National Governments

4.1   INTRODUCTION

This chapter explores the role and nature of networks as vehicles for cities and regions to go international in their attempt to participate in, and influence, emerging global governance. As discussed in Chaps. 2 and 3, networks and their diverse motivations and functions vary when it comes to their role in serving as connectors between sub-national actors and the international arena. Those networks claiming a stake in the international realm may reflect local or regional economic drivers (and Chap. 5 will focus in depth on examples), or may have wider motivations and a broader range of thematic purpose, such as environmental issues for example.

City networks differ quite clearly by agenda, their geographic reach, and their composition, that is, in the types and range of cities involved. In addition, these three descriptors may focus on a broader, more general agenda of strategic development, or follow more specific, thematically narrower and selective interests. This variation circumscribes the likely nature and number of interested players: a wider range of city sizes, or a narrower focus on large metropolitan areas or global cities, for instance. The examples discussed in Chaps. 5 and 6 illustrate that difference. Jensen (2014), based on comparing 13 sustainability-oriented city networks, distinguishes networks in terms of three characteristics: mission, scale, and actors. These are reflected in the variation in their primary agendas which include knowledge transfer through learning of good practice, and

© The Author(s) 2017   107
T. Herrschel, P. Newman, *Cities as International Actors*,
DOI 10.1057/978-1-137-39617-4_4

meetings, conferences etc. around specific aspects of common challenges or opportunities. Since the late 1980s, in the face of a growing orientation to the concept of globalisation, which was accompanied by an increasing acceptance of neo-liberalism as political-economic doctrine, cities have increasingly been expected to step outside of established comfort zones of spheres of governance. Instead, they were encouraged, and expected, to become more entrepreneurial (e.g. Hall and Hubbard 1996, 1998) and to develop new policy agendas and initiatives to promote growth by engaging in a new 'politics of flows' (Hubbard 2001). Such more enterprising and innovative city politics were imagined as promoters of local advantages through devising novel policies. This included international engagement—either individually on a one-by-one basis, or collectively, as part of a network. The result is a 'perforated', to borrow Duchachek's term in relation to borders (2001), division between the local and the international. While much of this was driven by a strengthening neo-liberal economic agenda of globalised free trade, 'since the 1990s we have observed an explosion in the activity and number of sustainability-related and web-based city networks' (Keiner and Kim 2007, p. 1369), growing from eight to 49 between 1982 and 2004 (ibid.), and has continued to grow since.

Networks varied in their degree of geographic focus and differed by type of member cities—e.g. size, function, historic linkages—and by topic/agenda as the rallying point for cooperation. Environmental tasks, perceived peripherality, or competitive pressures are potential drivers of such collaborations. Geographically, networks may be limited to a particular region, such as the Baltic Sea (UBC, BaltMet), Mediterranean (MEDCITIES), individual global regions (Eurocities City-net (Europe and Asia)) or to cities with specific characteristics, such as size or economic features. The second main purpose of such networks was found to be lobbying higher tier governments and other agencies/organisations/actors by speaking with a concerted voice and thus gaining more visibility and impact in politics. In such instances, which are particularly evident outside the European Union, such as in North America, local interests in lobbying are very much trained on the respective central government as traditional primary actor in the international arena. Lobbying is thus an expression of reliance on an agent to represent local interests internationally. And the state is held to this as a matter of adhering to its traditional role. International engagement by sub-national governments in North America appears thus most often to be merely indirect. The third purpose of using networks as sounding boards for individual agendas is image projection. Participating in an internationally operating policy network gives the impression of connectedness to, and participation in, global affairs, and thus a certain level of relevance. This matters in a competitive environment, where seeming peripherality on the basis of sheer geographic position or size, may lead to a vicious downward spiral of further marginalisation.

Consequently, the number of sub-national forms of collaboration expanded from eight to 49 networks between 1982 and 2006 (Keiner and Kim 2007) as international city networks dealing with urban development aspects have experienced a boom (Smith and Timberlake 2001). The main driver was the increasingly ubiquitous combination of neo-liberalism driving urban competitiveness and entrepreneurialism, on the one hand, and a more locally engaged sustainability agenda that makes local actors a part of identified global solutions (Bulkeley and Betsill 2005; Prugh et al. 2000), on the other. And this globalised challenge legitimises—even demands—local governments make the effort to enter the global arena. This may be through either direct one-to-one engagement, or through indirect involvement as mediated participation via networks, or lobbying of IOs as presumed more effective and experienced international actors. Examples include such transnational initiatives as the Sustainable Cities Programme of Habitat, or the Healthy Cities Programme of the WHO (Dahiya and Pugh 2000). Particularly in Europe, with its varying geography, history and political-administrative cultures, the density of networking is exceptional, as will be discussed later in this, as well as in the subsequent, chapter (see also Fig. 4.1).

In the past, most international links between local governments were organised through national associations, which possessed limited ambitions beyond national borders on the part of their individual cities and regions. Outside Europe, such as in North America, this view seems to have remained in the background (see Chap. 6), while in Europe, local interests have found a much more supportive environment for going international. For instance, more recently, international connections in Europe appear to have grown through a range of networked associations. Metropolis, the European city network organisation (http://www.metropolis.org), for instance, started with a few city members in 1985 on the initiative of the Paris regional government; London joined at a time when the metropolitan government could find few friends elsewhere and was about to be abolished by a hostile conservative government keen on removing highly visible platforms for opposition politics

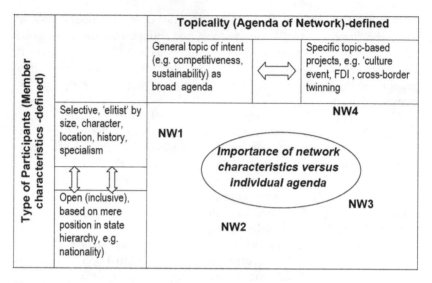

Fig. 4.1 International city network types: based on membership characteristics and/or topicality of agenda

(O'Leary 1987). Metropolis has subsequently expanded to more than 130 members currently, enjoying a more broadened role now in the much wider international local government network of United Cities and Local Governments (UCLG) which has over a thousand affiliated sub-national governments. Now, international networking ranges from links with neighbours across borders to regional and global groupings stretching further afield. Many networks have grown around shared political concerns (peace, human rights, solidarity, etc.) as political rallying points, with most activity focused on environmental issues and questions about urban development. We could see this growth of international networks as a response to global challenges and the desire to share experience, learn from others and to be more able to voice urban and regional concerns on the world stage. Local Agenda 21 as a localised version of the international agreement of Agenda 21 agreed at the Rio Earth Summit in 1992, illustrates this reaching out to sub-national governments from a global angle. But if sub-national networks are a response to global challenges they, in turn, create substantial coordination challenges in the emerging global governance arena, as they each also pursue their particular local agendas (Fig. 4.2).

UCLG- Subsections by Geography
Africa Section/UCLG-Africa
Asia-Pacific Section/UCLG-ASPAC
Eurasia Section/ UCLG-Eurasia
Europe Section/Council of European Municipalities and Regions CEMR
Forum of Regions/UCLG Regions
Latin America Section/Federación Latinoamericana de Ciudades/ Municipos y Asociaciones FLACMA
Metropolitan Section/ Metropolis
Middle East and West Asia Section UCLG-MEWA
UCLG North America Section/ Noram

Fig. 4.2 UCLG—organisation by geography and agendas/missions. *Source:* Based on information from UCLG website, uclg.org

The core themes of this chapter focus on the growth and organisation of these networks of sub-national governments, and their global and regionally based relationships with IOs (including the special case of the EU). Chapter 5 will elaborate on this further by looking at a range of illustrative examples. In so doing, a number of important issues arise, such as questions about the capacity of local governments to interact internationally, and the relative contributions of local governments in global forua. How are agreements achieved and what are the effects of signing up to international policy statements? An important focus here is on the institutional capacities of IOs as partners in many network initiatives to shape global agendas, and on the potentially constraining effects of international norms and agendas on the new, sub-national actors on the world stage. Chapter 3 looked briefly at theories of 'regime complexes' and ideas about the 'cognitive authority' generated by IOs. The resulting suggestion is that complexity may be a better descriptor of the international scene than the perhaps simplistic prospect of coherent regimes embracing both sub-national and international interests. Under the impact of the resulting overlapping and variegated relationships between actors at different scales, state authority may be difficult to orchestrate, so that the state may appear weakened. This leads to a wider discussion of the outcomes in particular of the allocation of authority in networks between several sub-national actors and IOs. And this matters because it affects the legitimacy of policy agreed through international networks and impacts on domestic politics. A question therefore arises about the significance of the achieved outputs on international networking in domestic politics and policy. What effects are the new sub-national actors on the world stage having on the work of IOs, and how do nation states relate to this increasingly complex world of networked knowledge, learning and lobbying? To gain a better understanding, we need to look beyond the easy argument about the 'natural' connectivity of cities that spontaneously create the 'bridging capital' (Barber 2013, p. 115) between local and international scales. Instead, we need to focus, on the gulf between economic or other functional interdependencies between cities, regions and the international arena, and look at the need for developing institutions for cooperation and coordination.

Much international work revolves around functional areas (see Fig. 4.3). For example, in transport planning, the group Cities for Mobility (UCLG 2009), established in 2003, has now 500 members in over 70 states. On environmental issues, ICLEI (International Council for Local Environmental Initiatives), formed in 1990, when more than 200 local governments from 43 countries came together at the World Congress of Local Governments for a Sustainable Future at the United Nations in New York, now counts 1,000 members. And the more recent C40 Climate Group, established by the former London Mayor, Ken Livingstone, in 2008, has now grown to an 'elite' membership of more than 80 self-defined 'global cities'. Meanwhile, a much older grouping focused on urban development, INTA (International Urban Development Association—formerly International New Towns Association), set up 40 years ago, in 1976, now counts 3,000 members, including not only local governments, but also professional and private sector members (http://www.inta.org/). In the

Committees	- Standing Committee on Gender Equality - Decentralization and Local Self-Government - Local Finance and Development - Culture - Development Cooperation and City Diplomacy Social Inclusion, Participative Democracy and Human Rights (CISDP) - Mediterranean Interregional Committee - Urban Health - Peripheral Cities - Urban Mobility - Digital and Knowledge-Based Cities - Urban Strategic Planning
Working Groups	- Capacity and Institution Building (CIB) - Intermediary Cities - Migration and Co-development - Responsible Tourism and Sustainable Development - Local Economic Development - Local governments and Cooperation in Middle-East
Task Forces	- Local Government Disaster Response - Urban Innovation Community

Fig. 4.3 UCLG—thematic committees and working groups. *Source:* Based on information from UCLG website, uclg.org

field of cultural policy, the League of Historical Cities, formed in 1994, lists now over 90 members. Its stated goals are to promote 'borderless and constructive dialogue among historical cities', taking on board the fact that 'Our present world is reaching an age where the "country" as a stronghold is being replaced by a greater, global society where individual countries are not the single entities they used to be' (http://www2.city.kyoto.lg.jp/somu/kokusai/lhcs/about/index.html). Other policy agendas, such as safety and security, however, seem to reside more firmly with nation states, reflecting traditional expectations of state power to enforce rules and protect state territory from an anarchic international realm as imagined by traditional, realist International Relations (Schmidt 1998; Gilpin 2002). Nevertheless, some networks, for example, Mayors for Peace, established in 1982 as an initiative by the Mayor of Hiroshima to push states towards endorsing complete abolition of all nuclear weapons, has now a 5,000-strong membership (http://www.mayorsforpeace.org). And there are some well-established bipartisan links such as that between

New York City and London, where the idea of global citizenship backed the concept of these two cities functioning as effectively one city. Their shared global city status and common Anglo-American background gave the moniker NYLON some credibility (Taylor 2012).

Developed networks operate through conferences and workshops as platforms for sharing experience, offering training and lobbying. Costs are shared, with leading members contributing greater sums, and member fees often transferred between networks. Members may bear the costs of hosting conferences and supporting secretariats. While entailing costs, there may be some prestige attached for individual cities in hosting headquarters as a sign of international connectedness and relevance. Indeed, internal corporate networks stretching across international borders may offer opportunities for cities to follow and build international policy networks (Hoyler 2011). For instance, UCLG is hosted in Barcelona, and is part of the city's energetic internationalisation strategy pursued since its preparations for the 1992 Summer Olympics. Meanwhile, other functions of this now high-profile international network are hosted by different cities to spread out prestige: its Committee on City Diplomacy resides in Lyon, and, as a sign of reaching out beyond the West, that on Urban and Strategic Planning is located in Durban and Porto Alegre. And, as a sign of cultural-linguistic competition and search for status, French cities take leading roles in many networks, often as a stand against too much *anglo-americanisme*.

Some functional areas are more crowded than others, reflecting their perceived political urgency and visibility, with environment, climate change, and energy garnering the largest memberships. In relation to climate change, for instance, multiple-city networks and networks engaging civil society, business and IOs, have developed. The density is particularly high in Europe, mainly a consequence of the UN's Agenda 21 programme following COP21 in Rio in 1992. The Åalborg Charter of European Cities and Towns towards Sustainability of 1994 can be regarded as the starting point for the direct engagement of cities and municipalities across Europe, with requirements imposed on local development policy under the Local Agenda 21 Charter serving as a mobilising factor. This Charter was the outcome of the First European Conference of Sustainable Cities and Towns in Åalborg, Denmark, and the inauguration of the European Cities and Towns Campaign. Some 80 municipalities signed up at the time, and this has now increased as a result of the Åalborg Charter's commitment to long-term action plans toward sustainability and implementing LA21 processes. To date, more than 2,700 local and regional authorities (http://sustainablecities.eu from more than 34 European countries have joined. 'The Campaign has played a key role in defining what a sustainable European city should look like and in setting out a process for making this vision a reality' across Europe (http://sustainablecities.eu).

We have already noted the claim for leadership in the field of climate change by the C40 (the descriptor of its website is Cities Climate Leadership Group), which stakes a claim to taking a lead role in relevant policy development. The C40 secretariat was set up in London with the then London Mayor its first Chair. The network was boosted in 2010 by the leadership of the Mayor of New York, Michael Bloomberg, whose foundation continues to support the network. Bloomberg sees cities clearly in the driving seat on environmental tasks: 'While international negotiations continue to make incremental progress, C40 cities are forging ahead. 'As innovators and practitioners, our cities are at the forefront of this issue' (http://www.c40.org/history). Across policy sectors local government networks are also linked with corporate partners.

A significant development in international networking beyond functional linkages is the expanding role of what we could term 'second-level', multi-function organisations with global reach. UCLG may be regarded as a re-launching of a century-old cooperative network of local governments, that according to Barber (2013, p. 111) no one (from a US perspective) had heard of. The re-launch in 2004 aimed to more actively 'represent and defend the interests of local governments on the world stage' (http://www.uclg.org/en/organisation/about). UCLG incorporates over 1,000 sub-national units and 155 national associations of sub-national governments (although conferences attract a small proportion of the membership). UCLG has well-developed links with the UN and other international 'partners'. Metropolis claims to represent the 'major metropolises' in UCLG, to give 'international political visibility to metropolitan interests' (http://www.metropolis.org/sites/default/files/pdf/plan_accion_2012-2014_en.pdf).

These networks of global reach have different histories, but overlapping functions, out of which new configurations of global alliances have emerged. For example, the Compact of Mayors is an agreement in 2014 by city networks focused on approaches to climate change mitigation and reducing vulnerability and enhancing resilience to climate change The Compact brought together UCLG, ICLEI-Local Governments for Sustainability (ICLEI; http://www.iclei.org), and the C40 Climate

Leadership Group (http://www.c40.org), with a dedicated secretariat. Again, in relation to climate change policy, a multiply networked association began in 2007 with the intention of mirroring the UN's work with states and to secure stronger sub-national representation. This increased institutional capacity adds to the global networks' visibility, and policy-making capacity and credibility. Also, over time, global networks see the need to redefine relations with each other. For example, in 2010, Metropolis redefined its relations with UCLG to clarify the respective roles in strategy making and avoid duplication of efforts through a better division of responsibilities. Similarly, Metropolis sought new links with INTA and reviewed its regional structures and links beyond city governments.

In addition to more general functional and global networks, there are also more interest-specific groupings, such as, for example, AIMF (Association Internationale des Maires Francophones) a network of elected leaders from 48 states with a small secretariat in Paris, and connection to other global sub-national networks. Given the high profile of some global cities in Metropolis and the C40 group, for example, other groupings have emerged to promote other scales and themes of interest to avoid head-on competition for attention. The R20 (Regions of Climate Action) network was promoted by the state of California and formed partnerships with global networks and other regional groupings (the German Länder for example) and now has 560 sub-national and local government members and corporate affiliates supporting its technical projects. Its stated mission is 'To help sub-national governments around the world to develop and communicate low-carbon and climate resilient economic development projects', working through knowledge transfer of successful policies among member cities in order 'to help build an effective green deal flow at sub-national level ... made possible by connecting Regions, Technology and Finance to build sustainable low-carbon projects' (http://regions20. org/about/mission). Again, in response to the perceived dominance of global cities, the FALP network was created by the Forum of Local Authorities for Social Inclusion in 2001 and the World Social Forum (WSF) in Porto Alegre in 2001 with the aim of 'promoting local initiatives for social inclusion and participatory democracy and expand the capacity of social and political intervention of locals governments'. This initial agenda was extended a year later to include the geographically defined problem of peripherality for cities within globalisation processes, and the associated obstacles for development (http://www.redefalp.com/ en/sobre). Accordingly, FALP is part of the broader UCLG Committee on 'Peripheral Cities' and titled its first meeting 'Another Look at the Metropolis from the Peripheries'.

Global networks have well-developed regional structures with connection to existing regionally organised groupings of sub-national governments. Metropolis for example, is structured into five Regional Secretariats (Africa, Asia Pacific, Europe, Latin America and the Caribbean, and North America), and through this can target network development within regions, currently for example in India, China and Brazil. Some of the membership fees of global networks can be channelled to regional sections that are in need of support and development, for example, in the case of Metropolis to ASPAC (Asia Pacific) and FLACMA (Latin American Federation of Cities, Municipalities and Municipal Associations), and the Compact of Mayors relies on coordination through regional associations—in Europe through the Council of European Municipalities and Regions (CCRE/CEMR founded in 1951). Regional structures have been expanding. In Latin America, FLACMA was established in 1999 out of regional associations created in the 1980s that subsequently joined together to organise the Latin American voice on the world stage. Since 2004 it has acted as the Latin American section of UCLG.

In Asia, CITYNET was established in 1987 with the support of UNESCAP, UNDP and UN-HABITAT to address the particular needs of the rapidly growing cities in the newly industrialising Asian Tiger states of the Asia Pacific. The network started with 27 members, and an independent secretariat set up in 1992 in Yokohama with the financial support of that city. CITYNET was created to 'promote cooperative links and partnerships throughout the Asia Pacific in order to improve the sustainability of our cities'. Its origins go back to 1982 and the 1st Regional Congress of Local Authorities for the Development of Human Settlements in the Asia Pacific, held in Yokohama. In 2015, there were 85 full and 45 associate members (http://citynet-ap.org/category/members-and-partners/associate-members/). 'The Congress stressed the need to build cooperative links between local level governments and urban stakeholders' (http://citynet-ap.org/category/about/history/).

From that point on, CITYNET has maintained cooperative links and partnerships throughout the Asia Pacific region with now 87 full members and the secretariat subsequently moved to Seoul in 2013 (http://citynet-ap.org/category/about/history/). The network has expanded, and more recently has targeted enhanced links with South Asia (where 40% of its members are located) through an MCGM-supported (Municipal

Corporation of Greater Mumbai) satellite office. Regional associations represent 'their' regions in the global networks and also maintain their own inter-regional connections. For example, FACMA receives some support from other local government federations, including advice, 'best practice' and support and development from the Federation of Canadian Local Authorities, and both FACMA and CITYNET are linked to European partners. There, the European Eurocities network has developed extensive connections in other global regions.

UCLG's 'world stage' is separated into numerous regional groupings of sub-national units, thus reflecting variations in cultures, agendas and ways of doing things. For example, UCLG Africa is a 'Pan African association of municipalities and national/regional local government associations in Africa' (http://www.awasla.org/uclg-africa), with 40 national associations of local governments and about 2,000 large cities (with populations over 100,000). Just as UCLG has done on the global scale, UCLG Africa is a reorganisation and unification of pre-existing groupings of local governments, and engages directly with organisations of African states and with IOs. The stated aim is 'seeking a paradigm shift for more sustainable, resilient and equitable urban water and sanitation practices in Africa' (http://www.awasla.org/uclg-africa). In 2015, UCLG Africa signed a partnership agreement on development cooperation with the European Commission, thus connecting the two global regions and establishing a North–South relationship between African cities and the EU as an international organisation with a strong urban voice.

In Chap. 3, we emphasised the enhanced capacity (Niederhafner 2013) of European cities for international work in the unique context of supportive higher level government. Chapters 5 and 6 will explore some of this work in detail, and here we just need to note the global connections of European networks. Eurocities, which began as a lobby organisation with six founding member cities in 1986, and now has over 130 full members and 40 partner cities, supported by some 50 staff in its Brussels office, opened in 1992 and works through engaging members in conferences, workshops, thematic forums and publications. The declared 'objective is to reinforce the important role that local governments should play in a multilevel governance structure. We aim to shape the opinions of Brussels stakeholders and ultimately shift the focus of EU legislation in a way which allows city governments to tackle strategic challenges at local level' (http://www.eurocities.eu/eurocities/about_us). Members argue that they are best able to deliver EU policy, not least on energy and social policy (Eurocities 2015), when working with wide networks and with EU and national institutions. In the unique European context, the consultative Committee of the Regions offers a formal place in policy-making since the Treaty of Lisbon (2009), contributing information, allowing knowledge transfer and providing a platform for articulating local voice. Despite this institutionally formalised status, the CoR brings only variable influence (162), depending on the issues involved, and the differing interests of nation states, on whose formal support city governments—and Eurocities—depend for gaining traction in the EU's political system.

The other main lobbying agent at the international (European) level is the Council of European Municipalities and Regions (CEMR) as a more inclusive local government lobbying network than Eurocities with its more 'elite', large city membership. Going right back to the origins of the European Union, CEMR was established in 1951 as an umbrella organisation for all national representations of sub-national government. Today, CEMR, through the national representations, represents the interests of European local authorities in more than 40 countries in the EU's policy-making machinery. In so doing, it 'promotes citizenship and exchange between elected representatives' in some 150,000 local governments (http://www.ccre.org/en/article/introducing_cemr). But CEMR also reaches beyond the EU, being part of the globally operating UCLG network which, through its main office in Barcelona, 'represents and defends the interests of local governments on the world stage, regardless of the size of the communities they serve'. Its declared mission is 'to be the united voice and world advocate of democratic local self-government, promoting its values, objectives and interests, through cooperation between local governments, and within the wider international community' (http://www.uclg.org/en/organisation/about).

Lobbying activity includes, of course, acting as platform for debate, working through several thematic policy committees as individual topical 'round tables' to coordinate agendas and also provide for knowledge transfer and exchanges of 'good practice'. And it is this role that offers particular opportunities to function as leader and agent in transnational, cross-border and inter-municipal connectivity/engagement, whether in tandem with corresponding action at state level, or less so, depending also on the need to bring on board national government to achieve influence on policy-making processes at the international level. It is, after all, (still) the nation states that ultimately wield the power to conclude international treaties to the standards of international law. The collectively oriented agenda is reflected in the CEMR's five main thematic areas, which reach beyond mere interaction between administrations, but also address policies that are closely related to the lives and interests of their citizens. This is an important element of attracting interest and support, and thus gaining legitimacy, for action beyond conventionally bounded responsibilities (http://www.ccre.org/en/article/introducing_cemr). For the sake of building political weight and credibility in lobbying, demonstrating representativeness of citizens' concerns and interests, and thus public legitimacy as speaking 'for the people' and not just the institutions, CEMR only considers applications for membership of countries and their municipal representations which fulfil the democratic conditions of the Council of Europe. This means first and foremost the holding of local free elections as a sign of at least some elements of local policy-making capacity, rather than merely being the local executive arm of central government.

Inclusiveness and representativeness of the variety of interests at the local level allow for more than one municipal representation per country to become members. For the same reason, national representation, be that through one or more municipal association, needs to represent at least one-third of a country's municipalities (http://www.ccre.org/en/article/introducing_cemr). In Europe, there is thus, in effect, a two-tier internationality—within and outside the EU. This differs from elsewhere, where there is a simpler two-tier differentiation between domestic (national) and international. In the North American context, for instance, the domestic (national) level is filled in the United States by the inclusive, 'catch all' League of Cities, which focuses on best practice for US cities, but also manages in close consultation with the White House extensive international connections, such as, for instance, with UCLG. As a more 'elite group' of larger cities with an inherently stronger interest in international opportunities, the US Conference of Mayors (http://usmayors.org) has maintained longstanding links with the even more elitist global association, Metropolis: 'for more than 30 years, Metropolis has had the mission of accompanying cities in mutual learning, innovation, governance, technical and financial assistance, international presence and debate' (http://www.metropolis.org/about-us#mission). All these various networks and engagements by local government illustrate the transscalar nature of international governance beyond the notion of uniform nation states: sub-national actors become increasingly 'restless' in the face of globalisation and the pressures for increased competitiveness and politically needed 'success'.

4.2   Sub-National Networks and International Organisations

Regional and global networks all have substantial interaction with IOs as an alternative indirect route to international presence and engagement next to collaborative networks as discussed above. In Chap. 3, we discussed some of the themes in the literature relating to networking and the outputs of international work, and considered the relations with IOs in the creation of policy norms and the relative influence of networks in global governance. We return to those debates here noting, as in Chap. 3, Alger's (2011, p. 1) perception of the 'escalating participation in the UN system' of governments other than states. Networks are not only engaged with UN agencies but also with the World Bank and other private actors on the world stage. What is clear from our review so far is the complexity of network links, the overlapping regional and global links and overlapping concerns and numerous joint initiatives. This leads to equally complex relationships between sub-national networks and IOs. It is in this complexity that we see some of the 'operating system' referred to by Stone (2013) underpinning global governance. Our initial review of the related IR literature in Chap. 3, highlighted ideas about the selective incentives offered by IOs, the circulation of policy ideas and establishment of governance norms and 'cognitive authority', a concept developed more than 30 years ago in relation to the construction of knowledge through second-hand information, such as through networks (Wilson 1983), rather than through primary information obtained from own direct experience. Given the density of sub-national networking, the orchestration of authority (Abbot and Snidal 2010) we discussed in Chap. 3, looks challenging if it is to be targeted and effective. In exploring the connections between networks and IOs we need to review these ideas about emerging global governance. The UN encourages non-state actors to engage with its Climate Change Summits as a way of gaining legitimacy and public support for its policy recommendations and thus build pressure on national governments to follow up agreed recommendation for policies. Global networks engaged with numerous meetings in preparation for COP21, the 2015 Paris Climate Conference, and reached across different tiers of government from local to international (Tollin 2015).

Much of this work is coordinated through the Compact of Mayors, an agreement in 2014 by city networks focused on approaches to climate change mitigation and reducing vulnerability and to enhance resilience to climate change. The Compact brought together ICLEI-Local Governments for Sustainability (http://www.iclei.org), the C40 Climate Leadership Group, and UCLG with a dedicated secretariat. The role of the C40 group is significant, and the city–IO relationship personified in former Mayor Bloomberg, now the UN Secretary-General's Special Envoy for Cities and Climate Change (http://www.compactofmayors.org/history/), symbolises the close link between global city and the UN as global organisation. Not surprisingly, seeking to boost its eminent international position, New York, now given extra voice by its former Mayor's international role, claimed global city leadership on climate change, and publicised efforts to reduce urban CO_2 levels through the 'PlaNYC' plan for a greener and less polluted city. After leaving office, Bloomberg's foundation continued to fund the C40 group and thus maintains its longer-term strategic input. Even so, sub-national representation at the UN Summit was not easily agreed. UN and sub-national leaders may share objectives, but the UN is a federation of nation states, and is often unable to reach agreements, such as at the previous COP World Climate Summit meetings.

A number of preparatory events, for example, six months before COP21, offered opportunities for all the major groups of non-state actors (sub-national and local governments, NGOs, business, workers and trade unions, youth, women, scientists) to make their voices heard (http://www.worldclimatesummit2015.org). The city case was headed by Bloomberg and the Mayor of Paris, both based in states that are relatively supportive of the COP agenda. This mattered, as they could work with added political credibility, rather than being constrained by the headwinds of national interest. France, in particular, with a historically integrated national/sub-national system, has perhaps shown less weariness in allowing other sub-national voices into policy debate. ICLEI organised a 'Cities and Regions Pavilion' at the COP21 meeting in Paris for cities (http://www.cities-and-regions.org/) to promote their roles and attempt to exercise some influence over national representatives. Through the jointly sponsored 'Climate Summit for Local Leaders' cities could claim much greater recognition at UN conferences. As a result of the combined resources of the host city and Bloomberg, and working through the global networks to mobilise interest and debate, sub-national activities at COP21 were extensive with over 1,000 governments represented. This resulted in a 'Paris City Hall Declaration' committing sub-national governments to further engagement with IOs, states, business and civil societies to deliver on their moral responsibility for action, given their role in contributing to the problem in the first place (http://www.uclg.org/sites/default/files/climate_summit_final_declaration.pdf).

The UN's Habitat III (United Nations Conference on Housing and Sustainable Urban Development), to be held in Quito in 2016, shows similar engagement of sub-national networks in preparatory work. The conference aims to set a new platform for nation states to formulate a global framework for urban policy, and local authorities can achieve representation in different ways. Thus, to be able to register for participation in Habitat III under the auspices of an NGO, or as members of a national delegation, the respective states need to approve such application. Member states thus act as de facto gatekeepers, although any negative decision would need to be justified to the Bureau, i.e. the body overseeing the Habitat III process within the UN (http://citiscope.org/habitatIII/news/2015/). Through a number of publications the UN has sought to define city roles, for example, in the 2014 'Action Area' for cities (http://www.un.org/climatechange/summit/action-areas),   including the UN's commitment to be doing more at sub-national scale through existing local government networks, or the UN Habitat's 'Urban Planning for City Leaders', launched in 2013. The presidents of Metropolis and UCLG sought a coordinated relationship with UN Habitat to minimise duplication of efforts and/or contradictory initiatives. And in Habitat III, we might expect the strongest case for orchestration (Blauberger and Rittberger 2015) in the alliance, as the UN welcomes other actors to counter the impasse of successive meetings of nation states by adding more alternative voices and pressures from outside the 'regular' national positions.

Yet, adding the sub-national voice is not always welcome by national governments. Thus, at preparatory meetings for Habitat III (in Nairobi in 2015) states failed to reach agreement on allowing a formal voice for local authorities and stakeholders in these negotiations. In the debate over a list of Sustainable Development Goals (SDGs) to guide global development work for the next 15 years, urban 'partners' had to mount a sustained campaign to include a specific goal related to urban development, and, eventually, after protests, language covering cities was inserted. Realist perspectives quite evidently still seem to have significant influence on national actors' perception of who matters in shaping international relations and agreements. Nevertheless, the UN's post-2015 development agenda continues sub-national involvement through extensive publications, conferences and a joint 'World Urban Campaign' with 'City Partners' promoting

UN objectives. The campaign for an urban SDG included UN SDSN, UN-Habitat, the World Urban Campaign, UCLG, Cities Alliance, ICLEI, the Coalition for Sustainable Cities and Regions, and many other such networks of sub-national actors. As a result, at the meeting in Rome, the Vatican, for instance, as a city state, could equally be considered both a state and a city actor. In addition to regional groupings, sub-national governments also make other links, for example, through common language. The *Réseau Habitat et Francophonie* (RHF), for example, was founded in 1987, linking sub-national governments in 17 francophone countries, and explicitly included relationships with the UN, as well as with other IOs, such as the World Bank.

Both global (UCLG, ICLEI, Metropolis, Compact of Mayors) and macro-regional networks (for example, Asia Pacific Urban Forum (APUF-6)) worked on the new urban agenda. Addressing wider development issues, the UN-Habitat World Urban Forum brings sub-national actors together around issues of equity, and thus builds links between private actors, civil society and sub-national governments. The 7th World Urban Forum, convened by UN-Habitat in Medellin, Colombia, brought together some 22,000 attendees, recruited from a mix of governments, private sector, IOs, academia, professionals and civil society (http://unhabitat. org/7th-world-urban-forum-medellin-declaration/). Other international partners have joined some of the initiatives in these fields, for example the UN-Habitat/World Bank Cities Alliance: Cities without Slums in Berlin in 1999, inaugurated in high-profile fashion by Nelson Mandela (http://www.citiesalliance.org/cws-action-plan), selecting those agendas that best fit with their respective local objectives. Across different policy fields, we can thus witness the 'escalating participation' of governments other than (nation) states. The UN also shapes sub-national participation in specific ways, for example by setting up an advisory Committee of Local Authorities in 2000 and through a 'Best Practice and Local Leadership' initiative (http://mirror.unhabitat.org/categories.asp?catid=508) that includes the World Urban Forum and Sustainable Cities programmes and working with the IULA and ICLEI in Cities for Change. Here, an explicit commitment to sub-national government involvement is made by pointing out that 'The main objective of the UN-Habitat Liaison Office in Madrid is to support local government in achieving the Millennium Development Goals' (http://mirror.unhabitat.org/categories.asp?catid=508).

Sub-national networks also contribute to the WSF, a form of counter-initiative to the annual World Economic Forum in Davos. Accordingly, the focus is on reducing inequality and increasing democratic control and equity by enlarging the scope for participation and giving a voice to a larger group of smaller, sub-national and NGOs—in a deliberate turn away from the established routine elite voices of IOs, such as the WTO, and the nation state governments (Campolina 2015). The very large numbers of participants, for example 155,000 in Porto Alegre in 2005, suggest a much broader-based debate and political process than traditional international meetings of states generate. Other global/urban priorities, migration for example, also generate IO/sub-national network cooperation. UCLG, for instance, participated in the project 'Mediterranean City-to-City Migration Profiles and Dialogue', alongside ICMPD (International Centre for Migration Policy Development) and UN-Habitat. Similarly, in relation to economic development, UCLG is active in global meetings for local government (World Forum of Local Economic Development (LED)). At its last meeting, in Turin in 2015, LED was hailed as a crucial avenue for more local involvement in global governance: 'Local Economic Development (LED) is suggested as a tool for implementing the future agenda at the local level and advises [*sic*] a reviewed global economic governance structure' (http://www.ledforumtorino2015.org/).

This new and expanding range of interactions has driven a need to reconsider relations among networks, and between networks and IOs. Connections between IOs bring private actors into global networks as partners, for example in the numerous cooperative programmes supported by UN-Habitat and the World Bank. The Cities Alliance (World Bank plus the UN, UCLG, ICLEI and some states and other private partners) works regionally, for example through Future Cities Africa. The World Bank's programmes in relation to local governments include strategy making and norm setting, as well as funding specific projects (http://www. worldbank.org/en/topic/urbandevelopment/overview). Metropolis has reviewed its inter-network relations as well as relations with UNACLA (United Nations Advisory Council for Local Authorities) and OECD and the World Bank. New World Bank initiatives—such as the creation of the FMDV (Global Fund for Cities Development)—were seen as offering the chance to enhance these relations with projects of particular importance for the future of the network. Adopting the IO vantage point, OECD supports the UCLG perspective of multi-level governance (http://www. uclg.org/en/media/news/uclg-and-oecd-sign-agreement-strengthen-collaboration#sthash.n7uo1eAG.dpuf), i.e. embracing the sub-national as well as supra-national level of governing. Such, in effect, supportive outreach by IOs to the local level to encourage participation in global governance can also be found with the Commonwealth Secretariat, for instance, as it supports a Local Government Forum to 'strengthen and promote local government' (http://thecommonwealth.org/organisation/commonwealth-local-government-forum-clgf). In addition, the Office also supports connections to city networks and sub-national governments through a 'developmental local government' programme which connects to the UN Global Forum, the regional Busan Partnership, Rio+20 EU and Habitat III (Habitat 2013 Conference Report).

IOs connect to city networks also through global or regional awards and competitions such as those of membership networks Metropolis (http://www.metropolis.org/awards) and Eurocities (http://www.eurocities.eu/eurocities/eurocities-awards) and those sponsored privately for example in the World Bank's IFC (International Finance Corporation)/Financial Times 'Excellence in City Transformation' awards. Collecting awards can be important for second cities or others not at the top of national priorities or international recognition. For example, Danang City was awarded 'Excellence in City Transformation' by the Financial Times and IFC in 2015 (http://aboutus.ft.com/2015/06/11/2015-ftifc-transformational-business-awards-winners-announced/#axzz3uOOokQUy), and recognised in the 'Smarter City' programme by IBM (https://www-03.ibm.com/press/us/en/pressrelease/41754.wss). Danang City was also selected from 400 cities in the world to join the Rockefeller Foundation's '100 Resilient Cities' in 2013 (https://www.rockefellerfoundation.org/our-work/initiatives/100-resilient-cities/). Competitions and awards help raise profiles and also ensure the transfer of lessons, while reinforcing the cognitive authority of IOs.

Connections and interrelationships create complexity and raise a series of questions about the impact of international work, not least in terms of political impact. As some IOs become more politicised (see Zürn et al. 2012), how do emerging policy conclusions and norms play out in the policy-making of global and regional networks and further in the domestic politics of sub-national governments? Around the politics of Habitat III, for example, and the visible interventions of global advocacy groups and shifts in public opinion, internationalism may look like a political necessity to achieve individual goals, especially in the fields of economic development and counteracting climate change. The rise of global activism, with growing numbers of representatives of NGOs finding their way into the centres of international governance such as Geneva (United Nations organisations) and Brussels (EU governing bodies), is evidence of the increasing politicisation of policy-making. But it also reflects a growing disquiet among individual interest groups at the sub-national level, that they are being listened to less, as globalisation seems to produce a growing inequality between those whose voice and interests matter, and those whose concerns do not, matter as much. This affects divisions within society across all geographic scales, as well as between cities and sub-national and supra-national regions.

As a result, there is increasingly less willingness to simply continue to rely on the nation state as negotiator and interlocutor between the interests within and outside a state. Globalised economic conditions and other complex issues, such as climate change, have become too competitive and pressing to just sit back and wait for opportunities to be handed down. The likelihood of political rewards, as well as a growing willingness and felt necessity to be more entrepreneurial about pursuing specific subnational interests beyond the borders of their own state and individual localities, have resulted in new forms and modes of operating in international/global politics and governance. The political opportunity structures (Tarrow 2005) provided by IOs, while being important reference points for such ambitions by sub-national actors, have also been changed by the growing complexity of interactions among sub-national actors and networks. For instance, IOs that are politicised may grant more generous access to civil society organisations in order to enhance their own legitimacy of action and decision-making. International work may no longer be undertaken behind closed doors but in more public struggles to also shape public opinion as potential political tailwind for IOs' own decisions and agendas.

4.3   Summary

This chapter looked at two of the three main avenues available to subnational actors, especially cities, for international engagement in governance mechanisms and processes—using intermediaries in the form of IOs or through collaborative networks. Their attraction is the increased capacity, competence and thus likely efficacy of such organisations, especially for cities with a less than 'global city' status. Network regimes and the cognitive authority of technocratic IOs suggest easy, simple and predictable uni-directional transfer of policy between scales from the international to the local. (For a discussion of recent debate on policy transfer see, for example, Benson and Jordan 2012.) The work of IOs in setting governance norms and circulating policy ideas, and, particularly in the EU, the offering of selective incentives to facilitate collective action, may be seen as features of the innate 'operating system' (Stone 2013) that constructs the 'informal governance' across new platforms, partnerships and alliances of policy-making. With the operating networks, by their nature, being relatively under-resourced in comparison with formal, institutionalised structures, an asymmetry of influence might be expected, placing the formal structures in a relatively advantaged position to promote their interests and agendas. And this is in addition to the already existing plurality of coordination challenges and their associated political manoeuvres.

In addition, we should expect consequences for practical governance at city level, such as changes in cities' organisational structures to facilitate effective engagement in international work. This includes, for instance, the dedication of secretariats to networks, or establishing representative (diplomatic) offices, to give the networks more presence and identity, and thus presumed capacity to act effectively and more visibly. IOs, in turn, need to resource increasingly diverse events and associated activities, and sustain pressure on policy-making processes and schedules, so as to produce successful outcomes to justify the resources needed to the organisation membership. Technocratic IOs, such as in public administration, have also to manage the charismatic authority of strong personalities in some policy fields, as these can easily develop their own political momentum and agency. In this respect, we could see the appointment of Bloomberg as special representative at the United Nations as both the co-option of a dominant voice, in close collaboration with the UN General Secretary, and the ceding of some initiative to sub-national networks. Here, the personality, rather than the organisation, has become the connector between sub-national and international/global interests and politics. IOs may have technocratic assets for policy development, but increasingly they have to engage in policy diplomacy which draws on personal relationships and diplomacy skills. Structures alone are not sufficient to achieve that.

The 'strategically situated agents', brokering between interests and agendas at the intersection of organisations involved in networked governance (Eccleston et al. 2013), as identified in Chap. 3, may appear from both IOs and collective networks of cities, as effective leaders or representatives that can achieve results which satisfy the membership. Power in complex arrangements and relationships, more or less regime-like, will be dispersed to a broader range of actors, and individual sub-national actors, especially the larger cities, are trying to avail themselves of a good stake in that. However, in developing overlapping interrelationships between networks, the secretariats of some IOs or networks may be able to secure and project more influence than others (Jinnah 2014), reflecting the range of actors involved, their political stature, and their capacities and capabilities in shaping governance. By the same token, IOs can have a constraining effect on sub-national actors by projecting a principle of order and procedure through their operational and discursive hegemony for one or more policy agenda, making it difficult for individual sub-national actors to ignore that and try to go their own ways. Cities and regions can also draw benefits from IOs in their role as nodes in an international system of network relations, where states continue to dominate as primary actors. It may have become less easy for IOs (including the EU after the euro crisis), however, as a result of a certain loss of credibility in their effectiveness in dealing with international/global crises, to co-opt sub-national 'partners' and 'orchestrate' authority.

International work includes determining the agenda, developing strategies and agendas, recruiting new and/or maintaining existing followers, while also paying for the realisation of proclaimed agendas to demonstrate effectiveness . There is some affinity here with the notion of a policy cycle or policy flow, described by Stone (2008, p. 13). This moves from agenda setting (after problem definition) or policy conceptualisation, via policy implementation, to policy monitoring for impact and/or achieved results (Kingah et al. 2015). This flow of stages can be seen as a consensus-based, informal decision-making process, rather than driven by provisions and procedures that are binding on the basis of legal treaties. Both the effectiveness and legitimacy of IOs and their global networks depend on their outputs, rather than the inherent quality of policy-making processes. In effect, results justify the means. Rousselin (2015, pp. 3–4) distinguishes between, on the one hand, legitimacy as an inherent property of the rules and processes of governance arrangements, and, on the other, the legitimation of solutions derived from debate and interaction of a variety of actors as an informal, implicit assent. Legitimate policy outcomes may well be the result of 'structural asymmetry' (Rousselin 2015, p. 13) among participants, where some participants are more influential than others, to the point of being hegemonic in terms of discursive and/or practical politics and power. Here, the perceived transparency and accountability of the decision process may help legitimate outcomes, but effective results will also be demanded. How well new global networks and IOs manage on the world stage, and thus justify their recognition as actors, depends on their understanding of the opportunities constructed through multiple and overlapping relationships, and the ability to utilise them in political agency and effective policy-making. Regime complexes may provide opportunities for venue-shopping, for example, but may also generate conflict and even turf wars about goals, agendas or best ways forward. But these are the processes and struggles that constitute emerging global governance. The following two chapters will look in more detail at the other main route of international engagement by sub-national actors to gain a foothold in international and/or global governance: 'going it alone' as an independent, individual actor, rather than (needing to) rely on mediators such as IOs or networks.

REFERENCES

Abbott, K.W. and Snidal, D., 2010. International regulation without international government: improving IO performance through orchestration. *The Review of International Organizations, 5*(3), 315–344.

Alger, C., 2011. Searching for Democratic Potential in Emerging Global Governance: What Are the Implications of Regional and Global Involvements of Local Governments? *International Journal of Peace Studies, 16*(2), 1–24.

Barber, B., 2013. *If Mayors Ruled the World. Dysfunctional Nations, Rising Cities.* New Haven: Yale University Press.

Benson, D. and Jordan, A., 2012. Policy transfer research: still evolving, not yet through? *Political Studies Review, 10*(3), 333–38.

Blauberger, M. and Rittberger, B., 2015. Orchestrating Policy Implementation: EU Governance through Regulatory Networks. *International Organizations as Orchestrators*, 39–64.

Bulkeley, H. and Betsill, M., 2005. Cities and climate change: urban sustainability and global environmental governance (Vol. 4). London: Routledge.

Campolina, A., 2015. World Social Forum can inspire activists to unite against the global power grab. In: *The Guardian*, 23 Mar 15.

Dahiya, B. and Pugh, C., 2000. *The localization of Agenda 21 and the sustainable cities programme. Sustainable Cities in Developing Countries: Theory and Practice at the Millennium.* London: Earthscan.

Eccleston, R., Kellow, A. and Carroll, P., 2013. G20 Endorsement in Post Crisis Global Governance: More than a Toothless Talking Shop? *British Journal of Politics and International Relations*, 1–20.

Eurocities 2015. Strategic Framework 2014 – 2020, http://nws.eurocities.eu/MediaShell/media/141218%20EUROCITIES%20strategic%20framework_FINAL.pdf (accessed 19/10/15)

Gilpin, R. 2002. A Realist Perspective on International Governance, In: D. Held and A. McGrew (eds.): *Governing Globalization: Power, Authority, and Global Governance*. Cambridge: Polity Press.

Hall, T. and Hubbard, P., 1996. The entrepreneurial city: new urban politics, new urban geographies? *Progress in human geography*, 20(2), 153–174.

Hall, T. and Hubbard, P. eds., 1998. *The entrepreneurial city: geographies of politics, regime, and representation*. John Wiley & Sons.

Hoyler, M., 2011. External relations of German cities through intra-firm networks—A global perspective. *Raumforschung und Raumordnung*, 69(3), 147–159.

Hubbard, P., 2001. The Politics of Flow: On Birmingham, Globalization and Competitiveness, Globalisation and World Cities, *GaWC Research Bulletin*, Available at *lboro.ac.uk/gawc*.

Keiner, M. and Kim, A., 2007. Transnational City Networks for Sustainability, *European Planning Studies*, 15(10), 1369–1395.

Kingah, S., Schmidt V. and Yong Wang., 2015. Setting the scene: the European Union's engagement with transnational policy networks, *Contemporary Politics*, 21(3), 231–244.

Jensen, M.D., 2014. Game Changing – Tracing the Positions, Strategies and Interaction Modes of the German Länder towards the (Ever Expanding?) *European Union, Regional & Federal Studies*, DOI: 10.1080/13597566.2014.911737.

Jinnah, S., 2014 *Post-treaty politics: secretariat influence in global environmental governance*. Cambridge, MA: MIT Press.

Niederhafner S., 2013. Comparing functions of transnational city networks in Europe and Asia, *Asia Europe Journal*, 11, 377–396.

O'Leary, B., 1987. Why was the GLC abolished?. *International Journal of Urban and Regional Research*, 11(2), 193–217.

Prugh, T., Costanza, R. and Daly, H.E., 2000. The local politics of global sustainability. Island Press.

Rousselin, M., 2015. The Power of Legitimation: The Role of Expert Networks in Global Environmental Governance. *Journal of Environmental Policy & Planning*, 1–17.

Schmidt, B.C., 1998. *The political discourse of anarchy: a disciplinary history of international relations*. New York: SUNY Press.

Smith, D.A. and Timberlake, M.F., 2001. World City Networks and Hierarchies, 1977–1997 An Empirical Analysis of Global Air Travel Links. *American Behavioral Scientist*, 44(10), 1656–1678.

Stone, D., 2008. Global Public Policy, Transnational Policy Communities, and Their Networks, *Policy Studies Journal*, 36(1), 19–38.

Stone, R., 2013. Informal governance in international organizations: Introduction to the special issue, *Review of International Organisations*, 8, 121–136.

Tarrow, S., 2005. The New Transnational Activism. Cambridge: Cambridge University Press.

Taylor, P.J., 2012. The interlocking network model. In: edited by B. Derudder, M. Hoyler, P. Taylor and F. Witlox (eds.): *International handbook of globalization and world cities.* Cheltenham: Edward Elgar, pp. 51–64.

Tollin, N., 2015. The role of cities and local authorities following COP21 and the Paris Agreement. Càtedra UNESCO de Sostenibilitat de la UPC [Universitat Politecnica Catalunya], available under: http://upcommons.upc.edu/handle/2117/82004, accessed 2 Apr 16.

UCLG (United Cities and Local Governments) 2009. Agenda21 for Urban Mobility. Cities for Mobility.

Wilson, P., 1983. *Second-hand knowledge: An inquiry into cognitive authority.* Westport, CT: Greenwood Press.

Zürn, M., Binderand, M. and Ecker-Erhardt, M., 2012. International Political Authority and Its Politicization, *International Theory,* 4(1), 69–106.

CHAPTER 5

Individual Initiatives by Cities in Europe

5.1   Introduction

City networks are not the only way of cities seeking to gain international visibility and access to policies, politics and economic developments at that scale. Individual cities may well 'go it alone', with the larger metropolitan areas and, especially, the 'global cities', primary candidates for singular city-to-city or city-to-international organisation engagement, because of their institutional capacity, likely economic foundations and ambitions. In this way, the EU offers a unique and distinctive context through its history of region-focused, i.e. sub-nationally oriented, policy measures. This is one of the decisive differences to the situation in North America, for instance, as discussed in Chap. 6. The growing focus on devolution of responsibilities as part of the multi-level governance discussed in Chap. 3, has encouraged cities to step out of their regional and national contexts and seek to utilise EU funding and administrative regimes to boost, and lobby for, their own interests outside national institutional straitjackets. This has taken two main avenues: (1) bilateral, at times, multi-lateral, action by cities, such as through 'town twinning', and (2) cities establishing international offices in Brussels, following in this effort by regions, to lobby EU institutions and act as marketing and communication offices for international business. While the former has developed since the 1950s, in response to the traumatic experiences of the Second World War, as well as an integral part of the EU's policies to foster integration, the second is

© The Author(s) 2017
T. Herrschel, P. Newman, *Cities as International Actors*,
DOI 10.1057/978-1-137-39617-4_5

a much more recent development. Driven by growing pressures for raised competitiveness under the impact of increasing globalisation, cities (and regions) have begun, since the mid to late 1990s, to enter the international—and global—arena of capitalism in an attempt to carve out new opportunities and stakes in economic development beyond those available as part of a nation state's economic space. This chapter will examine the two main policy frameworks within which cities establish direct international relations with other cities of IOs: the city twinning scheme and the EU's European Capital of Culture scheme.

Under the first route of individual urban engagement, bilateral arrangements, town twinning and, in Europe, 'Capital of Culture' nominations, have become important vehicles for the EU to facilitate cross-border and cross-national relationships, 'get-to-knows' and, of course, integration as the ultimate objective. The idea and scheme of 'twinning' have been copied elsewhere. Examples include the transatlantic city partnerships of US cities engaged with European partners, or the US–South Korea Sister Cities Relationships (http://www.asiamattersforamerica.org/south-korea/data/sistercities). Both, like the European scheme, are a policy of building peace-time relationships following a major war. In the case of US–South Korea Sister Cities Relationships, some 60 city pairs exist on the back of bilateral agreements between cities across international borders, which both advertise and facilitate links between cities as an expression and utilisation of collaboration between the partner states. Such agreements about city partnerships are also seen as symbolic statements that the two countries 'matter' to each other (http://www.asiamattersfora-merica.org/southkorea/data/sistercities). National strategic geo-political and geo-economic interests between the United States and South Korea, including South Korea's security needs, have thus, in effect, been projected onto these city partnerships as visible ties between both countries.

Although limited to Europe and less geo-politically loaded than the US–South Korean city twinning scheme, the EU scheme 'European Capital of Culture' seeks to build new international awareness of cities and their countries, and, increasingly, those which are struggling with peripherality or structural economic change. Starting off as a display of great European art and culture, as a manifestation of common European cultural values, this scheme has increasingly become a vehicle for lesser known, more peripheral places to step into the limelight of internationality, at least for the year-long nomination (see Fig. 5.1). This is to counteract a likely growing divide between the traditionally more outward-oriented

Single city initiatives post War until c1990	Single city initiative 1990 on
1945	2016
Main features: - bridging borders to 'heal' divisions (especially in Europe) - driving new internationality with lesser 'risk' at lower profile than state level - acting as 'ambassadors' of states - cities seen as integral to state territory, - state represented through cities	**Main features:** - overcoming borders to pursue new opportunities on international arena - enhancing local (and national) economic competitiveness and opportunities - reaching beyond state borders to joining city networks - 'freeing' from state territorial ties (as hindrances) and pursue presumed greater opportunities individually
Examples: - European City of Culture - Sister Cities International (SCI) - United Towns Organization (UTO), (Fédération mondiale des villes jumelées) - Council of European Municipalities and Regions (CEMR)	**Examples:** - European Capital of Culture - Brussels International Offices - United Cities and Local Government (UCLG)

Fig. 5.1   International activities by individual cities

cities, such as port cities or, of course, national capitals, and 'lesser' cities in more distant and peripheral locations, suffering from limited economic development prospects. Egality in spatial development and opportunity is an important consideration here (Kiran et al. 2012), rooted in post-war Keynesianism as driver of public policy, especially in Europe.

Bilateral city-to-city engagement may be divided into two phases: firstly, the Keynesian period of reconciliation and integration (see Fig. 5.1), very much shaped by a combination of social market economy and attempts at bridging and healing the often deep divisions—and distrust—between countries, especially in Europe. And then, secondly, beginning roughly with the 1980s, the period of a growing globalisation discourse with rising emphasis on neo-liberal, small state economics and competitiveness between places. Connectivity between, and visibility of, cities has become a sign of economic opportunity and 'success' as well as 'prospects', and thus increasingly an essential activity to avoid marginalisation and exclusion from this 'opportunity scenario'. In both periods, state engagement matters, aimed at overcoming borders and divisions, albeit for quite different reasons. 'Reaching out' as a sign of reconciliation and 'opening up' to neighbouring countries, for instance, has involved 'sending out' cities (and municipalities generally) as lower profile and thus potentially less conflictual ambassadors to spearhead this agenda. This contrasts with the role and understanding of cities as competitors, with alliances built for opportunistic, self-interested reasons, be that as agents of a national economic agenda, or, increasingly, outside the framework of such national considerations.

5.2   City-to-City Pairing Through Town Twinning

City-twinning, founded after the Second World War, is probably the most widely known and practised way for individual cities to link up—either as singular or multiple pairs. Their reach is essentially global, as cities from around the world can pair, with individual cities potentially able to have more than one 'partner'. The very purpose of this programme was to overcome post-war divisions and build greater understanding and trust between nations across international borders. And cities were seen as the primary locales of engagement in the sense of contact points. Beyond Europe, still under the impact of the traumatic experiences of the Second World War and its deep-running divisions between states, relevant post-war international city networks include Sister Cities International (SCI), inaugurated in 1956, and, a year later, the United Towns Organization (UTO) as a global organisation of sister cities (also FMVJ, as in the French name 'Fédération mondiale des villes jumelées'). In Europe, at a time when post-war conditions were dominated by the destruction, distrust and traumatic experience of the war, reaching out across borders—in a more or less tentative way as such, trust-building activity was left to subnational authorities—occurred well ahead of the founding of the EU in 1958 through the Treaty of Rome. Just six years after the end of the Second World War, in 1951, the Council of European Municipalities and Regions (CEMR) was brought into existence, seeking to facilitate a network of inter-linkages as part of international, cross-border, meetings and gradual trust building as a step towards healing the deep rifts and traumas dominating Europe in the 1950s.

Cities have a long tradition acting as distinct centres of power and economic centrality well before the territorial nation state was established in the nineteenth century (Short et al. 2000; Marston et al. 2002; Guibernau 2013). Port cities have here been of particular importance, not least through their functional connectedness well beyond 'their' regions and states. Building individual city partnerships as selective, strategic alliances to strengthen and advance positions and prospects, often tailored and restricted to particular objectives/policies, is one strategy to follow. In some instances, agendas may favour multi-lateral, multi-city relationships pursuing more or less specific objectives. Lobbying IOs and/or national governments—or the EU—are primary targets of collective multi-city (network) action. Yet, there are other, more immediately localist agendas—such as civic boosterism (Boyle 1997), specific, competitiveness-driven profiling (e.g. 'tech city', 'wired city', 'smart city') or focusing on sustainability as 'branding' (e.g., 'green city', etc.). For these objectives, demonstrating publicly international links is a useful device of raising a city's profile, and this may be, as part of one-to-one city partnerships, established for particular policy agendas or as part of a tailor-made network. Such networks, however, are by their very nature based on collective, rather than specific individual, interests. They are also selectively exclusive: to join, a city needs to offer an advantage to the other partners. On the other hand, individual cities may be sufficiently visible already to make them risk to 'go it alone', or they may prefer selective bilateral, rather than multi-lateral, collaboration to pursue a locality- or topic-specific agenda. Such moves may be triggered by particular challenges, such as identified strengths or weaknesses, or opportunities on the basis of political-economic context. This includes state support, or, in Europe, support by the EU to establish city partnerships as a way of fostering cross-border engagement and thus integration across spatial scales.

Bilateral engagement may involve launching specific projects with another city as partner, whereby cross-border relations are particularly effective for public political discourse. In such instances, 'city twinning', *Städtepartnerschaften* (city partnerships), *jumelages*, etc. have become an important strategic approach to promote individual cities. Nation states remain important players in this, as trans-border local relations are international in statutory nature and thus require the toleration—at least—by the respective national governments. The current re-imposition of Swedish border controls on the Øresund Bridge (Crouch 2016), after 50 years of open borders in Scandinavia, illustrates the latent capacity of states to cut through, and thus disrupt, relations between cities—by very visibly re-imposing their claim to territorial control—and all that is considered part of that. The state may thus, on the one hand, orchestrate such city-to-city links, not least from a perspective of furthering national interest, or, on the other, undermine, inhibit, or even reverse, such linkages and engagement.

Accordingly, cities may thus be instrumentalised as 'ambassadors' of a possible inter-state rapprochement, or cementing of friendly inter-state relations. Or, they may be 'captured' by the respective state and tied down to the state's territory with surrounding borders being the limit for engagement. This may go as far as turning city-to-city communication and engagement into a major international diplomatic event. A particularly 'extreme' case was relations across the former Iron Curtain. There, any cross-border city/town twinning was only possible by explicit permission by the respective communist states, as such connections amounted to a de facto perforation, and thus feared softening up, of the vigorously guarded Iron Curtain. Thus, it was only in 1986, 30 years after the sister cities idea had been launched in Western Europe, that German–German town twinning across the Iron Curtain was made possible after an agreement to such local-level interaction by the East German state. Such engagement remained suspiciously watched by the communist regime as was potentially subversive and system-threatening. East German cities quite clearly were no more than mere locales within a very visibly and formidably bordered and strictly centrally governed territory.

Cities are competing for influence in economic relations at the international and global level, but that is never really far away from national politics, as the current re-bordering of the Øresund region—now rebranded as Greater Copenhagen and Skåne—well illustrates. This may include sharing experiences and thus boosting own capacities to act effectively by joining and using networks around common policy agendas (Baycan-Levent et al. 2008, 2010). Networks may be constructed bottom-up through collective action by like-interested cities, or orchestrated—more or less hands-on—from above by one or more states seeking to use inter-urban linkages as a vehicle for their own—national/regional—political agendas. The main attraction of networks is their provision of economies of scale and synergies to individual cities through collaborative action in pursuit of common (Capello 2000; van den Berg et al. 2001).

The image of city twinning as building bridges is closely associated with that of cities acting as 'bridgeheads' across obstacles, be that physical barriers such as rivers, or political divisions, such as international borders.

Such may cut right through a shared urban area as a result of historic changes. The City Twin Association (CTA) addresses such circumstances by fostering international trans-border collaboration between cities separated by a border, which therefore represent primary contact—and contrast—points between social and economic developments and structures either side of an international border. Especially the politically important EU outer border, as well as the contrast between Nordic and Central European countries, highlights the potential bridging function that twin cities can take, not least in cases where the divisive effect of an international border is felt particularly strongly. This immediate 'bridging borders' role matters especially within the EU and its integrationist, 'de-bordering' agenda. Twin cities, separated by an international border, are viewed as a particularly symbolic, and thus instructive, example of outreach in de-bordering Europe, and bringing nation states closer together, especially after the end of the Cold War with its legacy of formidable and deep-seated divisions (Herrschel 2011). Accordingly, much of the focus of CTA is lobbying for the interests of border regions at EU level, and seeking funding under INTERREG programmes to boost communication through joint projects, such as cross-border mobility for employment. Such initiatives are much less difficult within the EU—although there, too, conditions may change, as we are currently learning from events within the EU surrounding the ongoing refugee and migration crisis and the politically rising issue of closing borders and asserting control. CTA grew out of the 'City Twins Cooperation Network' (2004–2006) and was set up after completion of a project linking the two 'twin cities' of Frankfurt/Oder and Slubice across the German–Polish border in late 2006. The goal in setting up CTA is to maintain some of the momentum and insights and experiences gained from that project (http://www.frankfurt-oder.eu), and transfer experiences gained to other such situations, rather than have it 'fizzle out' after the end of the funding period.

Pursuing immediate relations across the outer EU border is much more difficult. But it is the affected cities that, being at the forefront of the border effect (Evans 2003), are also the potentially most effective starting points for overcoming divisive border effects. This includes sharing experiences with trans-border regimes and initiatives and projects to reach across divisions and make policies to overcome these more effective. The main focus is on practical collaboration in administrative questions, local economic development, mobility of the workforce, education and local cross-border movements and culture. They are thus mostly 'soft' policy fields which do not interfere with national policies related to border security, law and order, etc. The whole policy is very much an example of 'orchestration', with EU funding under the INTERREG III programme encouraging small trans-border projects (Herrschel 2011). As such, this is very similar in intent to the Euro regions policies.

In Europe, city twinning is a form of incentivised internationalisation by sub-national actors (Baycan-Levent et al. 2010) as a way to facilitate reconciliation and tentative integration at a more grassroots level, that can also be experienced directly by people, rather than engaging in grand treaty-signing events at the national level. City twinning as a political agenda also involved transatlantic relations as a post-war expression of Western Europe's new friendship with North America as part of the Cold War era settlement. Sister City International (SCI) has provided an informal membership organisation since 1956 for those US cities with international connections. SCI was created at President Eisenhower's 1956 White House summit on 'citizen diplomacy', where he envisioned a network that would be a champion for peace and prosperity by fostering bonds between people from different communities around the world (http://www.sister-cities. org/about-sister-cities-international). International city engagement was thus clearly directed by the state to act as an agent of national geo-political and economic interests in the post-war world order. Perhaps a bit exaggeratedly, one might say that the cities have been 'wheeled out' by the state onto the international arena, to do something that traditionally has been the task and prerogative of states, although that was done only by consent. For cities it was a 'win', as they could utilise the national framework of support to also pursue their own interests. 'Citizen diplomacy' (Nye 2010), has become an important descriptor of SCI's role and purpose: fostering democracy through grassroots engagement and allowing 'people power'. This was an important element in the strategic arsenal of post-war competition between the two Cold War regimes of communism and market democracy (http://www.sister-cities.org/about-sister-cities-international).

Similarly, more geographically specific city twinning arrangements exist between the United states and individual global regions, including, increasingly, Asia (e.g. ASEAN). Just as in Europe during the Cold War, such arrangements serve as a low-key opportunity to establish linkages and 'get to knows' at the more (for the general public) accessible local level, than nationally proclaimed mutual 'friendships'. Such city-to-city connections, as we have seen were, even permitted to create a bit of perforation in the Iron Curtain between East and West, including between East and

West Germany. In the post-war period, in Europe, town twinning (Saunier 2001) served to initiate improvements in trans-border relations to start overcoming the deep divisions in post-war Europe. As a consequence, meetings between people through shared social events and exchange of local delegations were the primary objective, rather than cooperating to boost economic competitiveness. That came only much later. Today, political and economic actors are just as much involved. For the cities and towns, being able to point to such connections is important as a way to demonstrate connectivity, i.e. relevance, and open-mindedness, particularly in the case of smaller and more peripheral places, and to contrast with the image of being rural backwaters.

City twinning is a formalised—and publicity-effective—policy to encourage outward-looking policies beyond immediate regional and national boundaries (O'Toole 2001; Perkmann and Sum 2002), sending a subliminal political message about 'friendship', reconciliation, openness and connectedness. In a way, cities—and sub-national para-diplomatic engagement/outreach generally—serve as a politically less risky activity in shaping relations between (neighbouring) countries, as there is less high-profile, and thus 'risky', political capital involved. Putting up billboards at city limits, which list the names of 'sister' cities in different countries, serves as an uncontroversial, 'easy', yet effective, advertising of local relevance also internationally. Especially in Europe, these urban networks are important sources of information and of knowledge transfer concerning experiences elsewhere and policy-relevant ideas and insights (Brussels Capital Region interview, 14 June 2015, see also Chapter 5.4). And this also challenges the hegemonic role of states in dispensing and facilitating such information. Learning processes about policy norms and styles (Le Gales 2002) are an important element in self-empowerment and building up confidence to venture onto new policy arenas. Effectively, such changes may be viewed as the first step by cities to pursue their own, defined interests at the international level (Vion 2002), and to seek to find out about effective strategies.

5.3   European Capital of Culture as EU-Sponsored Route to International Engagement

'European Capital of Culture' (ECoC) is a title granted to a European city by the European Commission as the result of an annual competition for the duration of one year. During that time, the designated cities—now two per year—receive European funding to develop and implement their submitted programme of measures and projects as part of their year-long plan to showcase city life and culture as expression of its qualities as an urban place. These activities are aimed explicitly at a European—i.e. international—audience. Winning this title is thus a useful way of gaining additional resources and an enhanced 'image' as being 'international' on the back of a captivating profile to an international audience. It is thus a way of raising (additional) awareness and and interests, through the positive, curiosity-raising, image of the title, as well as extra financial support from the state. ECoC is clearly a programme aimed at individual cities to encourage and allow them to develop, sharpen and advertise their profiles, using 'culture' as the vehicle and theme to gain—or enhance—international attention, credibility and standing.

This urban outreach was not so much part of a competitiveness agenda as is so widespread today vis-à-vis globalisation, but rather an instrument to drive European integration at a more local, 'hands-on' level of engagement—including the public. The scheme was devised in 1985, i.e. in the very early years of the emerging neo-liberal globalisation discourse, and had the explicit goal of bringing together the peoples of the EU. The programme started out as European City of Culture, but was given its current, more ambitious and 'metropolitan' label 'capital of culture' in 1999. While at first, there was one 'city of culture' per year winning the competition, now there are at least two per year to boost the impact of the programme. The first city to be awarded the title was Athens in 1985, based on the fact that the whole idea for this title originated in Greece and its status as the cradle of European culture. Since then, the range of cities has become broader, going beyond the main metropolises and also including smaller and peripheral cities.

The programme, and thus also the selection process, has changed somewhat since its inauguration: while at first the existing cultural significance—and tradition—of a city was the main criterion, such as in the case of Athens, Florence or Paris, the emphasis shifted to a more integrationist, egalitarian approach, where they are now chosen on specific, innovative characteristics/features of the proposal in its approach to, and understanding and representation of, culture. 'The founding principles, then, were to do with the capacity of culture to act as a source of cohesion, and with the distinctive role which cities have played, and continue to play, as sites of cultural exchange and innovation' (Griffiths, 2007 p. 417). And this has to address two main features: firstly, a European and thus inherently international, outward-looking dimension, highlighting the role the city in the wider European cultural context, and, secondly, a direct relevance of activities for the local population as well as European audience. So it is about the duality of a city as both a local place, but also an international interlocutor and actor. Since the designation of Athens as first European City of Culture, the title has moved between cities around the member states, embracing at first well-established artistic and cultural centres: Florence (1986), Amsterdam (1987), Berlin (1988) and Paris (1989). With some local variations, the focus was generally on portraying the fine arts as, in effect, self-promoting qualities that needed little extra planning, projects or budgets to 'make an impact' (Richards 2000).

The designation of Glasgow in 1990 changed that view, as a city with limited international recognition—certainly in terms of established perception of 'culture'. Glasgow was certainly of considerable cultural importance for Scotland, but there was little in terms of international recognition and profile, and in that it differed from the earlier title-holders in a number of ways. The external image was one of a rather gritty industrial city in decline with extensive run-down housing estates and endemic social problems of deprivation. Its nomination was supported by the UK government largely because of the city's compliance with the then Conservative government's push for a greater role of the private sector in urban regeneration, based especially around property development. And this included a change in image to attract future investors. Plans to use the year as cultural capital as a vehicle to achieve that—and thus improve the prospects for directing private investment to the city—were thus appealing, not least as politically useful evidence of the success of the then nationally championed use of public–private partnerships to facilitate urban development.

'Glasgow's experience was widely seen as a major success, and has been a significant factor in encouraging other de-industrializing cities to try the cultural capital route to a more secure post-industrial future' (Griffiths 2008, p. 418). Subsequently, a host of post-industrial cities with great pressure and ambition to reinvent themselves for post-industrial era competition, gained ECoC status. None had established high profile 'culture status': Antwerp (1993), Rotterdam (2001) and Lille (2004). Motivations and declared objectives of ECoC candidates have varied between cities, with a growing shift towards listing a catalogue of objectives (Palmer 2004, p. 13) as a reflection of their strategic, place-making, more comprehensive regeneration and repositioning strategies that went well beyond the original idea of presenting a city's existing cultural assets.

And so economic gains have been high on the list of agendas, 'associated with increased numbers of visitors, image enhancement, urban revitalization and expansion of the creative industries' (Palmer 2004, p. 18).

The successful city is chosen by a selection panel, examining and evaluating national bids (based on earlier national competitions for the title). The Council of Ministers then grants the ECoC title to the successful city, based on the recommendation of the selection panel. So it is fundamentally a European initiative that empowers/enables the selected cities to go international as a deliberate and desired activity and strategy for cities to act as the connection points across the international realm. While under the initial programme, European Cities of Culture had been selected by member states on an intergovernmental basis, the revised selection process introduced in 2005 emphasises its new European dimension more explicitly and formally, by including central EU institutions in the process. This explicit Europeanisation of the ECoC programme and status serves to reinforce the European dimension of internationality, and as a sign of integration and trans-border reach (Aiello and Thurlow 2006). In this context, visual discourse functions as a complex marker of 'local' (i.e. city and/or national) identity as well as a mechanism to formulate and propagate Europeanness—rather than nationality—of a city's/country's identity. The nature of visual discourse seems to be such that it is well suited to managing this dialectic (cf. Aiello and Thurlow 2006) between 'local' and European 'internationality', because it allows it to be experienced by people. This makes it therefore also very much a shop window for European policies and agendas. ECoC status thus allows for the abstract nature of the European integration idea to become more 'hands-on', being expressed through an individual city's presentation and representation to both itself (and its population) and the outside world in form of its visitors. In this way, 'visual discourse manages the coexistence of difference and similarity, specificity and generality, and the local and the global' (Aiello and Thurlow 2006, p. 159).

The growing emphasis on a raised international profile for cities through large projects has also sought to utilise the International EXPO series as a way of not just showcasing national images, initially in a modernist, technologically oriented spirit, but increasingly as a vehicle for large-scale urban regeneration, repositioning in international competition, and rebranding. While the outcomes of such projects are being debated for their 'successfulness' (Locatelli and Mancini 2010), what they do demonstrate is the growing (primary) use of such projects by the relevant host cities to boost their international visibility and standing, ideally in conjunction with other such initiatives—such as 'Capital of Culture', to maximise the scope and long-term effectiveness of such a strategy. In Lisbon, for instance, the 1998 EXPO project goes under the name of 'The Nations' Park', i.e. a clear reference to nation-based internationalism. Linking the city's image to that of conventional, state-based internationality was intended to boost the city's image and likely competitive success by highlighting and reinforcing its status as national capital and the influence that comes with that using the large-scale redevelopment of an old industrial site as image-changing and -making, 'the overall aim is to give the capital a bigger international influence by promoting its Atlantic coastal position' (Carrière and Demazière 2002, p. 71). The project sought to redevelop a large tract of industrial docklands and turn it into a new urban centre for Lisbon. The nature and scope of the project, jointly funded by the EU and the Portuguese state, combines international ambition with local place-making, so that the project may be described as 'a great international event in a town or a process of urban redevelopment which includes an exhibition' (Matias Ferreira 1997, p. 9. cited in Carrière and Demazière 2002). Events since the exhibition increasingly point to the latter description (Carrière and Demazière 2002, p. 73). In some instances, cities were able to obtain two or more such high profile projects and thus gained extra and more sustained impetus for their international ambitions. Examples include Lisbon (City of Culture 1994 and EXPO 1998) or Barcelona (1992 Olympics and UNESCO Cultural Forum 2004), or, in a more political role, Riga as Capital of Culture 2014, immediately followed by its 'Europeanised' role as national capital during the Latvian presidency of the EU in the first half-year of 2015.

Looking at the outcome of these one-year higher profile images for cities, the picture is somewhat mixed. Palmer (2004), for instance found that a longer-term strategy, into which individual projects fit, is important for a longer-term impact of individual ECoC initiatives. Only then can they turn out to be more than a mere 'flash in the pan'. Nevertheless, as he discovered, ECoC cities often concentrate their efforts on funding one-off events and projects, rather than considering a longer-term effect and utility (Palmer, 2004). The availability of extra funding from the EU—limited to the year of a city's designation—will encourage such short-term perspectives, with little time and investment given to projecting effects into the future, i.e. when the additional funding will no longer be available. And in this, 'leadership appears to be a fundamental ingredient for credibility to be established at city, national and international levels. The absence of a powerful voice can therefore disadvantage the less well-heeled and less connected groups and communities' (Palmer 2004, p. 970). Instead, there is some evidence of uniformity in such cultural events, driven by a growing international outlook by local planners and policy-makers, seeking to follow 'good practice' and 'success' elsewhere, and wanting to copy it. Often, this is encouraged by equally internationally operating consultants who may 'sell' similar ideas to their clients for developing and implementing an ECoC strategy and programme. Hosting ECoC events may well involve a considerable financial outlay for cities, although dedicated spending has stretched from €8 million to €74 million, with capital spending on physical projects varying from around €10 million to over €220 million (Palmer-Rae 2004). Varying city sizes, but also ambitiousness of projects and agendas, account for these variations, as do disparities in cost levels in different countries and localities. 'Culture' has increasingly become more than the traditional understanding of 'arts'-based cultural institutions and events, but evolved into a wider concept of local social milieu and capacity for innovation and entrepreneurialism, just as propagated by Florida's 'creative class'.

Culture and creativity have, effectively, become two sides of the same coin, and 'capital of culture' policy agendas reflect that. Using this to raise a city's profile as a unique place in a competitive, globalised setting has given the title a strategic, 'boosterist' (Hiller 2000) meaning. Presenting a city as unique and competitively attractive has become a central element of 'liveability' and quality of life, both important indicators of competitiveness, in which being 'considered part of the international cultural circuit and creative industry hubs' (Evans 2005, p. 972) has become a main a driver of urban policy-making. The international dimension of the 'liveability' parameter has emerged out of international policy initiatives, such as Agenda 21, and as Local Agenda (LA) 21, its local application. It now serves as a broadly adopted reference point for 'liveability' indicators (FCM 2001). 'This game is played out in cities in the earlier stages of culture and regeneration, such as Singapore "Global City of the Arts" (Chang 2000), Adelaide (Montgomery 2004) and Helsinki (Verwijnen and Lehtovuori 1999), and many others who wish to be considered part of the international cultural circuit and creative industry hubs' (Evans 2005, p. 973). So, with local competitiveness in a global setting becoming the main driver of cities' higher profile engagement with 'culture' as a profiling strategy, it may not be entirely surprising that ECoC has become less about promoting and manifesting

European integration and commonality, as envisioned by the European Commission, but rather more about local differentiation in the pursuit of a distinct profile (Palmer-Rae Associates 2004) within the context of global competitiveness.

In the earlier phase of the programme, when 'culture' was much more associated with the 'artistic', Myerscough (1994) complained that the ECoC programme had 'achieved more in highlighting differences than in bringing the European dimension to the fore' (p. 20). Greater emphasis was placed on culture-related networking and international exchanges as possible avenues to more effective insertion into the international business arena and that of global urban competitiveness. 'The richness but also the challenge of ECOC is that there is no agreed formula for a cultural programme, and the unique historical, economic, social and political context of each city cannot be ignored' (Palmer-Rae Associates 2004, p. 14). Internationality clearly matters in one way or the other, i.e. as part of European integration or the bigger stage of the global economy. Nearly 20 years later, McAteer et al. (2014) point to the fact that ECoC activities get noticed and reported when there is a European and/or international dimension to them, such as trans-border activities, international arts/culture actors (individuals and organisations), or, seemingly of particular importance, transnational partnerships. So, being associated with internationality seems to give a locality immediate additional recognition and appeal as a relevant place, be it for 'liveablity' or economic opportunity. Having none of this, by contrast, insinuates a sense of disconnectedness and localist introspection.

This instrumental functionalism is at least partially driven by a continued adherence to the values of the new public management-inspired rationale in local policy-making and definition of agendas, which prioritises specific results and value for money. Under such a regime, short-term economic—and thus immediate political—advantages move to the top of the priority list, rather than longer-term outcomes. More immediate results are easier to 'sell' to the local electorate as 'gain', while longer-term or less immediately significant 'local' activities may be less welcome. Economic outcomes have therefore clearly become the main drivers of the form and nature of cities' international engagement as part of urban policies, whether as part of the ECoC or the sister cities movement, and whether in Europe or elsewhere (O'Toole 2001). They have become a tool to promote individuality and 'attractiveness'—including 'trendiness'—as a way to appealing to the famously billed 'creative class' as an indication of innovativeness and focusing on the future as a route to success.

This outward orientation and effort at raising visibility through ECoC nomination is illustrated by the outcomes that were expected by Stavanger's population of their forthcoming city's ECoC status in 2008. On the one hand, the majority didn't expect much impact on their own lives during 2008, while expecting that the city would gain in external/international visibility and recognition. The vision for Stavanger as Capital of Culture revolved around the 'Open Port' concept (http://www.stavanger2008. no), emphasising connectivity and welcome to the outside world. This corresponds with a large majority among the city's population of nearly 90% expecting a positive impact of the year's Capital of Culture status on the city's cultural life, and a similarly large majority anticipating 'important new impulses' for the region by making it 'better known' both in Norway and in Europe (Rommetvedt 2008).

Glasgow's nomination as European City of Culture marks the shift of the programme from the propagation of existing urban cultural assets and reputation to an outside international audience as a celebration of existing European culture and art, to an instrumentalisation of the notion of 'culture' as place-based innovativeness, entrepreneurialism and reinvention of a struggling post-industrial city. This plays to an international realm, supported by supra-national, rather than national funding (Mooney 2004). Subsequently, 'Glasgow continues to be mobilised as both a model and a reference point for other disadvantaged cities' to follow (Mooney 2004, p. 328). The success of the Glasgow ECoC campaign effectively established this approach (and its outcome) as a main criterion for subsequent nominations. It allowed less well-known, disadvantaged and struggling cities undergoing structural changes, or being affected by marginality/peripherality, to turn a passive role into a more proactive one and look for—and propose—a new direction of development. '"Doing a Glasgow" has now become a recurring theme in discussions of urban cultural policy and place marketing in many of Europe's older industrial cities' (Mooney 2004, p. 328). 'Flagship' arts and cultural projects as beacons to signal change and new qualities and agendas are used to attract attention. This is much like US-style urban boosterism as sheer image marketing (see Kantor 2002; Short et al. 1993). Yet, the longer-term value of such projects is not necessarily so clear (Garcia 2005). The nature of 'successful transformation' in terms of increased competitiveness and adjustment to the requirements of a neo-liberal economy may blend out other, 'shadow' effects. Thus, while overwhelmingly the dominant narrative from accounts of Glasgow's period as ECOC, and of cultural-led regeneration in the city, is that it was 'good for Glasgow' and that 1990 helped to 'transform' it, there is, however, a danger that such a focus on a city's image reduces it to just one homogeneous entity, with all actors and citizens being rolled into one, reified as one single product name.

In Liverpool, which sought to follow the Glasgow approach, the new city leadership of 1998 wanted to 'make a break' with the past and pursue a more strategic and integrated approach to the city's governance. To underline this commitment, marginalisation in terms the council published a "strategic vision" which talked of turning Liverpool into a "premier European city"' (Griffiths 2006, p. 322). This was an attempt to take the city out of its long-established introspective politically localist, defensive left-wing perspective, and place it into a European context so as to—also—overcome its narrow political-ideological self-obsession (of the leadership). The aim was to project a 'new start' with a new ambitious perspective that went beyond the ideological battles with the Conservative government in Downing Street. The availability of European funding through its Objective 1 status (restructuring old industrial areas) was crucial in mustering a new strategic agenda, as it offered extra resources that would allow the city to circumvent the national government with its restrictive fiscal policy that sought to control all forms of local expenditure as part of 'shrinking the state'. The city council thus took a very hands-on approach to shaping the bid and organising its preparation, including raising—and demonstrating—sufficiently broad local political support behind the bid to convince jurors. And that, in turn, produced a stronger identification with the city among residents and a sense of more collective awareness.

A different form of disadvantage than that of old industrial decline is illustrated by the case of the provincial Swedish city of Umeå. Here, geographic peripherality and thus danger of marginalisation in terms of globalised economic competition is the major challenge to future development prospects. Seeking to overcome, or escape from, competitive weaknesses through international profiling may also involve seeking to leave 'obscurity'. For this, cities may use ECoC status to step out of geographic peripherality and, from an outside perspective, even invisibility. Umeå, as the recent ECoC of 2014, is such a case. Located in north-east Sweden on the Bothnian coast of the Baltic Sea, some 600 km north of Stockholm, it is quite a distance from other larger urban centres. The city, however, is an important centre for this rural part of northern Sweden, and as such has been actively developed by national policies. This includes a distinct international dimension in the form of attracting foreign students to the city's university which has been funded by the Swedish government since the mid-1960s as a likely bridgehead to the outside world. Such connectivity includes encouragement of, and financial support for, academic staff to establish international networks through indirect engagement (interview at the Department of Politics, University of Umeå, 7 April 2014). This state-driven and state-enabled policy of locating and developing higher education as a 'lifeline' for the city to overcome its disconnected location seems to be working. And this has been the result not least through effective complementary local policies. In the local (trendy) coffee places and restaurants, one can hear a variety of different languages beyond Swedish as students of different nationalities mingle. The focus on arts and culture has attracted young people to Umeå where, according to the self-promoting claim by the city, more creative things are possible than in other, perhaps bigger cities, where their ideas would be just one among many (see also Umeå 2009).

The city's ECoC campaign built on that and sought to boost its effect by touring Europe in autumn 2013 with a road show to advertise, and raise international awareness for, its forthcoming status. This international road show around major European cities included Hamburg, London, Paris and Barcelona, all cities with strong international presence and image, not least also in the cultural scene. This effort at promoting openness and 'outreach' has been encapsulated by the whole Umeå 2014 campaign, seeking to raise attention and awareness. And this approach is now in itself competing for an award for the innovativeness of the road show. The glass pyramid on the main square in front of the old city hall, serving as a public information and debating space linked to Umeå 2014 events, nicely manifested the intended strategic 'open mind' and 'open place' idea. Such structures and geographic features do not necessarily lead by themselves to a natural affinity and collaboration in policy agendas and modes of operation. Here, wider networks, allowing for a broader range of not just types of places, but also types of political and strategic visions and agendas, may be more effective in offering scope for collaborative action—and an international interest.

The idea of competing for ECoC status goes back to a longer tradition of using culture as a means for economic development in the city (Umeå city council interview, 9 April 2014). This form of communicative, rather than physical, connectivity through infrastructure projects is the result of a review of likely future scenarios for the city's further development in the 1990s, in response to evident structural economic problems (traditional resource economy—timber, fishing, etc). It was realised that growth was needed to survive as a locality, so as to by generate sufficient local fiscal revenue (local taxes from the resident population and businesses, etc) to provide needed services. Culture became the new focus, effectively rediscovering 1970s policies about culture as a driver of local development— then in the form of education. The then new university was the starting point of this shift to looking beyond the region with its limited economic capacity. This was clearly a conventional state-led structural policy. The credibility of university project in terms of its leading role in culture within the city, and the now observed internationality in the city's streets in form of a diverse student body suggest the success of this attempt to link the city to the outside world through the vehicle of culture.

But it could be successful only with outside help—national government investment and European support and granted status. The city also tried to learn from other examples, of culture-led revitalisation and efforts at stemming an actual or perceived tide of decline, such as Liverpool or Glasgow (interview Umeå 2014 office 9 April 14). Creativity is considered crucial for bringing about growth, and that includes policy learning and innovation. This has involved reaching to the international arena as source of opportunity—on the back of national and European support as facilitation. In this process, the mayor has played a central role as a key actor by, teaming up with other mayors of cities with which exchanges and policy learning are intended. And these mutual 'support networks' reach across international borders. Important in this process, as was emphasised in the Umeå 2014 office, is the confidence which was boosted in Umeå through its status as 'capital of culture'. The need for such was highlighted by a consultant who was hired upon gaining ECoC status, and who conducted a SWOT analysis of the city. This showed the need for self-belief, and awareness and belief in what the city is good at, so as to support proactive and innovative policies that reach beyond established national/regional horizons. For this, greater institutional and fiscal capacity is also necessary, sought through a planned doubling of the population by 2050 (interview Umeå 2014 Office, 9 April 2014), together with closer collaboration with other municipalities in the region to provide a broader basis for further-reaching new international policy links. After some initial unease, collaboration now exists through the realisation among the other municipalities in the region that they can benefit from collaborative engagement with the regional centre. For instance, Sundsvall, a smaller town south of Umeå, sought to tie in with the Umeå 2014 project and thus attach itself to Umeå's growing international reach and likely positive spin-off effects. The town even has a small office for Umeå 2014 as a clear statement of its active stakeholding.

National borders and cultures still matter, however, as the communicational 'gap' with the Finnish city of Vaasa, across the Bothnian Sea, demonstrates. Vaasa apparently did not approach Umeå, from which it is separated by a four-hour ferry ride, about possible co-creation of activities under the ECoC umbrella. Also important seems to be 'status', such as reflected in city size and function. Capital cities (national capitals), for instance, seem to have a sense of elitism, just as larger cities seem to view smaller (or more peripheral ones) as 'below par' and thus less interesting as partners. The creation of 'elite clubs' for large member cities in the Canadian and North American municipal associations (see Chap. 6), is one such example. The somewhat distant relationship between Umeå and Riga, both ECoC cities in 2014, and both located in the eastern Baltic, seems to confirm that. In Riga's case, Umeå sensed a degree of 'snobbism', as Riga, Latvia's capital city, was felt to be looking down on the peripheral town in the 'wilds' of northern Sweden. The sense in Umeå therefore was that Riga seemed to think that there wasn't much to be gained from linking up with a peripheral, provincial town (interview, Umeå 2014 office, 9 April 2014). As a result, there was no active engagement, no mutual marketing as concurrent 'Cities of Culture', despite the shared wider regional context on the margins of north-eastern Europe. For instance, there was no explicit acknowledgement of each other as the 'second half' of the joint award, just a very inconspicuous link to each other's websites. But, interestingly, both Vaasa and Riga have used the 'Umea 2014' glass pyramid on the city's main square in front of the old town hall to market themselves (interview Umeå 2014 office, 9 April 2014). Nevertheless, and perhaps surprisingly, there seems to have been no joint discussion about likely legacies and how to approach that question. Instead, Umeå 2014 actors of the region have travelled to Marseille to learn about how best to ensure a positive legacy from ECoC status (interview Umeå 2014 office, 9 April 2014).

In Riga, meanwhile, evidence of ECoC status was striking by its all but absence in public space. In fact, there were no flags and hardly any signs advertising this year-long European status, or events relating to it. On a visit in early June 2014, without previous knowledge, one would not have noticed 'Riga 2014' at all. Yet, the recognition of the city is deemed important by those associated with ECoC status. At the Riga 2014 office, in the austere communist era town hall building, it was stressed that Riga's status as ECoC is important not just for the city, but also, and in particular, the country as a whole. This applies especially to boosting international contacts which already concentrate on the city as the capital. But 'more was needed again and again' (interview Riga 2014 office, 2 June 2014). Riga's interests and policies are thus quite evidently seen by default as also those of the state and the nation.

Clearly, therefore, the city's outreach and international representation is viewed as a vehicle for bringing the whole country from the 'edge of Europe' to greater international recognition, while helping boost Riga's competitiveness (interview Riga 2014 office, 2 June 2014). One of the key advantages of ECoC status was seen in people, including journalists, taking notice, visiting the city and gathering first-hand experiences, 'rather than relying on prejudices and presumptions'. 'It's only when people can be spoken to that Latvia's advantages can become evident' (interview Riga 2014 office, 2 June 2014). The city's higher profile internationally is also viewed as an important facilitator and support of a stronger sense of national identity, of national self-worth. Just 'as important is the possibility to re-assert national identity to "ourselves"' (interview Riga 2014 office, 2 June 2014). So, the city becomes the reference point for, and shaper of, national identity for the whole of Latvia, clearly manifesting Riga's pre-eminent status in the country. This close link between the city and the state became symbolically evident when a long human chain was built to move books from the old to the new national library in Riga as an act of national engagement (interview Riga 2014 office, 2 June 2014). Dealing with its own history also involves the former KGB house which has now been turned into a museum, after it had lain empty for some seven years. So, ECoC status here is very much also about a national self-discovery and reassurance, a decade after joining the EU. The city acts as interlocutor between the national self and the outside world based on the city's international connections and recognition. This adds a new dimension to conventional city marketing, as it is also aimed at the 'inside', not merely the local, but also, as national capital, the national population. The multitude of cultural events, and their live broadcast across the country, was very much part of the nation building and reaffirming mission by reinforcing 'Latvian citizens' sense of belonging to what is happening in the Latvian cultural space' (Timermane-Moora, curator of Riga 2014, http://riga2014.org/eng/news/57444-european-capital-of-culture-in-riga-a-resounding-success). The low-key nature of the ECoC status, with relatively modest events, is partly a result of playing mostly to a domestic audience, and partly a legacy of the 2008 financial crisis which seriously affected Latvia—much more so than Sweden (interview Riga 2014 office, 2 June 2014). It is the resulting 'no nonsense' approach that also helps explain the absence of any physical markers of Riga 2014.

The international representations in the city (embassies) are important traditional points of international connectivity, thus tying the city to the international arena. This international role is seen as a continuous task and opportunity: so, as was pointed out in the interview at the Riga 2014 offices, the international attention also served as preparation for Latvia's subsequent taking over of the leadership of the EU Council at the beginning of 2015. The close link between the city's internationality and that of the whole nation is also reflected in the fact that '"Riga 2014", working in partnership with the Ministry of Foreign Affairs and Latvian embassies abroad, held 190 different public diplomacy events in 2013 and 2014, in 39 countries around the world, telling Riga's European Capital of Culture story' (http://riga2014.org/eng/news/57444-european-capital-of-culture-in-riga-a-resounding-success). But despite this outward engagement, ECoC status and events were very much tuned to the national 'inside', while being relatively undersold to the independent external observer.

So it may not come as a complete surprise that an a ex-post assessment of Riga's ECoC year conducted for the European Commission (Fox and Rampton 2015) found that internationalisation efforts had rather limited results, because of a 'lack of activity linked to raising the international profile of the city in order to attract visitors from abroad to attend and visit ECoC activities'. Only a very small share of audiences attending Riga 2014 events came from outside Latvia. This seems to confirm the primarily inward-oriented nature of the event, providing a platform and stage for national arts and culture to boost national confidence and identity. It is this, rather than any physical evidence as 'legacy' to associate with the event, the absence of which was also noted in the report, that seems to have been the primary objective. Fostering and affirming Latvian-ness, rather than slogan-driven competitiveness, appear as the primary objective of Riga's ECoC status in 2014.

Umeå 2014, by contrast, had a lead slogan—'Curiosity and Passion'—to summarise and position its agenda which revolved around three objectives: human growth, sustainable development, and international relations. The cultural programme was based on the overarching concept of Umeå as the 'Northern Room' in the European 'house' (see inter alia Fox and Rampton 2015). So, there is a distinct outward-looking, international ambition, where characteristics of the 'inside' are 'packaged' and marketed to the wider world to attract attention and recognition. In its application for ECoC nomination, Umeå pointed out the European outlook—of course, also in response to the evaluation criteria. But rather than making 'wild' promises, the proposed growth in internationality is based on existing relations and experiences. In its application for the ECoC title in 2014, the city stated—of course also playing to the jurors—'Umeå 2014 is a window to all of Europe. We will use it to show that we are one of the foremost culture-driven cities in Europe. Before, during and after 2014 cultural exchanges between Umeå and the rest of Europe will increase. This means that Europe has an opportunity to become acquainted with Umeå's cultural scene. It is also an opportunity to establish bonds with new European friends for us … And when 2014 ends, what we have created will continue to be put to use—for many years to come.' In order to achieve that, the application continues, 'The European Capital of Culture programme will largely be built up through international collaborative projects. We have long-standing experience of cooperation between the universities and the various institution of the EU. Both Umeå University and the Swedish University of Agricultural Sciences in Umeå participate in different EU programmes, including in the cultural sector. This is a strength that we wish to build upon in our future developmental work' (Umeå 2009, p. 26).

Umeå's more actively outward-looking and acting approach to promoting its European status, such as the international 'Caught by Umeå' promotional tour of several European cities in 2013 (see above) seemed to have some success in terms of placing it on the tourist map. The city attracted around 57,000 visitors (Fox and Rampton 2015), probably helped by positive coverage in the international press, including the *New York Times*, and a listing in the Rough Guide's 'Top Ten Cities' in the world for 2014, alongside places like Liverpool, Sarajevo and Rio de Janeiro (http://www.roughguides.com/best-places/2014/top-10-cities/). The guide's predominant focus on younger travellers fits into the image of Umeå's internationality being largely built around young artists/students, and a 20%increase in hotel bookings from 2013 to 2014 (Fox and Rampton 2015) seems to confirm this perception. The question then is, however, how this momentum can be maintained and utilised in a longer-term strategy, without the extra funding that came with ECoC status. The city sought to capture some of this in its 2010–2020 cultural development strategy. The application for the European Green Capital Award 2017, for which it was shortlisted among four finalists (European Commission 2016), points to the city's maintaining a degree of continuity and momentum in the attempts at internationalisation as a way of escaping peripherality and relative invisibility. One way may be to strengthen work through its existing link-up with 'sister cities' which currently are mainly in Northern Europe, with the odd one in Mexico and Canada. Yet, in line with many other cities, regions and states, further expansion is under way especially into China and East Asia, not least also from the perspective of economic opportunity as part of the city's ongoing internationalisation strategy.

Single city internationalisation also operates outside, or in combination with, rather than just through, ECoC nominations, and can be driven by an intra-national competition for recognition and resources, such as between Åarhus, the second city in Denmark with its some 300,000 inhabitants (the city-region has more than 500,000), and the capital city of Copenhagen. Åarhus, and, indeed, the rural Jutland region as a whole, competes as 'second city' with the Copenhagen capital city-region for political influence and economic development and investment opportunities. And so it may not come as a surprise that Åarhus has sought to boost its standing through international engagement, utilising the EU's focus on regional scale policies in general, as well as its programme of ECoC in particular. Åarhus also uses the sister city programme to project connectedness to the world, and direct lobbying through an 'ambassadorial' office for representation of its interests at the EU in Brussels. The city's English version of its website offers a quite detailed account of international activities, with International Activities listed as one of the five categories on its home page (http://www.aarhus.dk/sitecore/content/Subsites/CityOfAarhus/Home). Here, the listed types of engagement include co-operation agreements, network activities, business development, sister cities, the Central Denmark EU Office and the Central Denmark Shanghai Office. The latter is an interesting step beyond the EU arena with its explicit for international engagement by sub-national actors. The Shanghai Office was opened in 2003 as a result of existing links, and thus established good relations, between the two cities through the sister cities programme. For Shanghai, of course, such engagement also provides important links to the EU and its economic opportunities. So it is a win-win arrangement. Trust building is an important part of this, and mutual visits by delegations of government and business representatives, especially in the fields of Energy/Environment, IT and Health/Life Sciences, contribute to that. This engagement has become a cornerstone of further ambitions concerning engagement with China, which now also include specific economy-related agreements, such as with Nanjing on clean technology. 'Aarhus is focused on China' proclaims the city's website, and quotes its mayor's observation that 'With the opportunities in China, it is natural for the City of Åarhus to expand the process of creating connections to benefit business opportunities. Close relations are imperative when doing business in China. When it comes to Åarhus and Nanjing, history has given Åarhus a special status and brought the two cities closer together. Both cities are eager to further develop this relationship' (http://www.aarhus.dk/sitecore/content/Subsites/CityOfAarhus/ Home/The-international-perspective/Co-operation-agreement.aspx?sc_ lang=da). This interest in China goes back to the very beginning of the new millennium, when this was articulated as part of the framing of the city's economic development strategy (interview Investment Location Åarhus, 10 December 2003).

Beyond this foray into globally reaching relations to China, the main focus of international activity has been Europe, especially the northern part of it. There is thus evidence of a growing geographic expansion of international ambitions further afield. The two main instruments of such engagement are the EU-supported sister city movement and direct representation to the EU machinery in Brussels. The former is the older policy and goes back to the immediate post-war year of 1946, extending to tie-ups with seven cities among the Nordic neighbours, and those on the Baltic Sea, such as Rostock (Germany) and St Petersburg (Russia). Much of the focus of these relations was (again) on economic opportunities, especially trade, including 'the sale of know-how, cooperation in the commercial area and business deals, where international partners place their trade in Åarhus or vice versa' (http://www.aarhus.dk/sitecore/content/ Subsites/CityOfAarhus/Home/The-international-perspective/Sister-cities.aspx?sc_lang=da). Inevitably, such exchanges also involve learning about policy practices, different ways of formulating and making policies. This is to achieve 'a boost in competencies and knowledge sharing, marketing and branding, as well as to build useful international networks and partnerships between the City of Åarhus and the sister cities' (ibid.).

The other main plank of Åarhus' outreach to the international arena, representation in Brussels, goes back to 1990, when the city was one of the very early adopters of this emerging direct representation approach by cities and regions in Brussels, encouraged by the EU's strong focus on regional policies under the new banner of 'Europe of the Regions' advocated by the Delors administration, as well as associated available funding that circumvented national governments. The European Regional Office is a joint representation with the Central Denmark (Jutland) region whose capital Åarhus is. Apart from improving collaboration between city and 'its' region, the 'overall aim of the office is to ensure that people, businesses and organisations in the region make the most out of the European Union. Again, economic interests are the primary driver' (http://www.aarhus.dk/sitecore/content/Subsites/CityOfAarhus/ Home/The-international-perspective/The-Central-Denmark-EU-Office. aspx?sc_lang=da). Activities revolve around this agenda and, in their nature, are very similar to those of other such city or regional representations in Brussels: advising on EU affairs, assisting with identifying funding opportunities and helping prepare applications, facilitating links to other European regions, and providing 'early warning' on emerging EU policy (ibid.).

As discussed in more detail below, opening a Brussels office to lobby European institutions and policy-makers has become an important instrument for European cities to by-pass their states to pursue local political and economic development ambitions. The economic development focus of the Åarhus EU Office in Brussels is reflected in its close link to the relevant department in the city administration (Department of Business and Industry in 2003) of Åarhus (www.Åarhus.dk, as on 1 N on 2003). The focus of the Brussels office since then has changed little, offering to provide access to the EU as a service for business and public institutions and organisations to boost the region's competitive standing. This included the explicit goal of promoting 'growth and job creation in the Region of Åarhus by maximising companies' and institutions' involvement in international funded projects and tender opportunities and identification and analysis of funding possibilities' (Åarhus municipal website, 1 November 2003). Proposal preparation and writing, searching for partners in bidding processes, and contacting the European Commission were just as much key activities then as they are now. 'The aim is to ensure that the Åarhus region, as such, utilizes the opportunities within the EU to the greatest advantage' (Åarhus municipal website, 1 November 2003).

But the city's ambitions went further already then, including a focus on China, as the existence—in 2003—of an internationalisation committee attests. This committee was, in effect, a public–private partnership, involving a variety of local stakeholders from the business community, civil society learning as well as public administration: three city councillors—including the council leader—and representatives from the business community, organisations, and knowledge and cultural institutions. So it is, essentially, a reflection of the triple helix concept. Set up initially for a two-year trial period, the stated objective was to develop the city's position as a global player by earmarking and coordinating such projects and initiatives that would 'strengthen Åarhus' international profile and attractiveness as a city to visit, study, work and invest in for foreign businessmen, students and tourists' (Åarhus municipalwebsite www.aarhus.dk, 2003), as the city's future growth and development was dependent on the city's business community, knowledge environments and cultural institutions, all of which would do well from the growing international competition. 'The Internationalisation Committee's task is to develop strategies and proposals for initiatives that can strengthen Åarhus' international attraction and impact. These actions will contribute in moving Åarhus from being *a city in Europe to be a European city*' (Åarhus municipal website 2003) by being able to attract, and retain, international employees. Looking at today's municipal website, the ambition for the still existing international committee reads: 'To develop the City of Åarhus as a *global player*'. There is thus a geographically more ambitious notion of 'international' that goes beyond the world of Brussels and the EU and claims a global horizon.

The third main plank of internationalisation, very much as a European project, is the city's designation in 2012 as ECoC for 2017. The city has thus been able to add this internationally visible status to its overall ambitions of stepping out of its provincial context at the 'opposite' end of the country from the capital Copenhagen. As ECoC 2017, Åarhus intends to offer a wide spectrum of cultural activities and projects to create 'Spectacle and Speculations' but also to bring the entire region together as part of the activities. This reaching out to the surrounding regional hinterland seeks to use the region's resources to boost the city's own standing and capacity to act and present itself to the outside world. This may involve the projection of a new image and/or qualities as a result of 'rethinking' as lead theme, under which Åarhus 2017 subsumes its intent to 'transform the Central Denmark Region into a cultural laboratory'. And this seeks to involve the region *and* the municipalities within it by boosting, and drawing on, close cooperation across the entire region (http://www.aarhus2017.dk/en). So, the strategy draws on existing policies and experiences and seeks to further develop and embed them, rather than creating something new altogether, which may not be sustainable beyond the extra funding available as an ECoC city and thus be of limited effect for the city's overall strategic agenda.

5.4   Single City Engagement Through
International Representation in Brussels

The second route to individual engagement for cities is an explicit 'foreign policy'—operated by a declared and formally established 'international relations' department or unit in the administration, and opening an international office in Brussels. Cities have begun opening their own representations, following earlier such processes by many regions from across Europe. Many cities, especially the metropolitan areas, want to be seen as more than a mere part of their respective regions. The result has been a growing 'thickness' of international representations in Brussels from the local to state level. Thus, in addition to its some 180 national embassies, there are nearly 250 regional and 175 EU representations and a large number of international and/or non-governmental organisations, lobbying bureaux and private sector bodies (Brussels Capital Region, cor.europa. eu/en/regions/Documents/regional-offices.xls). This is a considerable increase from the 54 'liaison offices' that Marks et al. (1996) identified for 1993. This growing population of the international realm—the traditional prerogative of the nation state (as also envisaged by the EU in form of the Council of Ministers as joint executive body)—by sub-national actors may be understood as supporting the MLG argument that such sub-national territorial entities of governance can transcend the scalar hierarchy and muster a relevant and effective presence at the supra-national level of the EU (Donas and Beyers 2012). This possibility offered by the nature and organisational structure of the EU is, however, uniquely supportive of such a new source of international agency. In addition, Brussels-based regional offices are distinct from other organised interests in the sense that they represent the public sector, democratically elected executives and territorial jurisdictions (Donas and Beyers 2012, p. 1).

Sub-national jurisdictions have opted for two main avenues to pursue their interests: through individual (singular) action (e.g. 'liaison offices', 'representations'), or through collective action as part of networks or bilateral and multi-lateral agreements (e.g. 'associations', 'unions')—built either on the basis of territorial belonging (regional/national/international networks), actor type (urban/non-urban, city/city-region/metropolis/region) or topic (environment/economic links/trans-border, port cities, peripherality). International groupings/networks built around particular topics or agendas (e.g. Association of Peripheral Maritime Regions, or Association of Border Regions) are particularly likely to wield influence on EU institutions and policy processes (Donas and Beyers 2012; Tatham 2008). Such associations are by nature selective and thus exclusive, and may include merely some of a national or regional entity, as the different categories overlap and intersect. Examples include the German Cities Association (excluding non-urban municipalities), or the English Core Cities Group (excluding non-urban municipalities and all those not among the main nine cities). By contrast, a territorial approach may include all municipalities 'encompassed' by a state, such as the Representation of the Free State of Bavaria, or may be assembled by all municipalities of one state as a bottom-up arrangement, or 'complete national association' (Donas and Beyers 2012), such as the Irish Regions Office, embracing all regions of Ireland.

The nature of the Brussels representations thus varies significantly in their rationale, agenda and legitimising justification. They reflect the statutory status of the represented regions: mere administrative entity which is essentially a construct by national government, or constitutionally recognised entities as representations of regional traditions, identity and even potential devolution, such as the German *Länder* or the Italian regions, the devolved Spanish regions (islands, Basque Country and Catalonia) with representations such as Delegacion del Gobierno de Canarias, or Délégation du pays Basque à Bruxelles, or UK regions, with their strong nationality underpinnings (e.g. the Scottish and Welsh Government EU Offices). But there are also strategic 'virtual' or 'new' regions, such as transborder Euro regions (e.g. Euro region Pyrenees-Mediterranean), and representations of municipalities, either as national or regional groupings, as well as representations of individual cities or groups of cities. Similarly, Corsica and Brittany take on a special status within France, which includes representations by individual larger cities/city-regions (Fig. 5.2).

Among these representations are some 40 which represent a city or city-region, based on their names, contrasting with those regions that make no reference in their names to any particular city—either as a deliberate strategy to emphasise the cohesive territoriality of a region, whether urban or not, in those cases where they are constructs for marketing or planning/administrative purposes, where an 'equal voice for all' is a deliberate political strategy. By contrast, on other occasions, the name of the main city is pushed into the foreground. Interesting here are the cases of Île de France, where Paris gets subsumed in the wider city-region's name, and the Capital Region of Denmark, which subsumes Copenhagen. Elsewhere, as in the case of Prague, the city and surrounding

City/City-Region	Stated Objectives/Purpose
Délégation de la Région de Bruxelles-Capitale (B)	- represents the Region at the European institutions - provides information on EU daft regulation programmes to the Region - coordinates local implementation of EU directives in Brussels - creates synergy between European policies and the international relations of the Region - develops relations with the other regional representations in Brussels (www. http://be.brussels/about-the-region/international-brussels)
EU office of Varna (BG)	"The EU office positions Varna at European level and promotes it as visitors and investments [sic] destination." (https://www.facebook.com/Varna-EU-Office), no web-address
Representation of the city of Kyustendil (BG)	No info found
Dubrovnik Neretva County Office (HR)	- has been actively engaged in the county's promotion at the centre of the European Union, - develops contacts with the EU's institutions in Brussels - cooperates with other European regions. - enhances collaboration within the County through joint office (www.dubrovnik-neretva.eu/about-us)
Delegation of Prague to the EU (CZ)	- increase awareness of Prague and its interests amongst the European institutions and other relevant organisations - .provide feedback on Prague's interests and activities back to Prague, - communicate European issues and the possibilities offered by the EU for other Prague institutions, associations and citizens (www.praha.eu)
Central Bohemia Region European Office (CZ)	- established 2004, promotes the region's interests - seeks to create opportunities, influence EU decision-makers & support region's engagement in Europe (http://www.czechreg.eu/)
CreoDK (Capital Region DK)	is the joint EU research office of the Univ. of Copenhagen, the Technical Univ. of Denmark & Capital Region of Denmark - The purpose ...is to enhance the influence of its three partners in the European research area (https://www.regionh.dk)
Kalundborg EU Office (DK)	No separate website, office space in 'House of the Cities', R de Luxem. 3 "Kalundborg Municipality is planning to develop an international strategy" (www. http://www.kl.dk)
Tallin European Office (EST)	No separate website, office space in 'House of the Cities', Rue de Luxembourg 3
Helsinki EU Office (FIN)	- supervises its stakeholders' interests and promotes their visibility at EU - provides information on the preparation of EU legislation, EU funding programmes, events, co-operation and networking opportunities. (http://euoffice.it.helsinki.fi)
Ile-de-France Europe (F)	- strategically monitors EU current affairs, especially European policies and programmes of interest to Ile-de-France Region. - early informs local and regional decision-makers and stakeholders to enable them to have their say in European decisions. - defends the interests of the Region on key topics - networking is paramount (www.iledefrance-europe.eu)

Fig. 5.2 Stated objectives by cities' Brussels offices. *Source*: Based on information from Committee of the Regions (http://www.cor.europa.eu) and information from regional office web pages

Büro des Landes Berlin (City of Berlin Office (D)	- 'early warning system' on EU policies for Berlin govt - feed Berlin's interests into EU decision-making and opinions - represent Berlin's interests at public events - support co-operation projects and network participation (www.berlin.de)
Hanse-Office, Hamburg (D)	- first regional office (1985), bis-state since 1987 - 'early warning' on EU policies, funding, etc - inform Hamburg citizens on EU processes - networking with other policy makers & interests (www.hanse-office.de)
Vertretung Bremen (Representation of Bremen) D	- founded in 1987 - represents Land Bremen at at European and int'l organisations in Brussels, Straßburg und Luxemburg. - main task: early warning on major EU decisions & policies
Representation of Budapest to the EU (HU)	Facebook site empty, no other info
Arnhem Nijmegen City Region (NL)	- promotes Arnhem Nijmegen City Region and find partners for European projects (mainly in economic development) - established 2006 - showcases how to collaborate within a triple helix structure and bring our stakeholders to Brussels (and vice-versa)
G-4 EU Office (Amsterdam, The Hague, Rotterdam, Utrecht) (NL)	- The EU Office is an integrated part of the national political and technical co-operation of the four cities aiming to promote their interests - The main objective is to monitor EU policy and legislative developments - focus on strengthening our network and intensifying effective relationships with Europe's political representatives, administrators etc
Representation of the City of Lódz in Brussels (PL)	- represent the City of Lodz by liaising with the EU institutions - promote the City by participating in exhibitions and public events - monitor EU legislation relating to urban policy, and competition - lobby for support of projects submitted by Lodz government/ institutions (http://en.uml.lodz.pl/)
Diputacio de Barcelona (E)	- Internat'l Relations Dept has two main objectives regarding EU: - provide for local govt info on funding, best pract, networks, EU partners .- represent municipalities and Province of Barcelona in EU legislatio processes with impact on local matters (www.diba.cat, Ctalan only)
City of Gothenburg EU Office (S)	- representing Gothenburg and its key stakeholders in Brussels. - monitoring the legislative initiative of the EU, - promoting Gothenburg and its actors at the European level, - supporting the development of strategic and long term EU projects. (http://international.goteborg.se)
City of Malmö EU Office (S)	- is a service-provision body for the City of Malmö's departments. - main tasks: monitor EU programmes and funds, - make and develop contacts, engage in lobbying - assist with project applications & project concepts with city depts. (http://malmo.se/English/EU-and-International-Cooperation-.html)

Fig. 5.2 (Continued)

City of London Office (GB)	- promotes and reinforces competitiveness of the Square Mile and in particular UK-based international financial services - works closely with practitioners, trade associations and other stakeholders to shape the future direction of financial services policy - focuses on issues created by EU and international regulative, fiscal and regulatory developments likely to impact on the City's operation. (https://www.cityoflondon.gov.uk/business/eu-and-regulation)
Greater Birmingham and West Midlands Office (GB)	- profile raising, promote Birmingham interests - gathering early intelligence on transnational European funding opps. - sustaining and enhancing relationships with key European stakeholders (http://www.birmingham.gov.uk/eia)
Greater Manchester Brussels Office (GB)	No longer on web, link greater-manchester.eu no longer working
London's European Office (GB)	- monitors and influences EU policy - identifies opportunities for London to obtain EU funding. - informs the GLA Group about relevant EU policies, legislation, funding - promotes the vision and work of the Mayor in Brussels to the EU - represents London's interests in the development of EU policies (https://www.london.gov.uk/about-us/mayor-london/public-affairs/londons-european-office)
Merseyside Brussels Office (GB)	- renamed Liverpool City Region Brussels Office (1 Jan 15) - represents Liverpool City Region (LCR) at the heart of EU - provides vital link between local public, business, voluntary orgs, EU institutions and other European regions. (www.lcrbrussels.eu)

Fig. 5.2   (Continued)

region (Central Bohemia) have separate representations, mirroring their administrative separateness as well as attitudinal divisions (Sýkora 2006). The opposite scenario is that of Bratislava, Brussels or Dubrovnik, where the city clearly stands for the wider region. Such urban dominance may draw on historic city-state status, as in the case of the Hanse Office, combining Hamburg as lead partner and the economically less potent and less well known adjoining federal state of Schleswig-Holstein. Quite evidently, Hamburg takes here the role of the internationally recognised and present lead partner. This confirms the observation made by Donas and Beyers (2012) that the more 'resourceful' sub-national authorities (SNAs) benefit from a high level of self-rule and/or harbour regionalist political parties. They are much more likely to establish larger liaison offices and occupy a prominent position in various trans-regional associations. Thus, for instance, the representations of the German *Länder* jointly employ more staff than the representation of the German state as a whole (embassy). 'Independent-minded' Bavaria, for instance, at more than 30 staff, is the largest, 'operating from its notable chateau' (Greenwood 2011, p. 187).

Its budget at some €0.5 million per annum is nearly four times that of the smallest representations, many of which occupy just one or two offices in an office suite shared with others (Marks et al. 2002). Many of those smaller ones are representations from the new Central European member states, where regions are an often unloved (Herrschel 2007) construct by central government decree to meet EU requirements for funding under the Structural Fund. They tend to be little more than territorial containers for spatial policies and subsidies. There are differences, however, with Poland's new regions which enjoy a relatively higher profile presence in Brussels with matching administrative capacities (Greenwood 2011, p. 187). Tatham (2008) thus observed that while the less powerful, 'second league' regions are using their offices to attract funding and subsidies—and achievement here is used to justify their existence—the more powerful, federated, 'first division' regions 'seek to influence European public policy itself' (Greenwood 2011, p. 188). Their presence in Brussels has thus become somewhat of a proxy latent power struggle in federated state systems between the centre and the devolved regions (Greenwood 2011, pp. 188–189).

Not surprisingly, in the early phase of these regional offices in Brussels— during the late 1980s and early 1990s—some nation states, especially those with strong, constitutionally empowered and protected regions (Spain, Germany, Italy), saw these foreign representations as challenges to their perceived exclusive right to represent the state internationally. Foreign policy and representation was to be a 'natural' national responsibility, including the right to deal with EU institutions. During these legal challenges about international representation, as the legal situation was not yet clear, the relevant regions refrained from using the label 'representation' for their Brussels offices, and named them less contentiously 'liaison bureaux'. Yet, as soon as the legal situation was clarified, and the name 'representation' was found permissible as long as it referred to 'inner state tasks', this label was swiftly re-adopted my many (Moore 2006; Greenwood 2011), especially those with strong self-confidence. In the case of Spain and Italy, for instance, regional representations had at first to remain low key and 'hide' behind the institutional presence of chambers of commerce or other non-state representation (Greenwood 2011), because the central states considered such representations as undue infringement of their traditional prerogative of international representation. Yet, since the legal clarification of the late 1990s, the regions feel confident enough to make strong statements about their institutional capacity and political agenda. Names such as 'Free State of ...' or 'Communidad Autonomas ...' or 'Autonomous Government of ...' (see Fig. 5.2) clearly illustrate the changing (and competitive) power relations in domestic governmental structures as they manifest themselves in these Brussels representations, as well as efforts to directly influence the Council of Ministers. Scotland, for instance, has increased its institutional presence through a concentration of a wide range of Scottish institutions and organisations, including trade unions and business representations, under one roof: 'Scotland Europa'. This avoids politicising the devolution debate further by being less formally challenging, and using instead 'institutional thickness' to boost presence and political impact and relevance in Brussels.

It is representations of that kind, where constitutional powers are more limited, and soft forms of diplomacy and policy-making become more important, that are deemed to be concerned about proving their democratic legitimacy to their respective population as a justification of their action. Greenwood (2011) distinguishes here 'medium devolution' countries, where regions are still within the process of finding the degree of devolution 'at home' and their action is still part of their political justification of continued devolution. In the case of the 'highly devolved' (Greenwood 2011) countries, where power distribution and devolution have been formally and territorially manifested and assured, regions seem more concerned about projecting their standing vis-à-vis their national governments as a show of strength. These offices have thus as much to do with positioning themselves in the domestic state hierarchy as with lobbying in Brussels. Generally, for these more politically ambitious regions, representative buildings in prestigious locations, flags and 'power names' have come to demonstrate their para-statal aspirations vis-à-vis their respective nation states. The line seems quite fine and somewhat fluid when it comes to defining 'internal affairs' as delimitation of these forms of international representation vis-à-vis conventional ambassadorial representations under international law. Much will also depend on personal connections, and political capability in lobbying and using soft forms of diplomacy.

The Netherlands offers an interesting example of different constellations of international engagement and interest lobbying by sub-national units (see Fig. 5.3). There is a collaborative bipolar city-region (Arnhem Nijmegen City Region), a collaborative 'elite' city network (G4 EU Offices—EU representation offices in Amsterdam, The Hague, Rotterdam and Utrecht—with each of the four cities having its own office within

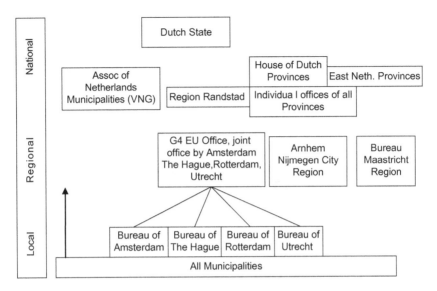

Fig. 5.3 Brussels offices by Dutch sub-national authorities

the common representation), single city-region representation (Bureau Maastricht Region in Brussels), representations of the regions (provinces), representation of the long-established state-defined region of Randstad (also province by role), and the national representation of all municipalities (Association of Netherlands Municipalities [VNG]).

The choice of name for these representations is also interesting to note as a signal of political intent and programme: liaison bureaux for Austrian regions, European Office (Central Bohemia), Representations (CZ), EU Office (Denmark), Contact and Information Point (German regions, Polish regions), Delegation (Spanish regions), Office of Government (Spain), or, in Belgium, the Ministry of the Region Capital Brussels. So, the picture is quite varied, with cities being represented either individually (in London's case even twofold—as a whole metropolis (Greater London), and then the finance centre of the Square Mile as the City of London), or as part of a functional city-region, a wider formalised region (e.g. Berlin city state), with or without referring to them by name. It is also interesting to note that there are wide differences in the size and international profile of cities seeking to 'go it alone', reaching from capital cities to, in some instances, provincial towns (e.g. in Bulgaria, see Fig. 5.2). Liverpool, in pursuit of its international agenda, which was given additional impetus by its status as ECoC, entertains a Brussels office of its own, with which it now shares the same building as that of its traditional rival Manchester. But at this international level, cooperation seems to be seen as opportune. 'Brussels is where the major EU institutions are located and where most European regions and sectors are represented, so it is the ideal place for Liverpool City Region to be making its voice heard. Liverpool City Region Brussels Office claims a good relationship with MEPs, the European Commission and the UK government's representation to the EU' (Liverpool City Region Brussels Office 2016).

Irrespectively, the sheer number of sub-national representations in Brussels makes for a formidable political arena between the sub-national and international, sitting in parallel to the conventional relationships between nation states and the international arena (here: Brussels). The unique nature of the EU offers particularly fertile ground for such a new space of internationality that reaches beneath the nation state level and is thus much 'thicker' and diverse in its composition of actors than traditional IR studies acknowledge, capturing all regional and local scales. Such local engagement combines with the regional scale in the instances of the larger cities/city-regions (as expressed in the very name), and speaks through municipal associations—some of which are exclusively reserved for urban municipalities (e.g. German Cities' Association, *Deutscher Städtetag*), although in collaboration with the more inclusive general municipal association *Deutscher Städte- und Gemeindebund* (interview, Deutscher Städtetag, Brussels Office, 8 July 2015)—or is organised at the regional level immediately beneath the national scale, including all subsequent scales of governing (municipalities, counties) as a matter of their hierarchically lower administrative position. In the case of the German Cities Association, there is a two-tier membership: 200 'direct members' as a form of 'first class' group, consisting of all unitary (and thus larger) cities and the three city-states of Berlin, Hamburg and Bremen, and the 'ordinary' membership of some 3,000 cities (qualified for membership through their formal city status), which are indirectly represented through their respective regional (federal state) groupings of the Association (http://www.staedtetag. de/mitglieder/index.html). The main tasks involve lobbying for the members' interests at national government, offering advice and helping knowledge transfer and policy exchanges. There is no explicit reference to international work, although such is carried out by its Brussels Office at EU level (Fig. 5.4).

		Type of International Representation	
		Formal	Informal
Scale (Level) of Actor & Governance	Regional	Formal regions (with varying powers, agents of centre or federalised devolved)	Informal regional associations (e.g. Baltic Sea Region, trans-border Euroregions)
		Formally established city-region	Collaborative, functional city regions (policy-based)
	Local	Municipality (city or non-urban) varying forms of engagement, based on municipal type & policy purpose	

Fig. 5.4 'Thickness' of international representations: intersection of scale and institutionalised formality

In 2007, Huysseune and Jans (2008) identified 165 regions, 17 local or sub-regional authorities, 26 networks of local and regional authorities, and 18 representations of mainly regional private-sector entities as accredited by the Brussels Capital Region, working from 226 accredited offices. The size and 'profile' of these offices varies, either being clustered in a dedicated building (Scotland House, House of the Dutch Provinces), or internationally shared to represent established political-economic collaborative engagement, such as the shared office suite of Copenhagen and Malmö as lead cities in the international Øresund region. The representation of individual cities may also be less visible, as they work through their respective regional offices, without having an officially accredited (by Brussels) office. Irrespectively, having a 'Brussels address' certainly seems de rigueur for European sub-national actors. These representations have thus become a significant group of players in the 'Brussels-based supranational policy community' (Huysseune and Jans 2008, p. 1). As a result, Brussels has become the main arena for regional and local lobbying at the European level of policy-making, but also a platform for marketing on the business and investment circuit.

Representations of sub-national authorities have their origins in the mid-1980s, when Birmingham opened an office in 1985 as the first city to do so. This was quite remarkable in that Birmingham, as a manufacturing city, has not been a traditionally particularly internationally engaged or visible city. This focus on the EU was driven by the fundamental structural changes the city and its engineering (automotive) based economy was undergoing at a time, in the 1980s, when national funding to local government was severely curtailed by the Thatcher government. Securing support from the EU's Structural Fund offered a source of revenue that reduced dependency on the centre and offered a chance to implement the new regeneration strategy that involved landmark projects, especially the canal-side development of the International Convention Centre as the beginning of a major city-centre redevelopment process to tackle industrial decline and boost the city's appeal and capacity beyond being the 'workshop of the nation'. Between 1988 and 1993, some £300 million in Structural Funding were obtained. The proactive and direct engagement with the EU and its funding opportunities for sub-national government was thus triggered by economic stress, major structural problems and limited national support, which mobilised a regional coalition of local and regional actors, including the government's own regional representation (Government Regional Office) as 'broker between the UK and Europe' (Bentley and Shutt 1997, p. 141), and between the public and private sector. Projects supported by ERDF monies thus also involved projects in other parts of the conurbation, such as the Warwick Science Park. Representing the whole conurbation of Greater Birmingham and the West Midlands, although run by Birmingham City Council since 2012, the stated objective continues to be explicitly about boosting the city-region's international competitiveness and helping secure funding from the EU through lobbying and providing 'early intelligence' on opportunities (http://www.errin.eu/content/greater-birmingham-west-midlands-brussels-office) for the various public and private actors in the region (http://www.greaterbirmingham.eu).

The other early adopters of a Brussels representation, the German *Länder*, represent quite a different state structure and power distribution at sub-national level. While also pursuing the agendas of lobbying and gathering intelligence on EU policies, especially those affecting their own policies increasingly more directly, this has also become a matter of status in a federal structure. The Brussels Offices present themselves as international representations and take up whole buildings in an ambassadorial style. Having an international representation boosts confidence and sends a signal to the federal government, which accepted in 1992 the presence of *Land* international policy-making in this form (Börzel 2002, p. 77). The earlier collective informal representation of their (i.e. the Western German) interests through a joint office in Brussels, which existed since the beginning of the EU, was deemed no longer adequate. Especially the bigger and economically more internationally integrated states sought to sharpen their profiles as independent entities within the German federal system. The post-1997 devolution in Britain, in many ways still a very centralised state in structural terms, has brought about similar efforts to achieve higher international visibility next to the British state by Scotland and Wales, for instance. There is evidence that more statutorily powerful regions, with greater policy-making capacity and scope, are more likely to seek to expand their influence at the European level, too, reflecting their greater confidence and ambition for more independent policy-making beyond their national circumferences (see Huysseune and Jans 2008).

The interest in a Brussels representation was boosted by the growing role of EU regional policy since the Single European Act in 1987, which sought to add new momentum to European integration, including completion of the internal Single Market (http://eur-lex.europa.eu/legal-content/SK/TXT/?uri=URISERV:xy0027). In addition, the EU gained some new powers in policy fields that often were (co-)responsibilities of regions and municipalities at the sub-national level: environment, social and economic policies to foster cohesion, and research and development as support for competitiveness. The increase in financial volume of regional policies encouraged the more independent-minded and powerful regions with an underlying nationalist agenda to boost financial support directly from the EU and thus circumvent their respective national governments with which they were in conflict about greater autonomy. Examples include the traditionally centralised states of Spain and the UK. 'Going to Brussels' offered a new route to boost the independence agenda in Catalonia, the Basque Country, Brittany, Scotland and Wales. So, while for some of the new regional representations it was about affirming and pushing further their existing powers in a federalised system (Germany, Austria, Italy), for others it was a route to gaining recognition in the first place, and challenging their centralised states about greater powers (Spain, UK). In the meantime, 'being in Brussels' has become a 'must have' for all regions to not be overlooked and underrepresented in the increasingly crowded arena of lobbying EU actors and decision-makers. As Fig. 5.2 (table) shows, regional representations are also widespread among Central European states, especially the Visegrad countries, Poland, the Czech Republic, Slovakia and Hungary, where regions largely have a tradition as administrative tools of a centralised state. But the more competitive nature of political lobbying and gaining funding from the EU encourages greater direct engagement by all regions to secure a 'slice of the pie'. And this requires a sufficient degree of flexibility and awareness of regional specificity to devise relevant and convincing strategies. The status of regions as more independent policy-makers gained a further boost through the growing formal acknowledgement of sub-national actors, especially regions, as an increasingly important level of EU policy-making and politics, as manifested inter alia in the explicit emphasis on the principle of subsidiarity.

As part of Europe's multi-level governance, the provision that region-based ministers may attend the Council of Ministers, and the European Committee of the Regions, suggests that regions are becoming part of the EU governance arrangements (Huysseune and Jans 2008).The CoR provides sub-national units their own institutional framework within the EU's machinery, albeit with few powers and a largely representational and lobbying role. And so, at least formally, EU politics does recognise the increased relevance of actors and interests at the sub-national level. Yet voices from within the CoR bemoan the limited impact and effectiveness of policy in terms of lobbying (Huysseune and Jans 2008). Much of the institution is about formal visibility, rather than governmental capacity (CoR visit, 22 January 2016), and its relevance and 'impact' largely depend on informal connections, lobbying and sheer visibility as a collective group and platform for joint gathering. Information flows and 'get-to-know' ability are important, as direct connections between regions and the EU Commission allow stepping aside from the formal hierarchy and circumventing national governments. The rhetoric of the 'Europe of the Regions' under Jacques Delors in the 1990s further fuelled the notion that nation states are less predominant. That this idea of using the regional scale to organise Europe was at least premature in political terms, is clearly illustrated by the rekindled self-centred nationalism we are currently witnessing with barbed wire and confrontational rhetoric having returned to daily political discourse in the face of the migration /refugee challenge of early 2016.

About one-sixth of all officially recognised sub-national representations (see Fig. 5.2) involves municipalities in the form of either municipal associations and collective groupings, or (mostly) larger cities or city-regions as individual actors with a designated office either within or separate from 'their' respective regional contexts. Indeed, as mentioned before, it was the Birmingham/West Midlands city-region that established the very first such representation as a new model of international engagement. The different rationales in engaging are also reflected in the 'task sheet' and evaluation of 'success'. While for the more empowered regions it is a matter of expressing their relative independence in some policy fields and their status vis-à-vis the nation state, for the administrative regions, depending on a benevolent view of their usefulness by the state, the pressure to deliver 'value for money' is greater. Here, some efforts may be merely experimental to evaluate the added benefit of stepping 'out' beyond conventional regional and, especially, national boundaries. This also applies to collaborative city networks where a utilitarian, rather than a representational, perspective prevails. Cities like London, Hamburg or Prague have their international Brussels representation as a matter of civic pride and course.

Based on their survey of the functions of the regional offices in Brussels, Huysseune and Jans (2008, p. 5) distinguish four policy fields/agendas: 'information management, networking, liaison between local and regional authorities and the EU, and the influencing of EU policy'. So it is primarily about 'soft' powers of lobbying, gathering intelligence and networking, although some sub-national representations will wield more cachet than others, based on their statutory and/or economic stature. They may thus be more effective in gaining access to the machinery of the Brussels bureaucracy. But, as pointed out earlier, these representations are also important sources of information of developmental needs and priorities at the regional scale, giving a more detailed picture than painted by national governments. They are thus considered to be more 'grassroots' and democratically representative, which gives regional interests added credibility and perceived democratic legitimacy.

In some instances, EU officials themselves may actively seek information and expertise, and the regional offices (as 'grassroots' or 'civil society' representatives) are being valued as valid and legitimate (public) sources of (regional) information and data. These offices are relevant partners for European Commission officials, because they enable the latter to develop programmes that meet the actual needs perceived at the grassroots level and thus give extra political cachet. As Huysseune and Jans (2008) discovered from their survey, acting as interlocutors between their region and EU institutions is considered a primary legitimating (and legitimate) task. Again, successful policy outcomes, especially when endorsed by the public, seem to justify political means that may not be entirely covered by formal 'procedure' as manifestation of legitimacy. But there is also considerable interest in horizontal networking with non-governmental and, especially, private sector actors in the pursuit of economic opportunities. And this may involve collaborative action for specific agendas. The location in Brussels allows combining sub-national and international interests, including EU policies and private sector investment interests, playing to both audiences—international and domestic.

The scope for exercising lobbying influence varies with the institutional capacity of the individual region, and here the formally institutionalised and empowered regions, such as in Germany, Belgium, Spain or Austria, may be able to 'make the most' of their direct access to the Council of Ministers, a route opened in the early 1990s. But regions with a less strong and protected position in their respective states, i.e. the administrative regions created and abolished by national government as mere agents of the centre, act more like interest groups, as they don't possess the confidence and institutional capacity to be more assertive and independent in their political agendas. They thus tend to concentrate on the 'soft power' of persuasion and lobbying. 'They contribute to the policy process by producing position papers, seek to establish issue-coalitions and networks to increase their credibility and impact on EU policy-makers, and participate in the wide array of consultation formats organized by the European Commission on important policy issues (e.g., expert groups, white and green papers, surveys, panels, public hearings, and Commission-sponsored conferences' (Huysseune and Jans 2008, p. 7).

Brussels, as Europe's capital, is an interesting case of city-regional internationality in its own right, as it combines the particular divisions within the Belgian state as a result of lingo-regionalism between Flemish and Walloons, with the capital region of Brussels the bilingual 'neutral ground'. Here, in its complex arrangement of meticulously institutionalised bilingualism in all public office, Brussels' engagement with the EU comes on the basis of acting on behalf of the Belgian state. The Belgian state's devolution situation gives the two main territorial regions, and the Brussels city-region, a particularly strong position as independent actors next to the state, rather than as subordinate to the state. This includes direct interaction with other states and IOs, as well as at state level within the EU (interview Brussels Capital Region, International Department, 8 July 2015). The three regions alternate as part of a rotating principle (each stays at the helm for 3–4 years), in their representative role of regionally devolved power *next* to the centre at the EU institutions. The regional level has to agree first, for the Belgian state then to be able to agree to EU policy measures, such as the Transatlantic Trade and Investment

Partnership (TTIP). The rotating regional leadership in Belgium requires agreement among all three regions, so as to speak with one voice and ensure interests of all three are taken into account (interview Brussels Capital Region, International Department, 8 July 2015).

Processes of negotiation are a constant feature of Belgian politics and provide cities and, especially, regions with considerable negotiating experience and skill, as well as confidence. This puts them at an advantage compared to many of their counterparts in other, less devolved states, where regions are used to being internationally represented by the state and relying on a hierarchical structure. In Belgium, no such hierarchy exists (any longer). Instead, linkages of devolved multi-level government operate sideways. Consequently, the Brussels city-region finds itself often better informed about EU policies (especially Cohesion Policy) than its city-/regional counterparts from other countries, as it deals directly in meetings with national ministers of the other EU countries and also the Commission. This provides direct access to top-level information and decision-making processes. Other—including bigger—city-regions, such as Île de France, for instance, approach Brussels for that reason so as to gain better information on the policies than they can obtain from the handed-down information from their national governments (interview Brussels Capital Region, International Department, 8 July 2015). The Brussels region, therefore, in effect, could stop an EU initiative/treaty from being ratified, although that rarely occurs, as policies will be pre-negotiated within Belgium first; the national ambassador comes to the region (the one 'in charge') to pre-negotiate the Belgian position in EU voting matters.

As a result, while the Capital Region of Brussels (i.e. Greater Brussels) collaborates with other municipalities and city networks, it also acts as host of the EU institutions as representative of the Belgian state. Thus, officials are focused on organisational formalities, such as preparing Council meetings in which Belgian regional ministers participate as representatives of the state and thus sit opposite other national representatives (interview Brussels Capital Region, International Department, 8 July 2015). This immediate proximity is unique, of course, but for other representations in Brussels, the physical and thus communicative proximity offers important opportunities for participating in, and influencing, EU decision-making on regionally relevant policies. Clearly (from a city-regional perspective), 'it is easier to access EU institutions being in Brussels than from Poland [for instance]' (interview Brussels Capital Region, International Department, 8 July 2015). Using the EU institutions is politically sensitive, as it suggests intent to by-pass the state. 'There are [still traditional] views in "traditional" internationally acting departments about the role sub-national actors ought to play, and there are national ministries that believe it is not something for cities to engage in. But this attitude is slowly changing, has been over last 15 years' (interview Brussels Capital Region, International Department, 8 July 2015).

This traditional view is illustrated by discussions in Tallinn about the benefits of opening an office in Brussels, when a former mayor, who advocated public sector austerity, and who came from a very conservative position, objected: 'It is a place to bury huge amounts of taxpayers' money, and as a result something will be left undone in the city ... Local municipalities have nothing to do with EU accession. It is a matter of [sic] states' (Kurm 2002). So, for many cities, gaining access to the EU-level political processes and negotiations is possible only through networks like Euro cities, which has been recognised by the EU as a relevant and important body and partner in policy-making. For the EU policy-makers, such partners also matter as democratic 'fig leaves' by demonstrating 'listening' to the local level and thus gaining democratic legitimacy from 'the people' for policy decisions. But attitudes are changing on the back of a realisation of the growing role of cities as drivers of economic development and competitiveness, which will also translate into greater political ambitions. 'While 15 years ago, it was difficult to get an urban dimension recognised in EU regional policies, it now is readily accepted, and this opens new doors, also at DG Regio' (interview Brussels Capital Region, International Department, 8 July 2015).

As host of the institutions of the EU, the government of the Brussels Capital Region founded the Brussels-Europe Liaison Office (BELO) in 1991 to 'promote the image of Brussels as capital of Europe and seat of key European institutions, and also promote the benefits of the EU for the well-being and prosperity of the Region' (Huysseune and Jans 2008, p. 8). Importantly, BELO has provided key support for these offices in Brussels by offering a formal certification to aid with administrative issues related to Brussels metropolitan bureaucracy. The regional offices, whether private entities or representatives of public authorities, have an unofficial status and can therefore be confronted with many complex administrative problems concerning their establishment in Brussels as a 'foreign' space, without being formally recognised as such. They do not possess diplomatic rights. A Regional Certificate was introduced in 1994, which acknowledges such a regional office as representation of an international, sub-national authority within the Brussels Capital Region. While not a legal document about status, it aids administrative and logistical tasks, such as access for public utilities or infrastructure projects that may need to pass through/under such locations.

This arrangement has now been given higher profile by giving BELO a greater role in the EU, as it effectively acts on behalf of the Belgian state as part of devolution. For that, the function has been divided into the 'Commissioner of Brussels—Europe and International' and 'Visit Brussels', the tourism marketing organisation. This arrangement also reflects the growing devolution of tasks from the state level downwards to the three main regions in Belgium. The installation of a Brussels Commissioner for Europe and International Organisations suggests a clearer, stronger commitment to an active international role for the city than implied by the characteristics associated with the name 'liaison office'. It appears much more proactive and committed than merely a passive 'go between'. This shift up a gear in international engagement by the city-region reflects both the particular internal dynamic of the Belgian state, moving towards maximum devolution to the two main ethnic regions plus Brussels, allowing the Brussels city-region's government to act as a proto-state and host nation, and an awareness of the potential that the numerous European and IOs in the city offer to access the arena of international politics, governance and economic decisions. As a consequence, the Brussels Commissioner has been granted the mandate to 'to take all necessary measures and thus consolidate the status of Brussels as capital of Europe and international decision-making centre worthy of the name' (http://www.commissioner. brussels). And this includes ensuring that the IOs' deployment is 'in harmony with the development of the Brussels Capital Region and the needs of its inhabitants' (ibid.). Quite clearly, a close link is created here between international engagement and local effects, the positive nature of which serves as legitimation of such engagement. But this also poses a dilemma for mayors and city decision-makers, as cities are local places as well as, increasingly, international actors with a different scale of perspective and agenda.

5.5 SUMMARY

This chapter explored in more detail local and regional strategies to 'go international' and the rationales behind this, within a European context. As outlined earlier in Chap. 4, three main strategic approaches were looked at: individual action, engagement with IOs, and joining, and working through, agenda-specific networks. The European context matters here quite evidently, as it shapes all three avenues to international engagement. Network-based policies concentrated on the 'flagship' programme of city twinning, the oldest programme in the EU. Aimed at local government international action as part of post-war reconciliation and integration strategies, the focus on reducing the divisive effects of borders has provided a fertile environment for cities and regions to step into the international arena. Increasingly, such twinning projects not only expand into a broader policy of transnational regionalism (Euro regions), but also expand beyond Europe. The attraction of such para-diplomatic activity rests in their lesser degree of political symbolism than work at state level. There is thus more scope for trial and error in politically riskier or unpredictable engagement.

Opening representations in Brussels has become another favoured route to international visibility and engagement. Driven by varying rationales, scope and capacity to open representations in Brussels to gain direct access to EU decision-making processes, such sub-ambassadorial visibility serves mainly two purposes: projecting presence and relevance to the outside world, while also showing international relevance and stature to the population 'at home'. National circumstances of state structure, such as federalism versus centralism, or a regionalist 'tradition' proved to be relevant for opting for either (or both) both avenues in response to the specific circumstances and their curtailing effects on feasible and promising options. And this, in turn, shapes the nature and operation of such a representation as a lobbying device at EU, and also global, level. For some regions, especially those harbouring more or less articulated dreams about independence, a Brussels office seems to serve as proto-embassy in a direct challenge to the respective nation state, thus projecting domestic politics onto the international circuit of European politics in Brussels.

Among individual, single city initiatives, the EU programme of ECoC offer interesting insights into the ways in which culture becomes an important vehicle for international local politics, but also of how economic competitiveness, as a universally effective outcome of globalisation, has produced a degree of standardisation of policies and strategies. Despite an initial focus on promoting distinct examples of 'high art' as part of a local tradition, much of ECoC strategy is about stepping out of international obscurity. Such may apply to an old industrial city with a negative image of decline and lost purpose, or a peripheral town off the radar screen of international political-economic awareness and interest. Yet, despite the decidedly local and place-specific focus of this European initiative, national circumstances and debates have remained clearly in the background—be that as context for state investment and thus scope for actual, physical connectivity or credible redevelopment, or as discourse about national identity, sense of 'togetherness' and purpose. A country's size in relation to the respective city also matters: whereas in Latvia events in the capital city of Riga automatically double up as national events or at least as events of national interest, such is less the case in a territorially expansive state such as Sweden, where there are considerable internal variations in regional (and local) affinities to the capital city.

For city mayors and regional leaders, this raises a question about whose interests they are expected to represent, and how they can serve those best: more neo-liberalism-inspired internationalisation versus social outreach, for instance? At a broader level, this is essentially also a question of ideology and political beliefs about the role of the state, the importance of international capitalism, and the most appropriate form of regulating the market to achieve agreed goals: neo-liberalism or the social market approach, central state intervention to counteract local and regional variations in opportunities versus local/regional individuality in strategic responses and sketching out of development pathways? How does engagement with the 'international', here the EU, benefit the city's population to justify choices made, such as international engagement through a Brussels office? Are there likely to be new divisions? And, if so, what does that say about the justification of such policies? Within the EU, the CoR is an important mediating platform for policy exchange, 'learning' and formulating, policy agendas and strategies.

There is thus a 'looking up' the multi-level hierarchy to the EU institutions and national governments (especially in the more centralised states), while also looking sideways to potential partners and strategic collaborators, especially the private sector and NGOs. All these considerations and negotiations need to take on board the different clienteles that city governments need to address as part of their democratic responsibilities: being competitive to deliver economic opportunities, but also cohesive, democratically legitimate, and 'just' (interview Brussels Capital Region, International Department, 8 July 2015). In effect, one might say, internationalisation stretches a city upwards (but with its feet tied to the ground), as it needs to remain a local place, addressing the needs and expectations of the local population, while also being extended outwardly (or 'upwardly') in its policy agendas and aspirations, and economic linkages, to the international sphere. The gap between the two (and even inherent contradictions) may thus be widening, making negotiations between the two potentially more contentious politically. As the number of actors increases, and the picture gets more diverse as a result, and with it individually held perspectives, interests and priorities, the task of negotiation, balancing and prioritising needs both careful articulation and negotiation to secure democratic legitimacy for the particular avenues chosen to connect the local to the international, and the success of such action to maintain economic viability and thus scope for providing local services and governmental structures and policies.

REFERENCES

Aiello, G and Thurlow, C., 2006. Symbolic Capitals: Visual Discourse and Intercultural Exchange in the European Capital of Culture Scheme. *Language and Intercultural Communication* Vol. 6, No. 2, 148–162.

Baycan-Levent, T., Nijkamp, P. and Sahin, M., 2008. New orientations in ethnic entrepreneurship: motivation, goals and strategies of new generation ethnic entrepreneurs. *International journal of foresight and innovation policy*, 5(1–3), 83–112.

Baycan-Levent, T., 2010. Diversity and creativity as seedbeds for urban and regional dynamics. *European Planning Studies*, 18(4), 565–594.

Bentley, G and Shutt, J., 1997. European Regional Policy in English Regions: The West Midlands and Yorkshire and Humberside. In: John Bachtler, Ivan Turok (eds, 1997): *The Coherence of EU Regional Policy: Contrasting Perspectives on the Structural Funds.* London: Jessica Kingsley Publishers, pp. 123–142.

Börzel T. A., 2002. *States and Regions in the European Union. Institutional Adaptation in Germany and Spain.* Cambridge: Cambridge University Press.

Boyle, M., 1997. Civic Boosterism in the Politics of Local Economic Development—'Institutional Positions'; and 'Strategic Orientations' in the Consumption of Hallmark Events. *Environment and Planning A,* 29(11), 1975–1997.

Capello, R., 2000. The city network paradigm: measuring urban network externalities. *Urban Studies,* 37(11), 1925–1945.

Carrière, J.P. and Demazière C., 2002. Urban Planning and Flagship Development Projects: Lessons from EXPO 98, Lisbon. *Planning Practice & Research,* Vol. 17, No. 1, 69– 79.

Chang, T.C., 2000. Renaissance revisited: Singapore as a 'global city for the arts'. *International journal of urban and regional research,* 24(4), 818–831.

Crouch, D., 2016. Swedish border controls hit Øresund bridge commuters as well as refugees . In: *The Guardian*, 4 Jan.

Donas, T. and Beyers, J., 2013. How regions assemble in Brussels: the organizational form of territorial representation in the European Union. *Publius: The Journal of Federalism*, *43*(4), 527–550.

European Commission., 2016. 2017 EGCA Shortlist, available under http://ec.europa.eu/environment/europeangreencapital/applying-for-the-award/2017-egca-applicant-cities/

Evans, C.L., 2003. The economic significance of national border effects. *American Economic Review*, 1291–1312.

Evans, G., 2005. Measure for Measure: Evaluating the Evidence of Culture's Contribution to Regeneration. In: *Urban Studies*, vol. 42, nos. 5/6, 1–25.

FCM (Federation of Canadian Municipalities), 2004. QUALITY OF LIFE IN CANADIAN COMMUNITIES, theme report no 3. Ottawa. Available under: https://www.fcm.ca/Documents/reports/Growth_the_Economy_and_the_Urban_Environment_EN.

Garcia, B., 2005. Deconstructing the city of culture: The long-term cultural legacies of Glasgow 1990. *Urban studies*, 42(5–6), 841–868.

Greenwood, J., 2011. *Interest representation in the European Union*. Houndsmill, Basingstoke: Palgrave Macmillan, 3rd ed.

Griffiths, R., 2006. City/Culture Discourses: Evidence from the Competition to Select the European Capital of Culture 2008. *European Planning Studies* Vol. 14, No. 4, 415–430.

Guibernau, M., 2013. *Nationalisms: The nation-state and nationalism in the twentieth century*. Oxford: Wiley.

Herrschel, T., 2007. Global Geographies of Post-socialist Transition. London: Routledge.

Herrschel T., 2011. *Borders in Post-Socialist Europe: Territory, Scale, Society*. Farnham: Ashgate.

Hiller, H.H., 2000. Mega-events, urban boosterism and growth strategies: an analysis of the objectives and legitimations of the Cape Town 2004 Olympic Bid. *International journal of urban and regional research*, 24(2), 449–458.

Huysseune, M. and Jans, M., 2008. Brussels as the capital of a Europe of the regions? Regional offices as European policy actors In: Brussels Studies (http://www.brusselsstudies.be Issue 16, 25 February 2008, pp 1–11)

Kantor, P., 2002. Terrorism and Governability in New York City Old Problem, New Dilemma. *Urban Affairs Review*, *38*(1), 120–127.

Kevin O'Toole., 2001. Kokusaika and Internationalisation: Australian and Japanese Sister City Type Relationships, Australian Journal of International Affairs, 55:3, pp. 403–419.

Kiran, E., Debenedetti, P.G. and Peters, C.J. eds., 2012. *Supercritical fluids: fundamentals and applications* (Vol. 366). Springer Science & Business Media.

Kurm, K., 2002. Tallin's Reps in Brussels under Fire. In: Baltic Times, 11 July 2002

Le Galès, P., 2002. *European cities: social conflicts and governance*. Oxford: OUP.

Liverpool City Region Brussels Office (2016): Bullet no. 20 (Feb); available under: http://www.lcrbrussels.eu/uploadedfiles/documents/Bulletin_Feb_2016.pdf.

Locatelli, G. and Mancini, M., 2010. Risk management in a mega-project: the Universal EXPO 2015 case. *International Journal of Project Organisation and Management*, 2(3), 236–253.

Marks, Gary, Francois Nielsen, Leonard Ray, and Jane E. Salk. 1996. Competencies, cracks and conflict: Regional mobilization in the European Union. In Governance in the European Organizational Form of Territorial Representation in the EU 23

Marks, G., Haesly, R. and Mbaye, H.A., 2002. What do subnational offices think they are doing in Brussels?. *Regional & Federal Studies*, 12(3), 1–23.

Marston, S.A., Knox, P.L. and Liverman, D.M., 2002. *World regions in global context: Peoples, places, and environments*. Prentice Hall.

McAteer, N., Rampton, J., France, J., Tajtáková, M. and Lehouelleur, S., 2014. Ex-post Evaluation of the 2013 European Capitals of Culture. Final Report for the European Commission DG Education and Culture. London: Emrys ltd.

Montgomery, J., 2004. Cultural quarters as mechanisms for urban regeneration. Part 2: A review of four cultural quarters in the UK, Ireland and Australia. *Planning, Practice & Research*, 19(1), 3–31.

Mooney, G., 2004. Cultural Policy as Urban Transformation? Critical Reflections on Glasgow, European City of Culture 1990. In: Local Economy, Vol. 19, No. 4, 327–340.

Moore, C., 2006. 'Schloss Neuwahnstein'? Why the Länder continue to strengthen their representations in Brussels. *German Politics*, 15(2), 192–205.

Myerscough, J., 1994. *European Cities of Culture and Cultural Months: Summary Report*. Network of Cultural Cities of Europe.

Nye, J.S., 2010. The pros and cons of citizen diplomacy. *New York Times*, 4 Oct.

Palmer/RAE Associates, 2004. European cities and capitals of culture. Study Prepared for the European Commission, Brussels., Parts 1, available under: https://ec.europa.eu/programmes/creativeeurope/sites/creative-europe/files/library/palmer-report-capitals-culture-1995-2004-i_en.pdf

Perkmann, M. and Sum, N.L., 2002. Globalization, regionalization and cross-border regions: scales, discourses and governance (pp. 3–21). Palgrave Macmillan UK.

Richards, G., 2000. The European cultural capital event: Strategic weapon in the cultural arms race?. *International Journal of Cultural Policy*, 6(2), 159–181.

Riga, 2014. European Capital of Culture in Riga – a resounding success. Press release. Available under: http://ttgnordic.com/european-capital-of-culture-in-riga-%E2%80%93-a-resounding-success/

Rommetvedt, H., 2008. Beliefs in culture as an instrument for regional development: The case of Stavanger, European Capital of Culture 2008. *Regional and Urban Regeneration in European Peripheries*, p. 59.

Saunier, P., 2001. Sketches from the Urban Internationale, 1910–50: Voluntary associations, international institutions and US philanthropic foundations. *International Journal of Urban and Regional Research*, 25(2), 380–403.

Short, J.R., Benton, L.M., Luce, W.B. and Walton, J., 1993. Reconstructing the image of an industrial city. Annals of the Association of American Geographers, 83(2), 207–224.

Short, J., Breitbach, C., Buckman, S. and Essex, J., 2000. From world cities to gateway cities: Extending the boundaries of globalization theory. *City*, 4(3), 317–340.

Sykora, L., 2006. Urban development, policy and planning in the Czech Republic and Prague. Spatial Planning and Urban Development in the New EU Member States: From Adjustment to Reinvention, Aldershot and Burlington: Ashgate, pp. 113–140.

Tatham, M., 2008. Going solo: Direct regional representation in the European Union. *Regional and Federal Studies*, 18(5), 493–515.

Fox, T and Rampton, J., 2015. Ex-post Evaluation of the European Capitals of Culture. Europ Commission.

Umeå., 2009. Curiosity and Passion – the Art of Co-Creation. Application for Nomination. Available under: http://umea2014.se/en/about-umea2014/european-capital-of-culture/umeas-bid/

Van den Berg, G.J., 2001. Duration models: specification, identification and multiple durations. *Handbook of econometrics*, 5, pp. 3381–3460.

Verwijnen, J. and Lehtovuori, P. eds., 1999. *Creative cities: cultural industries, urban development and the information society*. University of Art and Design Helsinki.

Vion, A., 2002. Europe from the bottom up: town twinning in France during the Cold War. *Contemporary European History*, 11(04), 623–640.

CHAPTER 6

Cities and Internationality in North America and Beyond

6.1 Introduction: Networks and Single City Action in the North American State Context

As shown in Chap. 5, the external context plays an important role in shaping the ways in which cities consider, and engage with, the international arena. The particular characteristics of multi-level governance in the European Union, including an explicit support for both sub-national political entities and trans-border relations as part of the integration agenda, have had a major impact on encouraging cities and regions to become international actors. There are obvious variations to that, reflecting size, economic and political capacity and political leadership as well as public interest in doing so. On that basis, an international sphere of various city networks—either as collaborative associations, or as individual bilateral or multi-lateral engagements, has developed. In general, a picture emerges that shows a tendency for larger, metropolitan actors to act separately from smaller urban and non-urban places, either individually, using their enhanced municipal political and economic capital to set out and pursued an independent strategy of international engagement, to or do so in forms of 'elitist' groupings, such as large cities.

In North America, the situation is unlike that in Europe, with much greater emphasis on businesses as shaper of local agendas and drivers of policies; particularly so in the United States. Entrepreneurialism has thus been much closer to local policy-making than in Europe with its more state-centric tradition (with the UK taking an intermediate position)

© The Author(s) 2017
T. Herrschel, P. Newman, *Cities as International Actors*,
DOI 10.1057/978-1-137-39617-4_6

(Herrschel 2014). As a result, the mechanisms and routes to international engagement by cities and other sub-national actors have differed: following international corporate business linkages and engagements on an otherwise huge domestic arena of continental scale in North America. The continental dimension of the United States provides a large domestic economic and political arena, beyond which not many municipalities feel the need—or urge—to reach. In Europe, by contrast, an 'internal internationality' across much of the continent under the auspices of the EU's institutionalised multi-national platform encouraged, even incentivised, an international engagement by urban players. In addition, in Europe, national economic spaces are much smaller than in the United States or Canada, inevitably requiring cross-border linkages and engagement in the pursuit of growth.

For the main, largest, metropolises, the situation is different, of course, as their international reputation, visibility and concentration of internationally interested and connected (economic, cultural and political) actors provides a platform of its own for engaging transnationally. New York, but also Los Angeles, Miami and, increasingly, Chicago, are clearly places of international interest and initiative. The situation is less prominent among the second tier cities, decreasing further as one looks down the municipal hierarchy. There, stepping out onto the international arena is much more challenging and 'remote' in scale and ambition from their usual local—at best regional—perspectives. This chapter looks at some examples from across the urban scale and settings—from the singular New York as one of the three traditional global cities, via Chicago as ambitious second tier city, or Seattle as home to major global corporations which drive the city's internationalisation, to Aurora as suburban city of the Denver metropolitan area. And in Canada, from Toronto as functional part of the US metropolitan Eastern Seaboard, via Hamilton as a smaller city in the wider Toronto metropolitan area, to Vancouver as a widely recognised internationalising city, where internationality is a major local economic asset for its competitiveness and appeal. The sample cities discussed in this chapter, just as in the previous chapter, cannot be representative in the narrower sense of the wide range of local conditions, strategic ambitions and political-economic positions. This would by far exceed the scope of this book. The purpose of their inclusion is to illustrate a variety of different local 'settings', of different 'placeness', as descriptor of policy choices when it comes to internationalisation strategies. Accordingly, as elaborated earlier (Chap. 3), cities or other sub-national actors may exercise a constraint choice about how best to go about and venture onto the international stage: individual action based on confidence and economic credibility and status, or collectively with others as part of a network, where individual action promises little scope, or where obstacles and risks of failure seem unreasonably high. Between these two options, of course, various combinations may exist, depending on the particular policy field or agenda. 'Going it alone' may, for instance, seem opportune for competitive acquisition of foreign direct investment (FDI), but much less so when it comes to policies of climate change, So, while 'size matters', agenda and objective of policies will also influence strategic choices between singular or collective international action.

Tentative, and, perhaps, also more experimental, internationalisation efforts work through collective organisations to boost efficacy and chances for likely success by drawing on a broader range of contacts, experiences and expertises. In the United States, the main vehicle for such network-based internationalisation is Sister City International. Founded by President Dwight D. Eisenhower in 1956 to reach out to, and 'mend fences' with, post-war Europe and countries affected by the Korean War, the organisation serves as the national membership platform for over 500 individual 'sister cities', counties and states across the United States, connected to some 2,000 municipalities in some 140 countries (Salomon and Klocksin 2014). This means considerable capacity to network and link up with like-interested partners across the world. Other nation states have similar programmes encouraging local government cooperation, such as the UK's support for the Commonwealth Local Government Forum Twinning agreements (DFID 2010). In the case of the United States, SCI has provided an increasingly more widely used platform for expanding policy horizons, starting from more minor cultural and educational exchanges and linkages, and moving to develop into broader economic interests and connections beyond the American market. These embrace economic development and transnational investment as rapidly growing agendas. So it is perhaps not so surprising to find that the idea of 'international' and 'cross-border' is as such much less frequently found in local development strategies of municipalities, but also those of the large 'regions', the states in the United States and provinces in Canada, than found in Europe. There, the smaller scale territoriality matters with its smaller grid of international borders making them much more present and economically and politically relevant. Consequently, the issue of spatial integration has become more pertinent in the wake of progressing globalisation (see Chap. 5). But the initial kickstart of European trans-bordering has been the political agenda of addressing war legacies of divisions and distrust, a process that then, gradually, gained an economic dimension as part of growing economic liberalisation as the predominant discourse since the late 1970s. So it is interesting to note the rather more limited number of hits when searching the internet for the combination of 'international' and 'city sub-national' in combination with North America, compared with adding 'Europe'.

The effect of state scale becomes also apparent in the focus of engagement. Both in Europe and North America, municipalities have a keen interest in lobbying 'their' respective government for their interests, with the major cities trying to do that the most effectively. Conditions to do so, however, vary, not least in terms of a readiness to consider such options. In Europe, Brussels is the main hub of such ambitions in the form of representational 'offices', making such engagements immediately international, even if the geographic distances to the represented cities may be rather short. In the United States and Canada, such distances often go much farther: Washington (Capitol Hill), or Ottawa, respectively, are the main destination and/or place of reference for further-reaching engagement, albeit restricted mainly to municipal associations as representational bodies, rather than individual city efforts. Here, administrative hierarchies matter, and there is no tradition of city-centric statehood and notions of urban political and economic autonomy, as in Europe (see the Hanseatic League and city-states, Chap. 2). And so, indeed, the very notion of what is embodied by 'city' and appropriate urban engagement, differs fundamentally. But having an office in Washington, albeit indirectly through 'club membership', such as the national (US) local government network NLC, is an important indication of status and thus attraction for cities to join. In Canada, the federal capital in Ottawa is equally important, although the sheer scale of activity is of course more limited in comparison to that in the United States. The provincial capitals matter here first and foremost as statutory higher tier centres for the municipal governments. The legal and fiscal framework for local action is defined there, as municipalities are effectively creatures of provincial legislation. This contrasts with the much stronger, statutorily protected and thus more autonomous position of local government in the United States (Herrschel 2014).

Subsequent sections in this chapter follow, in principle, the structure of the previous Chap. 5, as it also distinguishes between network-based, collective, and individual, city strategies for engagement at the higher level government, let alone internationally, and explores the nature, operation and ambition/agenda of both. Much of the chapter deals with North America, because of its particular New World nature of 'urban', its continental scale, with Canada and Mexico offering 'internationality' from a US perspective, and globally important economic role and visibility. Canada and the United States, together with Mexico, share in NAFTA as an economically focused free trade area that aims to encourage international— economic—connections. And so it seems that economic ambitions are the main drivers of such activity, albeit in a relatively earlier stage than found in Europe. References will also be made to Australia and South Africa to add different cultural-historic contexts as variables which influence cities' engagement with the international sphere.

Ten years ago, Kresl and Frey (2005, p. 140) postulated that 'given this reality of frustration when cities look to superior levels of government for assistance, it is quite natural for them to create structures which, in their concerns and issues, will be the sole driving force'. As a result, there is a danger, of course, of a separation between scales of perspectives and policy approaches, with urban lenses, based on locally perceived urgencies and effects, and policy-making scope, shaping national interests and political decisions. Again, this would reinforce a widespread distinction between the 'urban' and the 'international' in terms of analysis, perceived priorities, and resulting preferences for responses. In North America, this distinction has remained much stronger than in Europe, where the EU's institutional, as well as ideological approach has been much more inter-scalar in nature, offering several arenas, as well as incentives, for local–national–international interaction and lobbying—and in a much more ad hoc and 'chaotic' way than the conventional hierarchy-following route, where national governments remain the primary interlocutors between the international and the sub-national. And in North America, there is a further distinction between the United States with constitutionally strong municipalities as expressions of the democratic will of local 'communities' (manifested in the provision of 'home rule'), and Canada, where as creatures of provincial governments, municipalities have a considerably weaker statutory standing vis-à-vis their respective central governments. Both countries share the relative remoteness between the national (federal) government level and the local. In terms of the differences in underlying constitutional arrangement for the multi-scalar state, the Canadian federal government has shown much less direct interest, such as through a dedicated minister for urban affairs, for instance, than their US counterparts (Kresl and Fry

2005), with the origins of the 2008 financial crisis, federally subsidised and secured home owners' mortgages clearly demonstrating this cross-scalar interdependence.

As a consequence of this tradition, most sub-national link-ups in the United States and in Canada are city-to-city relationships—although here there are variations in impact between the 'big players' and the 'rest', which may cause frictions about elitist 'big city' interests dominating federal–local relations and—therefore—policies (Kresl and Fry 2005). Such engagement has generally been associated first and foremost with 'sister city' schemes as the most prominent such example, and with national associations of municipalities—mainly to lobby national government. Yet, a select group of well-established cities with internationally recognised names, such as New York, Los Angeles or Chicago, also more recent entries onto the international scene, such as Toronto, Seattle or Vancouver, seek to go beyond that. Yet, these are not primarily driven by economic rationales alone, but also socio-cultural links (romanticised, perhaps), such as particular ethnic groups among a city's residents seeking to rekindle connections with their respective historic 'homelands' (Kresl and Fry 2005). The case of the suburban city of Aurora in the Denver metropolitan area (city-region) illustrates this factor as a driver of locally-defined international engagement. The outcome is an engagement of a rather more specific, limited nature than that driven primarily by economic opportunism, as a city's culture and social activities are of primary interest, and not so much hard economic factors of global competitiveness, although those are never far away. In fact, they have gained in importance on the back of a strong sense of municipal governments' duty to follow and serve their citizens' interests ('home rule'). And this includes boosting economic development as a perceived driver of growth and prosperity. The main platforms for formulating collective urban policies include the Federation of Canadian Municipalities—i.e. including all local governments, not just those of urban areas—and, in the United States, the National League of Cities and the US Conference of Mayors. In both countries, there are also 'big city' elite groupings of these organisations, representing metropolitan interests (e.g. the Big Cities Mayors' Caucus). 'City', of course, has a broader meaning than in Europe, and is largely based on population numbers, rather than historic notions of city status and physiognomy. They may thus include localities with just a few hundred inhabitants, and thus are, in essence, a municipality, rather than a 'city' (see also Herrschel 2014).

In Canada, only few cities have the stature to engage on the international arena independently, with Toronto and, increasingly also, Montreal and Vancouver as internationally oriented—and recognised—metropolitan areas, with both economic clout and also the socio-cultural factor—Francophone Montréal, and Vancouver and Toronto with sizeable Far Eastern populations. But also the 'second tier' cities matter, including the respective capital cities of the provinces and their metropolitan areas, drawing on their political links to the national capital and thus likely avenues for lobbying by local, especially economic, interests. Most cities concentrate on representing their respective regions as administrative and economic centres, rather than seeking to step out of that context and representing themselves independently on a wider scale. Only a few, mainly Toronto and Montreal, and, increasingly also Calgary and Vancouver, are seeking to reach to the international arena (and that obviously includes the United States, but, as a step further, also goes beyond) independent of national government.

6.2   Network-Based Action in the United States

In the United States, cities have largely been defined by national (federal) politics and policies which encouraged suburbanisation as a way of boosting home ownership and thus the idea of house building as a sign of achievement and democratisation. The sub-prime mortgage crisis as trigger of the 2008 financial meltdown, and its aftermath until today, highlighted this interdependency. 'As a consequence, much of the federal government's urban policy has worked to the detriment of the social and economic interest and strength of the nation's cities' (Kresl and Fry 2005, p. 139). This policy shifted the main focus of development to the suburbs, with the cities increasingly seen as a legacy, rather than as a driver, of future-oriented strategic agendas. This, and the encouragement of individual, car-based transport, facilitated the urban sprawl as an ever-expanding suburbanisation of cities (Champion 2001; Dierwechter 2008). The flight to the suburbs has weakened the cities by creating the notion of their being part of the past, rather than the (suburban) future, a notion reinforced by ethnic divisions. In contrast to Europe, there is a mostly small historic 'gap' between central cities and suburbs of mostly only a few decades (except in the relatively oldest New England states). In that way, 'city' does not necessarily mean a contrast to 'suburban' or 'semi-rural' in terms of a culture of 'localness', civic pride and political authority. Societal and economic characteristics matter as descriptors of policies (Herrschel 2014). This matters, because it provides for the political context of public attitudes to local policy-makers seeking to reach 'abroad', especially so when this is to happen at the wider city-regional level, where localist and collective instincts intersect.

Only more recently have the larger cities been experiencing a rediscovery of 'urbanity' as a life-style choice by people either prior to, or after, the family period of the life cycle. The narrative of cities being given competitive advantage through the 'creative class', as propagated by Richard Florida, may also play a role in this. This more recent development challenges established divisions between 'core urban' and 'suburban' ways of life, with the core city experiencing a revitalised and political-economic environment that pushes for a more outward-looking, international perspective as part of a cosmopolitan 'creative class' as presumed driver of new (innovative) opportunities. While this creates new divisions between the newly gentrifying, and the struggling sections of a metropolitan area, it rebalances the relationship between 'old core' and 'younger suburb' in terms of economic opportunity and thus policy orientation and agenda setting (see e.g. Greater Detroit, or the Greater Vancouver region, Herrschel 2014). In the former case, the core city has been shrinking in real terms both in terms of population as well as economic relevance, while in the latter case the 'old' city Vancouver faces challenges in terms of size and economic dynamic from the suburban city of Surrey. In both countries, the United States and Canada, the growing importance of cities as places to live and be economically active is widely acknowledged. In the United States, large US cities (greater than 150,000 inhabitants) generated almost 85% of national GDP in 2010, compared with 65% for those in Western Europe. And over the next 10–15 years, the 259 'large' US cities are expected to generate more than 10% of global GDP growth (Manyika et al. 2012). In Canada, some 80% of the population live in urban areas (Kresl and Frey 2005). And this gives city mayors and policy-makers the confidence—and political ammunition—to lobby for more consideration in national politics and decision-making at the national and provincial level.

To achieve greater lobbying capacity and influence in political decisions affecting local matters, as in Europe, North American cities have mobilised to build associations and joint actions for various agendas, so as to boost their policy effectiveness and standing and allow them to 'punch above their (individual) weight'. In contrast to Europe, this network engagement aims primarily at their respective central governments at state/provincial level, and also, and increasingly so, the national governments in Ottawa and Washington respectively. The local view outward to the international arena is thus still, in essence, one of a hierarchical nature, where the national government is still viewed as the main connector to the outside, representing sub-national interests as part of national policies. At the same time, a more direct engagement between 'local' and 'international' has been developing in the world of business as part of incoming (or outgoing) FDI. Not surprisingly, therefore, internationally operating businesses have thus become the primary drivers of the internationalisation of urban policies. Political structures and perceptions of hierarchically organised scalar spheres or responsibility have been challenged by these new relations, and needed to respond. A good part of external political engagements by cities works through city associations as platforms for, and agents of, individual cities' interests, but also, increasingly, by individual cities acting individually on their own. In the United States, the post-war initiative Sister Cities International (see Chap. 5) acting as a pendant to such an initiative in Europe, equally serves as a starting point of such activities. This means shifting from the initial focus on cultural and social programmes and contacts as a means of reaching out beyond national borders and thus mental and political divisions, to promoting economic development and increased competitiveness through collaborative action. The main organisations include (see Fig. 3.2 above): the National League of Cities (NLC, United States), US Conference of Mayors, Federation of Canadian Municipalities (including the 'elite' Big Cities Mayors' Caucus), and Sister Cities International (in the United States and Canada).

6.2.1   The National League of Cities (NLC)

The NLC was founded in 1924 and with over 1,700 city members is the largest city organisation in the United States, and sits as joint national organisation next to the 49 state-based municipal leagues with together over 18,000 cities. So it is about 10% of the organised municipalities that have an interest in nation-wide agendas, including lobbying at the federal level in Washington. The 'elite' NLC emerged through combining ten state municipal associations, or leagues, for the specific purpose of enhancing policy learning through sharing research and information, and mustering advocacy at federal government level. 'City', of course, means many more things in North America than in Europe, with legal status as a municipality, rather than functional or physiognomic features, or 'urban-ity', as descriptors. Often, such 'cities' show nothing like what is expected in a European context. Merely suburban 'sprawl' may be seen. The US Census Bureau defines 'urban' for the 1990 census as being 'urbanised', without further specification of what that entails. The other main criteria include being more than 2,500 population in size, and being 'incorpo-rated', i.e. independent municipalities in their own right (http://www.census.gov/population/censusdata/urdef.txt). So, 'city', as a municipal entity, is thus entirely technocratic in definition, referring merely to their administrative 'independence' from the next higher level in the administra-tive hierarchy, the county, while saying nothing much about institutional or fiscal capacity to muster own policy agendas beyond an immediate delivery of local services as a primary task. As 'incorporated' city, they may enjoy their own tax-raising powers and thus greater potential individual-ity in local policy-making—although size here, and popular willingness to pay higher taxes for an increased range of policies, ultimately decides on viability and administrative capacity to frame political agendas and turn them into action. But there are, of course, differences between a place in the Midwest with a population of 3500 and the large metropolitan areas joined up to the continuous urban band of Megalopolis (Herrschel 2014) along the East Coast. While for the smaller 'cities' participation in a net-work and association is crucial for gaining access to relevant information and lobbying capacity within their respective states, for instance, for the larger, metropolitan entities, individual action in choosing international collaborators may be more likely, not least as a profiling effort. Thus, in Canada, for instance, within the municipal association FCM, the 'Big City Mayors' Caucus', and in the United States, the US Conference of Mayors, were set up as elite groupings of large and therefore economically and politically more relevant and ambitious places (see below).

The main interests of the NLC revolve around domestic issues, espe-cially lobbying at national and state level. Its main standing committees involve 'community and economic development', 'energy and environ-ment', 'human development', ' information technology and communica-tion', 'public safety and crime prevention', and 'transport and infrastructure services' (http://www.nlc.org). These are typical municipal concerns and agendas. The NLC's strategic priorities for 2016 include typical munici-pal concerns, such as economic development, infrastructure and public safety, and 'providing a framework to empower cities to address the chal-lenges we face and move our nation forward'. Quite clearly, the NLC sees itself as an advocacy group for local government at the national level—and not beyond. There is no explicit section on 'international relations', for instance. The federal government in Washington is the primary focus of political engagement. Thus, the 2015 Annual Report lists the following primary objectives: 'Proactively drive federal policy', 'Promote innovation and provide proven strategies and valuable resources', 'Raise the profile of city governments as key leaders and partners in improving the quality of life for our nation', 'Expand the capacity of city officials to serve as ethical, effective and engaged leaders', and 'Transform our organization so that it is focused on top priorities, fully aligned, nimble, accountable and transparent' (NLC 2015). And so it proclaims: 'With the strength of a growing advocacy network of city leaders, NLC made significant progress on legislation that matters most to cities, keeping city priorities front and center in Washington' (NLC 2015).

The clear focus on day-to-day urban governance tasks and challenges faced by member states is also reflected in the NLC's strategic plan 'City of the Future' as also outlined in the 2015 Annual Report, which focuses on specific policy fields for which information, experiences and strategic options are to be outlined. They include: current and future trends in technology, economics, climate, culture and demographics through a city-centric legislation. This very much reflects the notion of providing a service for the fee-paying membership, which revolves around policy learning, exchange of experience, and advice. Topics include such standard-bearers of local development policy as the 'interrelationship of technology and mobility'. Future reports will explore issues including housing, economic development and transportation, all aimed at 'increasing the capacity of city leaders' (NLC 2015).

Perhaps not entirely surprisingly when taking into account the inherent local agendas dominating among local governments, internationality does not feature at all among the strategic goals, or even as a field of likely activity of the network. This reflects the fact that many of the member cities may be quite small and 'provincial'—in a continent-wide context, with functional and political connections and interests firmly rooted in a national/North American arena. And this represents much of the outlook among the respective residents as electors of local politicians. Lobbying at national—rather than international—level is therefore the primary concern, while for many the rest of the world turns hazy beyond the boundaries of the North American continent. Thus, the 2015 Annual Report points to the opening of a new office near Capitol Hill as a base for more effective lobbying activities. In that way, it is similar to the representative offices in Brussels—only there, through the nature of the EU, it is a multinational arena. In the United States, the federal level seems to mark the pinnacle of municipal lobbying, with associations at state level serving as 'intermediate' level of organising and lobbying, with most day-to-day local policy-making circumscribed by legislation from there. So, the NLC's Annual Report highlights the fact that 'NLC has selected a new office location within walking distance of the U.S. Capitol, reflecting the League's increased focus on strengthening the voice of cities in Washington. NLC and the National Association of Counties (NAC) will move into the same new building in the summer of 2016' (NLC 2015).

6.2.2   The US Conference of Mayors

The second main representation of municipal interests in the United States is the US Conference of Mayors, a more 'elitist' club in that it represents cities of at least 30,000 inhabitants. This may still seem comparatively small, but it establishes an important floor in terms of size and thus institutional and political capacity. Given the different population densities across the United States, 30,000 inhabitants may represent a fairly important (statutory) city in terms of centrality, similar to the Scandinavian countries, perhaps. The fact that it is the mayors who are representing the member cities adds to the sense of political relevance and efficacy, but also points to the political dimension of such engagement, as mayors are directly elected. The Conference's primary objectives, therefore, perhaps not so surprisingly, are very much shaped by local issues and interests in managerial aptitude, to be enhanced through learning from good practice, and lobbying the federal government in Washington on the cities' behalf. The primary roles of the US Conference of Mayors include

- promote the development of effective national urban/suburban policy;
- strengthen federal–city relationships;
- ensure that federal policy meets urban needs;
- provide mayors with leadership and management tools; and
- create a forum in which mayors can share ideas and information. (http://www.usmayors.org/about/overview.asp)

Mayors contribute to the development of national urban policy—the main arena for the Conference's engagement—by serving on one or more of the Conference's standing committees. Conference policies and programmes are developed and guided by an Executive Committee and Advisory Board, as well as a number of topical standing committees, such as exports, innovation, homelessness or brownfield development. The developed policy agendas represent the views of the nation's mayors as advocated at the federal level.

The Mayors' Conference was put in place in 1932, i.e. during the Great Depression by the then President Edgar Hoover, in response to the mayors of three leading cities, seeking assistance from the national government for the challenges of social costs of mass unemployment, which went beyond municipal capacity. So, the policy focus has very much been on domestic agendas and concerns. Yet, there has also emerged an international dimension to its policies, although with a different focus from that of European cities. Thus, among the topics of the 2015 Adopted Resolutions with headings such as Children, Health and Human Services, Community Development and Housing, or Criminal and Social Justice and Energy/Environment, one can also find International Affairs. Yet, these are not so much about economic competitiveness and place marketing, as in Europe, but rather of a campaigning, more symbolic nature: 'In Support of Somali Communities to Continue Remittance to Somalia and the Horn of Africa', or 'Calling for the Effective Implementation of the Nuclear Non-Proliferation Treaty', or 'Disarmament Obligation and Redirection of Nuclear Weapons Spending to Meet the Needs of Cities'. Yet there are also new policies aiming at specifically economic agendas, such as 'In Support of Expanding Exports and Twenty-First Century Trade Agreements', 'Restoring a Level Playing Field Through Open Skies Policy' or 'Metro Economies'. At the same time, much of the focus is on practical policy issues and exchanges of experiences and 'good practice'. In 2015, the different programmes pursued are very much day-to-day issues, such as City Livability, Community Policing, Clean Air, Mayors Climate Protection Center, or Recycling at Work (http://usmayors.org/legislationprograms/).

Two things become obvious in this list: the small scale and detail of initiatives, and the fundamental tendency to primarily look to Washington and the federal government. Indeed, the declared purpose of the joint platform for mayors is to 'collectively represent the views of the nation's mayors' and influence national urban policy. Views beyond that are of a more symbolic nature, seeking to make a political statement, which may also be aimed at the federal government as a form of declaring 'opposition' to national foreign agendas. Yet, no explicit direct action at international level is envisaged, such as through collaboration with other actors of a similar kind to shape and pursue an international agenda. Such seems still considered the prerogative of the state, at least as far as the membership of this organisation is concerned. So it is down to individual cities to become actors in their own right by stepping into the international arena and connecting with other, like-minded cities from elsewhere to establish effective lobbying at that level, especially also IOs, such as UN Habitat.

6.2.3   Sister Cities International

Sister Cities International and the recent project Global Cities Initiative are the two main platforms for the international engagement of American cities. While the former first focused on social and cultural links to cities outside the United States and only later also engaged in economic development, the latter project is much more explicitly economically oriented. Despite the common reference in their names, Sister Cities International is from its stated objectives much less about pioneering international understanding and relations between states than the European concern with city twinning (see Chap. 5), where the war experience has driven a reconciliation and integration agenda. Yet, Sister Cities International offers the opportunity for a wide range of cities—irrespective of their size and existing status and visibility—to adopt an international agenda. Chicago and Aurora (Denver) are interesting examples, by their very difference in a typical American way, between metropolitan core city with an international economy, and a 'suburban city' in the middle of the Great Plains.

A sister city relationship establishes a long-term, cooperative relationship between a US city and a city in another country, based on 'similar demographics as well as cultural, educational, business and technical characteristics and opportunities for alignment.' (http://cities-today. com/how-sister-city-partnerships-can-play-a-new-role-in-a-global-economy/). Such a relationship is formalised through a memorandum of understanding signed between the mayors or elected city representatives (leaders) of the relevant cities, and involves activities by different types of actors from governmental and non-governmental backgrounds. There is no formal limit to the number of sister cities for any one city. Such engagement is considered beneficial, because 'we must not only understand and engage our highly diverse local community, but we must also connect with international partners to exchange information, ideas and economic opportunity' (Aurora Mayor Steve Hogan, Aurora Sister Cities International website).

'While sister city relationships have traditionally been developed for diplomatic, cultural or educational purposes, in today's economic climate there is a growing need for cities to expand and leverage sister city partnerships for economic development' (http://cities-today.com/how-sister-city-partnerships-can-play-a-new-role-in-a-global-economy/). Business interests and local (municipal) interests are closely intertwined, leading to a more corporatist situation than in Europe (Herrschel 2014; Pierre 2011). Organisations like the Chambers of Commerce, or other local business interests, are typical examples. Their influence will vary with the policy agenda, as well as the importance of the business community in the expectations of local government. In contrast to Europe, in North America, an inherently stronger emphasis on entrepreneurialism and business involvement in service delivery, policy formulation and delivery gives business connections a particular relevance for the representation of a locality's links to the 'outside'—and here whether it is nationally confined or reaching beyond. The other main driver—and foundation/justification—of a city's reach to the 'outside' is societal networks through ethnic communities as a result of immigration. Social and economic links through cross-border family connections provide an important network of internationality. The example of the city of Aurora in Colorado illustrates this quite well—a low profile place in a low profile state develops an international agenda based on social connections, and uses those to boost its profile and recognition as investment in improved business opportunities/prospects.

Aurora, a new, suburban city of 350,000 inhabitants in the Denver city-region engages in Sister Cities International because it realises the local economic relevance of an international outlook: 'communities that engage globally thrive locally'. This global outlook is portrayed as drawing on the city's 'diverse and international community[,] while striving to improve the city's international business and trade ties' (https://aurorasistercities.org/about/). Accordingly, 'the mission of Aurora Sister Cities International is to promote mutually beneficial local and global partnerships centered on international trade, and cultural and educational exchange'. This agenda corresponds in its general outlook with that of its European counterpart of 'city twinning' and its original cultural-educational focus. Yet, 'additionally, Aurora Sister Cities International aims to serve as *the* liaison, facilitator and guide to foster international trade opportunities between Aurora, Colorado and its sister and friendship cities' (https://aurorasistercities.org/about/). The international engagement within the network thus suggests different levels 'of strategic relationships with our international partners'. These levels differ in the degree of formality of the partnerships and the 'officialness' of the agreement:

- Sister Cities—the mayor and city council of each city vote and agree to a formal partnership.
- Friendship Cities—the mayor of each city agrees to a variably formal format of partnership.
- Strategic Exchanges—initiatives to boost economic opportunities are facilitated by the network organisation of Aurora Sister Cities International, rather than the individual member cities. Such initiatives may lead to a more formal 'friendship' or 'sister city' relationship (https://aurorasistercities.org/about/).

Their programs and initiatives include conventional arts and culture projects which tie in with the city population's ethnic groupings, such as Ethiopian and Korean cultural projects: a collaborative exhibit with the Aurora History Museum highlighting Aurora's Ethiopian-born communities, seeking to showcase 'the culture, traditions and history of Aurora Ethiopians' (https://aurorasistercities.org/about/). Yet, there are also explicit plans to use city partnerships to foster economic exchanges (trade and tourism) through reciprocal trade and tourism missions with South Korean partners, such as in Seongnam City, and a few further 'friendship cities' (https://aurorasistercities.org/about/). Other international links involve more 'traditional' (for such city partnership schemes) forms of collaboration, such as between medical and public health school partners in Aurora and Adama in Ethiopia. The city views these links through its Sister City International status as an important specialisation factor in gaining competitiveness, including promoting 'global partnerships for the city of Aurora and its citizens', engaging 'Aurora's highly diverse international community through our local committees and other cultural and educational exchange initiatives' and enhancing 'international trade through our relationships with cities across the world', by helping local businesses dealing with partners abroad, 'particularly those located in our sister and friendship cities' (https://aurorasistercities.org/about/).

'Aurora is poised to step into the global arena, and bring the diversity of our communities to the center of our international initiatives', says the executive director for Aurora Sister Cities International, in relation to building a link to the new Ethiopian sister city of Adama, a city similar in size to Aurora, yet in a quite different regional setting. To develop that new relationship, Aurora Sister Cities International will seek to develop joint initiatives, using a committee that brings together Aurora residents to help identify goals and planning to support the relationship with Adama. This public involvement serves to boost public support for subsequent policies—and related expenditure—so as to secure political advantages from such international policy outreach. Planned activities 'include educational exchanges, municipal collaboration, medical, energy and technology projects, and international trade and development' (https://aurorasistercities.org/about/). Interestingly, pointing to the somewhat avant-garde nature of such city-to-city engagement from North America to Africa, this initiative was possible only via the Ethiopian embassy in Washington as a 'go between', and so followed conventional channels of communication between states when it comes to international relations. After an expression of interest in establishing such a sister city relationship with the second largest city in Ethiopia, Aurora's Ethiopian community and the Ethiopian ambassador in Washington facilitated the link-up. 'The Ethiopian Embassy took the lead to discuss the proposal with federal channels in Ethiopia, and provided the recommendation for the city of Aurora to consider partnering with Adama' Ethiosports.

Aurora's further international ambitions are outlined in the city's Comprehensive Strategic Plan 2015–18, in which it stipulates under the category 'International and Immigrant Affairs', that 'like many cities and towns across the United States, Aurora is becoming a more diverse and international city' (https://aurorasistercities.org/about/). So, internationality is not just about 'reaching out' into the international arena, but also about the nature of the locality per se, i.e. here the multicultural composition of the local community. And, reflecting the omnipresent globalisation-driven understanding of the world as a marketplace, international engagement is viewed in terms of 'competitiveness' and economic opportunity, as 'immigrant integration is essential to the vibrancy, safety, economic prosperity and cultural richness of their cities'. So, it is about the human resource dimension of cultural diversity. And it is in light of this strategic goal of integration that 'the city has established the Aurora Immigrant and Refugee Task Force, the International Roundtable, Global Fest, and reestablished Aurora Sister Cities International' (https://aurorasistercities.org/about/). Internationalisation is thus here about using local multiculturalism as a connecting point of reference to 'matching' cultures abroad, and thus gain international connectivity as a 'launch pad' for expected subsequent economic opportunities. So, while 'the primary objectives of the plan are to maximize resources, develop innovative efforts, and avoid duplication of programs and services aimed at the local immigrant and refugee community', the immediate local goal is integration. And to facilitate that, the city council created in 2015an Office of International Initiatives to bundle services and initiatives aimed at the 'international, immigrant, refugee, and newcomer communities.' (http://metroafrican.com/2014/06/aurora-colorado-forms-sister-city-partnership-with-adama-ethiopia/). The Strategic Plan makes it explicitly clear that 'internationality' is considered a 'driving force for economic development', as it says in one of its strategy headings. And this includes as a goal 'to improve Aurora's appeal to entrepreneurs from all over the world and to further expand our international relationships in the field of science and business'. And so, the strategy points out, 'in order to continue to grow and become a key player at the international level, international strategic partnerships and collaborations in the areas of economics, culture, medicine, and business must be developed' (https://aurorasistercities. org/about/).

This is to be achieved through a variety of smaller, yet well coordinated lobbying and outreach activities, including:

- Define and promote international trade and investment in the city.
- Develop relationships with foreign consulates, foreign governments, World Denver IIE, the World Trade Center and Aurora Sister Cities to promote Aurora as an international destination for business and tourism.
- Promote the retention of foreign students attending colleges and universities in Aurora.
- Monitor business activities of foreign companies in the Denver greater area and promote the participation of local companies in international trade and business missions.
- Partner with Aurora Sister Cities and the Office of the Mayor/ Council to participate in and plan trade/exchange missions with cities abroad.
- Support business and economic partnerships with our current Sister Cities.
- Strengthen and expand the work and mission of the Aurora International Roundtable.
- Expand current city branding efforts to promote Aurora as a business friendly, international city (City of Aurora 2015).

So, to conclude on this particular, and perhaps somewhat unexpected, locale of internationalisation, Aurora's international strategy is clearly drawing on the international dimension of its population, including the student body of its university—something that corresponds with the efforts of Umeå in north-eastern Sweden (see Chap. 5). The city seeks to use this local internationality as a shared starting point for 're-tracing' links to the various countries of origins of many of its residents, and to use that in developing an international network. Existing internationally oriented organisations in the region, but also at national level, such as embassies, serve as 'relay stations' to build connections with like-interested cities further afield. In addition, the multinational background of its population is used to project an image of an open, outward-looking and internationally aware and engaged city to boost its appeal to potential external investors. This emphasis on diversity bears clear references to the image of Richard Florida's 'creative class'. So, there are some echoes to the efforts made by European cities, but there is not the more accessible international platform for institutional lobbying as found in the EU with its institutions in Brussels and the scope to open up international local and regional representations. Instead, the more traditional way via embassies, and thus the nation state-based international links, are being used as the most likely route to build individual international relationships.

6.2.4   The Global Cities Initiative (GCI)

The Global Cities Initiative is a very recent attempt at boosting the international engagement of US cities beyond that of a few established 'global' cities, following the aftermath of the financial crash of 2008 and the subsequent global economic recession with severe impact on the US economy (Borbely 2009). The GCI was set up in 2012 as a joined venture between J.P. Morgan as private financier and the Brookings Institution as academic adviser to aid and encourage internationalisation strategies and actual engagement by larger (metropolitan) cities. Focus and intent is thus quite different from that of municipal (city) associations as discussed earlier. The explicit purpose is to encourage and support US cities to individually engage effectively in the international arena to boost their economic prospects vis-à-vis globalisation. For this purpose, GCI 'equips urban leaders with the practical knowledge and thus capability and policy-making entrepreneurialism to devise effective strategies to become more globally connected and competitive' ('About the Global Cities Initiative: Economic Development/Salt Lake City': http://slco.org/economic-development/about-global-cities-initiative/). This includes helping 'city and metropolitan leaders better leverage their global assets', while providing 'metropolitan area leaders with proven, actionable ideas for how to expand the global reach of their economies, building on best practices and policy innovations from across the nation and around the world' and 'creates a network of U.S. and international cities interested in partnering together to advance global trade and commerce' (ibid.).

Interestingly, GCI clearly emphasises the increasingly pre-eminent role of cities, especially metropolitan regions, as 'the centers of global trade and commerce', implicitly standing next to nation states as the conventional international actors—as evident in the much more restrained and cautious efforts of municipalities to 'go international' than in Europe. For that purpose, 'through a competitive application process, economic development practitioners in both U.S. and international cities are selected to receive hands-on guidance on the development and implementation of actionable strategies to enhance global trade and commerce and strengthen regional economies' (http://slco.org/economic-development/about-global-cities-initiative/).

Support to cities is provided to those selected in a competitive bid, with 28 cities chosen in total. One of the main objectives is to facilitate the GCI's Exchange as a 'peer learning network'. Degree of 'readiness and commitment to pursue the Exchange's global competitiveness principles' were the main selection criteria (https://www.jpmorganchase.com). Cities participating in the GCI Exchange include many of the largest US cities, such as Baltimore, Fresno, Houston, Kansas City, Philadelphia, Salt Lake City, Seattle, Portland, St. Louis, Atlanta, Chicago and Los Angeles ('Eight New Cities Selected to Join Global Cities Initiative's Exchange Network': https://www.jpmorganchase.com). So it becomes quite evident that this programme seeks to help those cities below the much quoted 'global cities' in the United States, the secondary cities with international ambitions and interests, to take that step and foster such linkages—individually, not as part of a network (which does not exist for that purpose) (Fig. 6.1).

City Name	Volume in International Trade, $bn
1. New York City	85.1
2. Houston, Texas	80.6
3. Los Angeles, California	62.2
4. Detroit, Michigan	44.0
5. Miami, Florida	35.9
6. Seattle, Washington	35.4
7. Chicago, Illinois	33.7
8. San Jose, California	26.3
9. Minneapolis, Michigan	23.2
10. Philadelphia, Pennsylvania	22.7

Fig. 6.1   Top ten internationally trading US cities. *Source*: Based on data from the Chicago Council on Global Affairs, http://www.thechicagocouncil.org

6.3   LOCAL INTERNATIONALISATION THROUGH NETWORKS IN CANADA

In Canada, local government is a creature of parliament and obtains all its powers through parliamentary acts by the provinces. These, and the municipal charters, define the powers and legitimate actions of a municipality (see Madison and Brunet-Jailly 2014). There are no protected, guaranteed powers at the local level that could be defended against the centre as, for instance, is the case in the United States. As a result, municipalities, including the large cities, possess no intrinsic right to engage internationally as a political option. However, recent reform to the municipal acts since 2000 has in most provinces broadened the constitutional basis for autonomous municipal action, and that may include international engagement, as illustrated by the case of Toronto below.

Political acumen may be expected to matter, so that the status of the capital city of a province (or, in the United States, federal state) exercises additional attraction and attention. Likewise, as centres of political decision-making, provincial capitals may be expected to be among the first off the mark as they also harbour the policy agendas of the provincial governments which have a longer tradition of also looking to the international realm. This, however, is not usually viewed as participating in national foreign policy of a traditional nature, such as being involved in relevant foreign negotiations or policy formations by provincial or federal government (Madison and Brunet-Jailly 2014). In some instances, however, such involvement occurs, such as between Halifax and 'its' province of Nova Scotia (Madison and Brunet-Jailly 2014). Similarly, Quebec seems to involve some of its cities, such as the capital Quebec City, in its foreign policy initiatives, albeit generally through informal, rather than 'official' exchanges. Of course, such engagement may be facilitated and supported through specific funding arrangements to support the city's participation in a foreign project by the province. In Quebec, of course, the politics of language and cultural identity fosters international engagement with other Francophone countries as part of its efforts to emphasise autonomy, and thus goes well beyond economic rationality in the context of globalism. Elsewhere, as in neighbouring Ontario, the capital city's (Toronto's) involvement with the province's, or even federal, foreign policies may involve informal consultations on, at times even involvement in, individual projects, such as the concerted involvement in El Salvador in 2001 (Madison and Brunet-Jailly 2014).The economic and political 'weight' of the main city, especially a large metropolitan area as Toronto, cannot be simply ignored by policy-makers, even if they are formally higher up in the governmental hierarchy. This applies in particular in instances with distinct urban relevance.

The Federation of Canadian Municipalities (FCM) is the national voice for Canada's local governments, representing nearly 2,000 other local governments and 90% of the Canadian population (http://www.fcm. ca/home/membership.htm), which range in size from a few thousand inhabitants to Toronto's 2.6 million. Formed in 1937, the FCM is a civic lobbying group which seeks access to national government, although primary responsibility as central government for municipalities rests with the provinces (Stevenson and Gilbert 2005). Given this multi-scalar engagement, much of its activity and effectiveness is based on 'soft diplomacy', i.e. informal engagement and lobbying, as it possesses no formal powers to request access to policy-making processes at either province or federal level. International engagement became more prominent with the establishment in 1987 of a dedicated office for international relations, with a third of its 120 staff working in this international office. So, quite clearly, the international arena has become a major playing field for the Association. Nevertheless, since the late 1980s, after a period of uncertainty about its role and modus operandi (Stevenson and Gilbert 2005), the FCM has focused its attention more to the provinces as statutory masters of the municipal level, rather than seeking to modify central–local relations and multi-level government structures in Canada as a whole. The difficult Quebec–Canada relationship as part of Quebec's explicit separatist agenda in the early 1980s, proved politically difficult (Stevenson and Gilbert 2005).

Growing autonomy for the larger cities in several provinces over the last 15 years has opened up the opportunity for new policy agendas and ventures for those cities (including, in particular, Montreal, Winnipeg and Vancouver), as they were expected to assume more responsibility for local economic, social and environmental welfare of their populations. The emergence of the Big Cities' Mayors Caucus within the FCM as an 'elite group' later in the 1980s reflected, and further enhanced, the evolving growing metropolitan focus of sub-national governance, mostly in response to the growing internationalisation of businesses and their relational flows and connections. Yet, in contrast to Europe with its particular emphasis on international—i.e. Europe-wide—regionalism, in North America, there is no tradition of, and no supportive platform for, a more proactive and innovative definition of local economic governance and policy, which may include a scaled-up engagement with the international. This includes the perceptions by the state of its own hegemonic status, as there is no supra-national governmental arena—unlike in Europe—which allowed lobbying opportunities for other than national actors. Local—and that means essentially urban/metropolitan—interests in international activities are thus much less politically and governmentally oriented than in Europe, and are mostly couched in terms of collective action through membership organisations. In Canada, this is primarily the FCM as a broad church for all municipalities, which advocates collective local interests at the provincial (regional) and national (federal) level, but not beyond, with the balancing between provincial and federal responsibilities and interests—including those of independent-minded Quebec—as part of ongoing tensions between a more or less centralised federalism (Hubbard and

Paquet 2010). The 'FCM represents the interests of all municipalities on policy and program matters within federal jurisdiction. Members include Canada's largest cities, small urban and rural communities' (http://www. fcm.ca/home.htm). The FCM is clearly contained by national borders— there are no international offices as representative 'consulates' maintained by it (Fig. 6.2).

The main focus of the organisation is connecting the local to the federal level, especially through lobbying to strengthen local voice at the national level, including the Prime Minister's Office, cabinet ministers, party leaders and Members of Parliament. In so doing, the FCM adds the municipal perspective to the Minister of Finance's annual pre-budget consultations and to parliamentary committees. Although not without its contestations, especially in relation to the role of the provinces as actual central government for municipalities and thus a more devolutionary agenda (much favoured by Quebec), this cross-scalar lobbying is one of three main agendas/services offered to the membership. This is next to offering a platform for inter-municipal networking, policy learning through the sharing of knowledge and learning from 'good practice', and promoting local initiatives, so as to aid the finding of policy solutions and good practices among member municipalities. Yet, indirectly and implicitly, there is an international dimension and agenda. But there is also a campaigning element to the FCM's agendas, such as promoting good governance and democratic values in developing countries as part of a rather ambitious and idealistic goal of 'improving the lives of people around the world' through direct collaboration with municipal governments and agencies across the globe to 'strengthen local governance and democracy, foster economic development, and promote gender equality and environmental sustainability' (http://www.fcm.ca/home.htm). 'Partnership' is thus an important buzzword when representing local government interests at the federal level, pushing for a recognition of the local effects of national foreign policy, as well as articulating local interests in, and expectation from, international engagement by the federal government. The FCM's current lobbying agendas include:

Continue to enhance the existing local–federal partnership in shaping and advancing Canada's international development and trade objectives.
Consider the municipal impacts of international trade agreements, e.g. between the EU and Canada.

'Large City' in Canada	Sister City
Brampton	Miami Beach, Florida; Plano, Texas, US
Calgary	Daejeon, South Korea Daqing, Heilongjiang province, China Jaipur, India
Edmonton	Gatineau, Quebec Harbin, Heilongjiang, China Nashville, TN, US
Gatineau	Burnaby, BC
Halifax	Campeche, Mexico Hakodate, Japan Liverpool, UK Norfolk, Virginia, US
Hamilton	Flint, Michigan, US Fukuyama, JPN
Kitchener	None listed
Laval	Klagenfurt, Austria Laval, Mayenne, France Nice, France Petah Tikva, Israel
London	Nanjing, China
Mississauga	Kariya, Japan
Montréal	Busan, South Korea (Hiroshima, Japan Lucknow, India Lyon, France Manila, Philippines
Ottawa	Beijing, China Buenos Aires, Argentina Catania, Italy Palermo, Italy Campobasso,, Italy Seoul, South Korea
Québec	Albany, New York, US Bordeaux, France Calgary, Canada Cannes, France Changchun, China Guanajuato, Mexico Huế, Vietnam Iaşi, Romania Liège, Belgium
Regina	Fujioka, Japan Jinan, China

Fig. 6.2   Large Canadian cities' sister cities. *Source*: Based on information from the FCM (http://www.fcm.ca), and Sister Cities of the World (http://en.sister-city.info)

Respect FCM's principles on free and fair trade when negotiating new
international trade agreements. (FCM n.d.)
Utilising municipal networks and economic competencies to boost
national economic competitiveness and development.
(http://www.fcm.ca/home.htm)

International interests of the FCM include its international programmes aimed at mobilising Canadian municipal leaders and experts
to engage with, and participate in, a global network of municipal governments. The FCM formulates its collective policies in several committees, on which individual cities from both linguistic groups now serve
(Stevenson and Gilbert 2005). And one of these committees is explicitly
for dealing with international relations as an agenda item. International
activities are not just about attracting FDI or shaping collaborative business links in response to globalisation, but also conducting active development policy, something usually associated with national governments.
So it does not come as a surprise, perhaps, that such activity is done in
association with the national government's foreign office as the conventionally legitimate international actor. Thus, the FCM has available $20
million per annum for international development work through dedicated
programmes: 'Municipal Partners for Economic Development' (MPED)
seeking to improve local governance and economic policy development in
Bolivia, Burkina Faso, Cambodia, Mali, Nicaragua, Tanzania and Vietnam;
'Caribbean Local Economic Development' (CARILED) aimed at helping
municipal governments in the Caribbean building the necessary skills to
attract new business investments to their communities; and 'Municipal
Local Economic Development' (MLED) which seeks to promote economic growth, strengthen intergovernmental cooperation and advance
gender equality in the city of Lviv and the region of Dnipropetrovsk in
Ukraine (http://www.fcm.ca/home.htm).
    Internationality may be expected to be primarily a task for, and interest
of, the larger municipalities, especially the bigger cities, with the necessary broader institutional capacity and political and economic horizons.
Indeed, the FCM includes an urban 'elite' club in the shape of the Big
City Mayors' Caucus (BCMC) as the voice of Canada's biggest cities
which, in turn, are considered (and consider themselves) to be the primary economic engines of the Canadian economy and hubs for innovation
(http://www.fcm.ca/home/membership.htm). The BCMS represents
21 of Canada's biggest cities, reaching from St John's in Newfoundland

with 100,000 inhabitants, to Toronto's 3 million population, and offers a primary platform for engagement with the central government in Ottawa (http://www.fcm.ca/home/about-us/big-city-mayors-caucus.htm) and deals with bigger policy issues than those of the day-to-day running of local government, where the provinces are the main partners for negotiation. It is here, at the big picture level, that the perennial questions about Québec's status within the Canadian federation can be more easily bridged, encouraging Montreal, in particular, to collaborate with the other metropolitan cities on the basis of being a metropolis, rather than being part of a nationalist agenda (Stevenson and Gilbert 2005). On that basis, international engagement mostly involves partnership with the federal government in Ottawa as traditional actor in international relations, rather than the province of Québec in its attempt to raise its profile and increase its autonomy. Thus, while Canadian municipalities are globally connected through multi-lateral economic links, as well as global challenges of climate change, they seek to do so through collective, network-based partnership and in cooperation with the federal government, to allow them to play a more effective and visible role on the international stage (http://www.fcm.ca/home/membership.htm), while also remaining to some degree true to the North American traditional convention that makes 'foreign' matters primarily a matter of national (federal) activity.

Outside the Big Cities elite group of the FCM, as in the United States, cities' international links work mostly through the national sister cities initiative as a well-established, politically uncontroversial programme of mainly symbolic meaning. All sizes of cities may be part of this outreach programme. So, for instance, Toronto embraces international city partnering through its International Alliance Programme which involves nine international city-to-city links in the form of more formalised 'partner cities', aimed at boosting economic development through specific collaboration, and more ceremonial 'friendship cities', where cultural exchanges are the primary focus. Montreal is particularly active in its internationalisation efforts through such partnerships. Currently it is in the process of boosting its existing five partnerships by 17 new ones (see Table 6.xx). The robust engagement of Québec (also found for Québec City with eight sister city agreements) fits into the generally active picture of foreign policy link-ups by the province and reflects the political efforts by the French-speaking part of Canada to achieve greater visibility as an independent actor on the back of its greater autonomy efforts within the Canadian Federation (Bothwell and Rothwell 1995; Stevenson and Gilbert 2005).

The type of engagement and nature of joint initiatives vary, reaching from basic exchanges of information as part of policy and staff exchanges to joint projects to boost economic competitiveness and visibility. The main driver behind forming specific pairings are historic structural similarities or shared experiences, such as Vancouver's assistance to Odessa (Ukraine) during the Second World War, making for the oldest city twinning pair in Canada (Madison and Brunet-Jailly 2014).

Summing up the picture for Canadian cities' international engagement, it becomes evident that, as in the United States, the particular continental scale of the state in political, economic and functional respects clearly has an effect on the perceived need to 'go international', but also the willingness to take the 'plunge' into the unknown. This is the case for smaller cities and towns which either are firmly integrated into the wider metropolitan structure of a leading city, or are located in less urbanised parts of the continent from where the world looks far away. It is in this different scalar perceptive and operating context that both Canada and the United States vary from the European situation where 'national' may, in geographic terms, not even be as much as one province or state, or much more than the size of a handful of counties. International cross-border movements and relationships are thus much more inevitable for European cities than for those on the North American continent. The other main factor, of course, is that of national constitutional arrangements and governmental culture and milieu. This includes the statutory power and autonomy granted to municipalities to act, including the need and scope to be more innovative and enterprising in catering for local interests and expectations through imaginative policies. In Canada, municipal powers are much more constrained by statute than in the United States, so that questions about 'appropriate' local policy interests and ambitions involve provincial politics and interests more than is the case in the United States. Also, in Canada, the underlying national ambitions of Quebec play an important role in shaping municipal policy interests, and here, in particular, the willingness to collaborate across the language divide. But such collaboration is, for the smaller and medium-sized cities the main avenue to reach out further geographically via municipal associations as interlocutor between the national and international arenas. For the bigger, metropolitan players, metropolitan interests and mindsets seem to become more important for shaping interests, and these seem more able to facilitate collaboration across national borders—often individually, or as more elitist 'big city' associations. So it seems that metropolitanisation is able to rise above national perspectives and scalar operations and follow a more independent-minded metropolitan-defined agenda which includes international activity as a matter of course. The degree of 'metropolitanism' in economic, but, especially, political terms, appears a primary driver and facilitator of multi-scalar operation by cities, right up to the global level.

6.4   INDIVIDUAL CITY INITIATIVES IN CANADA AND THE UNITED STATES

When referring to international urbanism in an American context, the names of New York, Chicago or Los Angeles immediately spring to mind, with New York as 'global city' clearly taking the top position. This is based on connectivity and connectedness in economic terms, especially in conjunction with globalisation and its emphasis on 'nodes' and 'flows', rather than territorial structure (Soja 2000; Sassen 1991). Quite clearly, these three cities are superbly connected and internationally engaged through their economic, political and societal connections. Yet, there are differences in the ways in which they utilise and project that position into proactive internationalisation policies and action. Internationality, or even globality, seems to follow economic relations, rather than being showcased through formal international offices as para-consulates, as found in Brussels (see Chap. 5). Such institutionalised international presence next to the state is not evident. Less visible personal networks and relationships seem to be preferred. Business leadership and representations are the main drivers of internationalisation at the urban/regional level, such as through business associations (often the Chambers of Commerce). This reflects their importance in shaping local policies, with municipal government in North America, and, especially, the United States, playing a central role. Municipalities are traditionally considered primarily responsible for local service delivery, rather than autonomous political activities that go beyond the immediate locality. Even at a 'mere' city-regional level that can become difficult. So it may not come as a complete surprise that one of the few projects seeking to foster international city engagement is a collaboration between the private sector (international investment bank J.P. Morgan and the academic think tank Brookings Institution, which have teamed up to foster the international engagement of cities, as explained in the previous section.

The examples discussed here include New York and Chicago, as well as Montreal and Toronto, to illustrate the role of the two national contexts as well as local factors for the internationalisation strategies of these leading cities in the United States and Canada respectively. New York City is probably *the* global city, not just by the strength and reach its functional interrelationships with the rest of the world, especially through its finance sector (similar to London), but also by its globally high recognition factor. This is reflected also in its administration and its outlook on the issue of international engagement and, of course, the political manoeuvres of its high-profile mayoral office.

> The Mayor's Office for International Affairs, through its services and unique programming, provides a global platform from which the City promotes its goals for a more equitable and inclusive society. The office cultivates critical partnerships with the international community that strengthen our abilities as a global leader. With one out of three New Yorkers foreign-born, and over 200 languages spoken in our homes and on our streets, we are honored to host the United Nations Headquarters and the largest diplomatic corps in the world, who play an important role in serving New York's vibrant and diverse communities. (http://www1.nyc.gov/site/international/index.page)

To underpin this international, global role, there is a dedicated NYC Mayor's Office for International Affairs, something akin to the city's Foreign Office. And so, in 2015, the programme 'Global Vision | Urban Action' was launched in a stage-managed city-global setting by bringing together leading representatives of the city and of the UN which, of course, has its headquarters in New York.

This new programme aims at bringing together cities from around the world to discuss and exchange knowledge of good and effective practice in tackling global challenges, especially climate change and sustainability—or possibly—practice to tackle climate change and sustainable development. 'Through our Connecting Local to Global (CL2G) programming, the Mayor's Office for International Affairs works to help connect NYC's diplomatic and consular community to the City they live in and serve', and through this 'New Yorkness of the UN', another initiative launched by the mayor in 2015, the city's government seeks to 'connect NYC's solutions to local problems to international efforts to tackle global issues, from climate change and disability rights to immigration and food insecurity' (http://www1.nyc.gov/site/international/index.page). The mayor's personality, personal network and political skills clearly matter in these policies to give them credibility and efficacy. The sheer size of the New York administration and thus its weight in the city's economy, and the resources available, add to the scope and capacity for New York to reach out globally and project influence—without underlying corresponding formal entitlement. Although 'Michael Bloomberg has no official mandates beyond Mayor of New York City … New York City's leadership gets more and more involved in American diplomacy—and pursues its own—every single day. With an annual budget of about $60 billion … the sheer scale of New York City governance dwarfs most sovereign nations' (Khanna and Joishy 2011). And this attitude and globally oriented political strategy and engagement continues to be followed by the current mayor Bill de Blasio: 'From income inequality to climate change, so many cities across the globe face similar challenges—and by working together, we can find innovative solutions that will lift up people in every community. Our administration is committed to working with other global cities on these issues through action-oriented partnerships, and Global Partners is a key tool for engaging in that critical work' ('Global Partners' webpage on the city's website: http://www1.nyc.gov/site/globalpartners/index.page). So, New York quite evidently plays a global role as may be expected, and operates at that level as a matter of course. Quite clearly, New York does not need to rely on any city network, on the back of which to pursue international ambition. Its unique position as one of the 'original' global cities gives it the advantage of being able to set the agenda on its own.

Chicago provides the second example of international engagement. America's globally aspiring 'third' city (see also JJP report) competes for international attention against the established 'global cities', such as New York and Los Angeles, and perhaps even San Francisco on the back of Silicon Valley's fame (Hartley 2015). Much of this has to do with its physical connectedness as historic 'gateway' to the American Midwest, with the second busiest airport in the United States and the highest density of major roads connecting it to the rest of the country (Rodríguez-Núñez et al. 2014). Chicago's domestic competitors, including also Toronto, have gained much of their global standing through strong leadership in industries with visibility and impact (Hartley 2015), So it the particular nature of an economic sector's global reach that has affected and helped to lift the cities to that eminent level, rather than political connectedness. That is something that is not (any longer) so readily available to Chicago, although the relocation of Boeing's headquarters from Seattle to Chicago has provided an important symbolic boost. The city's broader economic specialism than, for instance, New York's outstanding specialism in financial services, requires other drivers to gain greater visibility and global recognition. This is where a very pro-active, outward-looking business community has become an important factor. This has a long-established tradition, going back to the business leaders' Commercial Club of some 100 years ago. There is thus a strong history of businesses' public involvement, in particular in civic leadership where individual personalities played an important part in achieving success for the city in economic terms (interview Chicago 2020, 13 July 2004). This tradition becomes evident in the continued clear presence of the business community in setting Chicago's policy agendas, including an outward-looking perspective connected to trading interests. This also includes the important role of the mayor's personality as driver of Chicago's public policy and presence. And it is this business focus, also among political leaders, that encourages concerted action and collaboration in order to contribute to, as well as benefit from, an internationally visible and attractive Chicago city-region. Consequently, the Chicago Chamber of Commerce was renamed some 25 years ago the Chicagoland Chamber of Commerce, and the suburban mayors around the city of Chicago initiated the Metropolitan Mayors' Caucus with the Chicago mayor in 1998. The prospect of increased power for joint lobbying drives this city-regional approach. For the Chicago mayor, the main insight was the realisation of the advantages of direct lobbying (interview Chicagoland Chamber of Commerce, 12 July 2004). And this is not just limited to the national government in Washington, but goes well beyond to the global arena.

Such international ambition is reflected in, and promoted by, the Chicago Center for Global Affairs (CCGA) which has been in place for nearly a century. When set up in 1922 as the Chicago Council for Foreign Affairs, this was in direct challenge to the return of the United States as a whole to isolationism in response to the experiences of the First World War (Kaplan 2015). The very name of this voluntary organisation, with close links to the Chicago city administration, is ambitiously programmatic. Its task is aimed at both the city-regional and the international realms at the same time, seeking to convince the city-regional public of the virtues of 'going global', and present the city and its region as an international place that is relevant and attractive to be located in from an outside perspective. This is trying to bridge the gap in discourse and public awareness: 'Everyone is talking about globalization. Everyone is talking about cities. But no one is talking [here] about global cities.' In fact, 'the Midwest still struggles to see itself as global'. To counteract that, the association tries to raise public awareness among residents and policy-makers alike for the city-region's existing global ties. 'We are expanding our role here in Chicago, trying to give a view of how globalization is affecting Chicago and how Chicago is affecting the rest of the world' (Richard Longworth, Chicago Council of Global Affairs, quoted in Kaplan 2015). Following historic cultural and economic links and interests, 'foreign' very much meant, in essence, a European outlook. This was true especially in the aftermath of the end of the Cold War, when strategic political agendas concentrated on development, economic change, integration and 'transition' to market democracies in Central Europe, inter alia through the facilitation of exchanges between young business and political leaders in the Midwest and Europe. At the same time, human rights emerged as a central topic as civil strife increased in countries around the globe, reflecting the Council's campaigning tradition beyond national policy agendas and efforts, but also beyond immediately economic considerations. This thus includes global economic issues, yet also democratisation, sovereignty and intervention, as well as global institutions. These are all 'traditional' topics of international politics conducted by states. Since the 9/11 events in 2001, this broader outlook has contrasted with the rapidly increasing national discourse about security and 'protection', with new isolationist undertones. This meant a shift from more idealistic agendas, 'such as nuclear proliferation to more economic issues such as trade and transportation', and, again, a renewed emphasis on public education about the virtues of maintaining an outward-looking perspective and interest for an export-oriented Midwestern economy. 'Additionally [the Council] did a lot on immigration and Chicago's immigrant community' (Longworth, CGGA, quoted in Kaplan 2015).

Increasingly, therefore, Chicago, as the speaker for a powerful economic region, has articulated an international policy that adds another voice to the political agendas and perspectives of the federal government in Washington. Economic capacity and a well-connected, internationally operating economy provide a strong driver for city politics to follow, including lobbying and seeking to influence national politics. 'There are big issues of American policy that affect us ... And when those policies are made, Chicago's voice ought to be heard. And we are Chicago's voice in this area' (Marshall Bouton, former president of CGGA, quoted in Kaplan 2015). And such policy interests include issues such as immigration and food security, topics traditionally associated with international policies shaped by national politics. 'Being a global city is really crucial economically. The Chicago Council is helping project the city on an international stage' (Henry Bienen, former president of CCGA, quoted in Kaplan 2015). And current CEO Ivo Daalder even contemplates publicly 'whether Chicago should have its own foreign policy' (quoted in Kaplan 2015). This aspiration to link the city to the global arena of international relations and diplomacy is also reflected in Chicago's economic development arm, the public–private partnership of World Business Chicago. Being chaired by the Chicago mayor, the importance of economic development as an international task for the city's politics and policy-making is underpinned. And this includes a global outlook, as World Business Chicago's CEO emphasises: 'We promote Chicago as a great global business city' (Kaplan 2015).

The international, global engagement and aspirations of Chicago's political and business leaders is given a high-profile international platform and audience in the shape of the Chicago Forum as a 'unique gathering, which for the first time ever brings together all the leaders that make global cities truly global—mayors and maestros, entrepreneurs and university presidents'. 'Global cities shape our world and our future,' observes Ivo H. Daalder, ambassador as well as president of the CCGA. To highlight the link between international relations and metropolitan politics and economic interests, the Chicago Forum's inaugural conference in May 2015 announced that it brings together 'leaders from the world's global cities—London, Shanghai, Rio, Dubai, Sydney and others' and former presidents and prime ministers of countries in different parts of the world to underpin the aspiration of Chicago policy-makers and business leaders to project Chicago as both a global city, right at the top level next to competitor New York, *and* also an international player on a par with national leaders.

The proposed agenda for the Chicago Forum's first conference in Chicago in May 2015 reflects this aspiration by referring to a number of traditional topics of international diplomacy and relations:

> The Chicago Forum on Global Cities will facilitate a new international dialogue around the key elements of urban life and other relevant topics, including: how urbanization and climate change are converging in challenging ways; how leading cities can help develop solutions addressing the scarcity of resources; how immigration trends affect global cities; how inequality is affecting underprivileged communities; how cities are driving

the global economy; how mayors are leading the fight against terrorism and twenty-first century security threats; how cities are implementing their own foreign policies; and how a global city's arts and culture offerings contribute to international diplomacy (CFGC 2015a).

Madeleine Albright, former US Secretary of State, another participant in this Forum, affirms: 'As global cities evolve into ever more vibrant hubs for commerce, education, culture and innovation, they will undoubtedly have a more pronounced influence, not only within their countries' borders, but also on an international level … This trend will only accelerate as global cities grow, so we need to better understand the dynamics between global cities of the future and traditional nation-states in order to tackle twenty-first century challenges' (CFGC 2015a).

Likewise, Saskia Sassen, against the background of her work on global cities, argued at the same meeting that 'by pursuing their own business ties, trade missions, cultural exchanges, and agreements with each other, global cities may even have the ability to disrupt the foreign policy agendas of their nations … Cities are more nimble [*sic*] and often less weighed down by national politics than central governments are, and that means they can push the envelope further and faster by working with other cities that share a similar set of social and economic issues and interests' (CFGC 2015a). This potentially opens up new diplomatic routes. '[W]ith countries struggling to reach basic agreements, city-to-city communication and coordination is not just innovative, it has the potential to change the nature of the conversation about international commitments,' stated Sam Scott, chairman of Chicago Sister Cities International, another participant at the Forum (CFGC 2015a). And so cities may counteract, or go well beyond, national policies which they think are inadequate or to their detriment. This applies in particular in relation to the climate change agenda. Thus, the CCAG postulated that 'In the years following COP21, American cities have the opportunity, and perhaps responsibility, to greatly exceed the national emissions reductions targets. It's an effort they must contribute if we are to have any hope of halting climate change' (Tiboris 2015).

Another important facilitator and avenue for international 'outreach' for Chicago's policy-makers is, as in the much less well known, smaller Aurora, the Sister Cities International network. Thus, in November 2013, the cities of Chicago and Mexico City formally established—through a contract—the 'Chicago–Mexico City Global Cities Economic Partnership'

(Jackson, 2013). This builds upon the relationship established in 1991 through mutual sister city status, as well as their shared economic assets and interest in a trade and investment relationship to mutual benefit. The context of a free trade area in the form of NAFTA aids such closer economic linkages of a city-to-city nature. The objective of the agreement about collaboration is aimed at formalising a 'bilateral relationship to expand job growth and economic opportunities in both cities, especially in advanced industries, through joint initiatives in trade, investment, and innovation'. This involves in particular coordinated initiatives and projects, such as in exports and foreign direct investment; innovation and research; and education and human capital—as circumscribed by respective national, regional and local regulation.

Overall, the aim is to produce a win-win situation for both cities in which they boost each other's economic competitiveness in a global setting, including their visibility and credibility as potential partners for other economic players in the international arena. It is interesting to note in Chicago Sister Cities International's mission statement the link between the 'internal' and the 'external' of the city, as it 'is committed to promoting Chicago as a global city, developing international partnerships and networks, and sharing best practices through citizen-to-citizen connections' (http://chicagosistercities.com/misson/). So it is not just about place-to-place connectivity, but dissolving places into individual citizens as a means to democratic representation and involvement.

This internationalisation strategy goes back to a more politically symbolic use of city-to-city partnerships at a time when the world became divided into 'East' and 'West' during the Cold War years until 1989. Thus, the first Sister Cities agreement was signed in 1960 with the capital city of Poland, Warsaw, by the then Chicago mayor. This was to signal an attempt to transgress the Iron Curtain at a sub-national and thus politically less sensitive level, given that such trans-Iron Curtain arrangements at state level were incomparably more difficult at that time (see Chap. 5). More city-to-city 'sister' arrangements followed on a case-by-case footing, until, in 1990, when the Iron Curtain finally came down, Chicago intensified such linkages by signing agreements with seven additional sister cities. This accelerated outreach internationally was pushed further by the mayor at the time (Richard M. Daley) who formalised this process by establishing a Board of Directors for Chicago Sister Cities International to enhance its political visibility and credibility as well as capability in boosting the sister city network. This organisational strengthening coincides with an expansion in community engagement through more publicity work, accompanied by a rapid increase in sister city relationships. As a result, Chicago established official relationships with 28 cities around the world, making it the most active Sister Cities organisation in the world. Clearly, building a city network, rather than direct lobbying through an own office, is the preferred route taken by Chicago to reach out internationally. This is an inherently less formal means of 'diplomacy' and thus seen as potentially in competition with similar national activities, as it is less physically 'representational' than an own 'international representation' in an office/building as found in Europe. Nevertheless, this network building is viewed by Chicago policy-makers as a way of boosting 'Chicago's international activity and its status as a leading global city' (http://chicagosistercities.com/misson/).

Internationalisation efforts were enhanced by merging Chicago Sister Cities International with the business-led international organisation, World Business Chicago. This public–private organisation reflects the long-established role of businesses in shaping Chicago's economic strategies and role (interviews Chicagoland Chamber of Commerce, 12 July 2004). Chaired by the mayor of the city, World Business Chicago is about promoting regional economic development within 'Chicagoland'. By merging the two organisations, the city-regional dimension as Chicago's economic power base is more explicitly internationalised as part of a city network that focuses on Chicago. This allows linking the 'internal' with the international 'external' as a means to 'put Chicago at the forefront of the global economy'. The combined organisation of sister city networking and international business engagement now operates under the auspices of the latter, World Business Chicago, Chicago's not-for-profit economic development agency, clearly highlighting the economic (and corporate) focus of Chicago's international ambitions (http://www.worldbusiness-chicago.com/who-we-are/). This reflects a general shift in focus from a traditional interest in diplomatic, cultural or educational agendas to a growing need for cities to expand and leverage sister city partnerships for economic development in a globalised, competitive environment.

Figure 6.3 shows the rapid expansion of the Chicago sister city network in the 1990s, as well as the political messages/statements implied by the various twinning processes, such as the collapse of communism in Eastern Europe. The increased twinning activity was also driven by the mayors' interests, with Mayor Richard M. Daley particularly pro-active, signing 21 of Chicago's 28 sister city agreements

Sister City Name	Global Region
Athens (Greece) **Birmingham** (UK) **Belgrade** (Serbia) **Gothenburg** (Sweden) **Galway** (Ireland) **Milan** (Italy) **Paris** (France) **Vilnius** (Lithuania) **Kyiv** (Ukraine) **Hamburg** (Germany) **Lucerne** (Switzerland) **Moscow** (Russia) **Prague** (Czech Republic)	Europe
Amman (Jordan) **Delhi** (India) **Busan** (South Korea) **Lahore** (Pakistan) **Shanghai** (China) **Shenyang** (China) **Osaka** (Japan) **Petach Tikva** (Israel)	Asia
Accra (Ghana) **Casablanca** (Morocco) **Durban** (South Africa)	Africa
Bogota (Colombia) **Mexico City** (Mexico) **Toronto** (Canada)	Americas

Fig. 6.3 Chicago's sister cities in the world. *Source*: Based on information from Chicago Sister Cities International (http://chicagosistercities.com/sister-cities/)

(https://www.wbez.org/shows/curious-city/sister-cities-chicagos-international-family/6f2c3b84-a21e-40f8-a0a7-97163164e161).

Development has become the main driving force for cities to join the network (https://www.wbez.org/shows/curious-city/sister-cities-chicagos-international-family/6f2c3b84-a21e-40f8-a0a7-97163164e161),   and these interests become also more substantial in 'hands-on' activities in terms of boosting the economic effects. Thus, in late 2013, the cities of Chicago and Mexico City entered into a city-to-city trade agreement, the first of its kind, taking the sister city agreement between the two cities of 20 years ago to a new level, while building on existing trust based on strong cultural and economic links between the two cities. The new trade agreement seeks to strengthen cooperation in FDI, trade, innovation, tourism and education to boost employment and strengthen global competitiveness (http://chicagosistercities.com).

This agreement was facilitated by the Global Cities Initiatives, the collaborative project between J.P. Morgan Chase and the Brookings Institution. This initiative was launched in Los Angeles in 2012 as a vehicle to help leaders of American metropolitan areas to strengthen their regional economies by raising their competitiveness in a 'global economy [which] is a network of metropolitan economies [and] ... home to most of the world's population, production, finance, and sources of innovation'. Over a five-year period, with $10 million a year, this joint initiative seeks to support inter alia the creation of 'an international network of leaders from global cities intent upon deepening global trade relationships' (http://www.brookings.edu/about/projects/global-cities/about). This was a multi-actor project that also involved the Chicagoland Chamber of Commerce and ProMexico, the Mexican government's 'outreach institution' tasked with strengthening Mexico's participation in the international economy. 'It was very important to all parties that this become a substantive, active partnership, not [a] ceremonial agreement that was signed and then filed for perpetuity' (http://cities-today.com/how-sister-city-partnerships-can-play-a-new-role-in-a-global-economy). These linkages, CSCI points out, go beyond the administrative entities of the two collaborating cities and individual actors within, but involve the wider city-regions and thus are of significant importance for economic development at the regional level and beyond ('How sister city partnerships can play a new role in a global economy', *Cities Today*, 27 May 2014: http://cities-today.com/how-sister-city-partnerships-can-play-a-new-role-in-a-global-economy/).

This matters, because it is the international standing and visibility of individual businesses and corporate actors that underpin the international—or global—status of a city. Globally, the average large metropolitan area receives FDI from more than 30 different countries and almost 80 different city-regions worldwide. Nevertheless, most of the investment by volume concentrates in the 'top ten' countries, with city-regions accounting for 75% of that volume. The focus of international investment interests on American city-regions means that the largest 100 metropolitan areas in the United States contain nearly three-quarters of all jobs in foreign-owned enterprises. In total, companies from 445 city-regions and 115 countries generate direct investment (Saha et al. 2014). For that, investors look for, and generate, connectivity to utilise a globalised division of production. Flexibility and responsiveness are crucial, especially also vis-à-vis quickly changing technologies and markets. 'In short, collaboration enables flexible capacity, while international collaboration taps a vastly more diverse and hungry talent pool' (Hartley 2015). It is not size alone that matters for influence and international engagement. Rather, it is the ability to be flexible, learn and innovate, including in policy terms (see Hartley 2016).

Toronto, at over 3 million the largest Canadian city within an agglomeration of some 8 million, used that shift in political perspective to devise its first internationally oriented policy agenda in 1999 (Madison and Brunet-Jailly 2014). This was driven by a combination of a post-recession recovery in the national economy, a pro-active, outward-looking mayor, and the new unitary structure of the city created by the province as consolidated local government (Metro Toronto) to achieve administrative efficiencies and cost savings (see Slack and Côté 2014). This provided added institutional capacity (Boudreau et al. 2006) especially also vis-à-vis the challenges of globalisation (Williams 1999), and a supportive, business-oriented government in the province of Ontario (City of Ontario 2000). So, in 1999, the city council approved and funded the implementation of the new International Alliance Program as a city-to-city initiative 'to foster relationships with international cities for economic development purposes' (City or Ontario 2000, p. 1). This is a city-to-city initiative, aimed at establishing partnerships with cities that show 'economic similarities and characteristics' (City or Ontario 2000, p. 1) with Toronto as the basis for intended economic exchanges and collaborative arrangements across national borders, without involvement of other tiers of government. Accordingly, the two key elements involve bilateral exchanges as win-win scenarios initiated by 'hosting incoming international business delegations and organizing outgoing missions' (City or Ontario 2000, p. 1). High profile trade missions by the mayor to US cities, Europe and the Middle East, are one important tool of Toronto's international engagement, thus combining political and economic networks and relations. This is thus a politically initiated outreach, rather than one on the back of existing business relations, with local government following more or less enthusiastically. In line with its origins, the 'International Alliance Programme' gives economic development a pre-eminent first position among its list of objectives (http://www1.toronto.ca). And internationalisation is a clear and explicit part of that. Under 'economic development', one stated goal is to 'Increase Toronto's profile on the world stage and help Toronto businesses increase the exposure of products and services' (http://www1.toronto.ca).

Promoting the city's economy is also the more or less indirect objective under the other headings, such as 'Cultural development', where the aim is to 'Promote Toronto as the Creative City of the future with robust cultural and creative industries' and 'Invigorate and promote Toronto's cultural tourist attractions' (http://www1.toronto.ca), thus reflecting Richard Florida's idea of a 'creative class', which became influential around that time (Florida 2002). Accordingly, under 'Cross-cultural community development', the multicultural nature of Toronto's population is also profiled as a 'human resource' in economic terms, not least to demonstrate existing internationality, rather than localist insularity. Following the model of sister cities or city twinning as in Europe (see Chap. 5), establishing 'partner cities' is a task 'driven by city staff and focus heavily on economic development goals such as building business links, increasing Toronto's profile, cultural exchanges, and promoting trade' (City of Toronto 2000a). Through these activities, the city council has sought to reduce the psychological barrier for incoming FDI clients 'to take the leap into unfamiliar, "foreign" territory', and 'gets this City onto the "long list" of potential sites' (City of Toronto 2000b).

Outside Toronto, other cities are part of the metropolis, such as Hamilton, with a population of half a million, located within the wider Toronto city-region on Lake Ontario. As home to McMaster University, the city benefits from the internationalisation effort of the institutions as part of its attempt to attract foreign students and seek internationally collaborative research, especially in science and technology (City of Hamilton 2010). The city's strategy, however, is much less internationally oriented, with much of its concerns focused on supporting the university-related science cluster and raising the attractiveness of the city to live in, so as to appeal to potential investors, employees and researchers (development strategy). Generally, 'internationality' barely features in the city's strategic development goals, and when it does, it is in relation to its international airport. The city's Vision 2020 strategy, for instance, makes no reference of any international ambitions (http://www.myhamilton.ca/myhamilton/CityandGovernment). The city benefits from being a part of the Greater Toronto area and the wider Atlantic seaboard metropolitan band. It is thus in a more advantageous position than, for instance, Aurora within the Denver agglomeration. Perhaps not surprisingly, the city's efforts to raise its international profile are somewhat limited, essentially restricted to a handful of sister city agreements. Under 'International Relations' the city council's website lists Saitama, Japan; Wuxi and Chengdu (China); Sacramento, United States; and Ypres, Belgium (http://www.hamilton.govt.nz/our-council/about-council/internationalrelationships/Pages/default.aspx). Beyond that, the main attraction is being near Toronto without Toronto costs. So, again, smaller, economically more regionally or nationally embedded cities seem much more hesitant in North America to engage independently beyond national borders. The sister city programme offers here a low key and 'safe' possibility to demonstrate some degree of internationality for the sake of image, without too many follow-up responsibilities or commitments. Alternatively, the city may engage through the Canadian municipal association, FCM (Federation of Canadian Municipalities).

6.5   Combining Individual and Network-Based Internationalisation: 'Cascadia' as Linear, Poly-Centric and Transnational City-Region

In North America, the idea of a linear polycentric metropolis has a long tradition, epitomised by Jean Gottmann's concept of Megalopolis on the US East Coast. This, however, had no transnational element, as it was entirely limited to US territory. In this respect more interesting is the much more recent idea of 'Cascadia' in the Pacific Northwest as an international city-region, stretching from Eugene, the capital of the state of Oregon, via Portland and Seattle, to Vancouver in Canada. Cascadia, as a politically imagined trans-border city network (Smith 2008), occupies quite a unique position in North America. The idea of a functional, but also value (lifestyle-) based city-region was brought together by the so-called I5-corridor, as it follows the main freeway (motorway) of that name along the western foothills of the Cascade Mountains. These provide not just a formidable topographic barrier to the east, but also a represent a transition to a sparsely populated, rural interior, thus emphasising the relative peripherality of the region to the rest of the North American continent. This shared sense of relative separateness from other metropolitan regions is reflected in a sense of shared fate and opportunity. In that sense, the notion of Cascadia may go beyond other such large polycentric regions, also conceptualised as mega-regions (Schafran 2014) of varying degrees of 'realness'. Looking outwardly, beyond national borders, and here, especially, to the Pacific Rim and China, has become an important strategic concern. Almost half of the region's exports go there (Clarke 2000). It is very much based on the urban politics and urban economies of the main cities as centres of high tech, innovative industries of global reach, with Boeing and Microsoft probably the stalwarts of that innovative technology focus with a global perspective. Other, more consumer-oriented global players now include Amazon and Starbucks (in Seattle) and Nike in Portland. On the other hand, especially in Vancouver, smaller businesses build the economic base, so that there is less of a globalisation impetus. In between are major international transport hubs: SeaTac airport, and bulk shipping ports in Vancouver (also a major airport hub) and Seattle-Tacoma (subsumed under Puget Sound; Herrschel 2013). There is thus a combination of local specialisms within this overall complementary band of metropolitan economies, with globally operating corporations providing a crucial push for 'going international' to city governments. Cascadia is a multi-scalar construct, connecting the international regionalism of free trade agreements to city-regional functional connectivity, giving rise to the image of Cascadia constituting 'the [American] 'Main Street' linking the NAFTA partners (Clarke 2000, p. 370). This main street of Cascadia refers to the 'inner core' of the region, imagined as the main cities connected by a high speed rail link to integrate this urban corridor even further (Smith 2008).

The underlying shared expectation of collective competitive gains via a globalised market, encouraged governments of the two affected US states, Oregon and Washington, and the Canadian province of British Columbia to become 'engaged in direct, primary relations with each other across international boundaries' (Clarke 2000, p. 371). But it is not just economic inter-linkages that provide the glue for this corridor-region. There are also shared values in terms of quality of life—quite in contrast to the interior parts to the east of the Cascades—and thus the accepted need for a joint approach to governance to produce effective environmentally-oriented policies (Clarke 2000). This further under-pinned the notion of a cross-border regional entity which transcends established administrative borders and boundaries, although the notions of an (older) ecological and a (more recent) economic Cascadia region are not spatially congruent (Smith 2008). Internationalisation has thus become a recognised necessity since the early 1990s to further, and pro-tect, a jointly valued way of life (Cold-Ravnkilde et al. 2004). But this was, of course, prior to the events of 9/11 in 2001, when the United States viewed its borders again as defence lines, rather than points of con-nection and communication.

The concept of Cascadia 'exemplifies responses to apparent gaps in the ability of national governments to control global and transnational eco-nomic processes' (Clark, 2000), and points to the need for a broader, multi-scalar range of actors populating the international arena of govern-ing cross-border functional relations through inter-jurisdictional engage-ment. Leaving this too often to distant national governments, as also in this case, cannot produce the required locally optimised answers. It is for that reason that cities and city-regions have become more pro-active either individually, collectively, or both, depending on their particular circum-stances and policy-making capacity and capability.

This economic space has prompted calls for establishing matching gov-ernance arrangements that overcome the administrative divisions that dis-sect the economic corridor of Cascadia (Clarke 2000; Brunet-Jailly 2008). The international dimension of the region, further emphasised by NAFTA and a subsequently stronger north–south flow of goods and economic interests (Clarke 2000; Cold-Ravnkilde et al. 2004), added to the felt urgency of more engagement across the US–Canadian border to coordi-nate and cooperate in economic governance. In particular, local businesses have moved to the forefront of promoting easier and less 'visible' border crossings (Cold-Ravnkilde et al. 2004), so that the business community has again been the main driver of more imaginative policies that go beyond established horizons and 'reaches'. There have been two drivers of local internationalism in this region: economic competitiveness and 'ecologi-cal and sustainability narratives in order to attract capital while creating an elite transnational group-identity' (Cold-Ravnkilde et al. 2004, p. 60).

National policies have been somewhat contradictory in this respect, reinforcing border controls on the one hand—post-September 2001—while seeking to create a common economic space through NAFTA (Cold-Ravnkilde et al. 2004).

Particularly the latter has encouraged bilateral alliances and collaborative governmental arrangements, with the Cascadia Project seeking to coordinate growth management and strategic planning in the Pacific Northwest. Economic competition in a global setting has become the main focus of Cascadia as a political-economic space (Clarke 2000). But Cascadia is more than an opportunistic tool for area marketing. There is a sense of shared values and qualities of life—different from other parts in North America—and this has led to some claims for greater—joint—autonomy within the respective nation states with their 'far-away' national governments (http://www.cascadianow.org/about-cascadia/). The term 'Cascadia' was introduced in 1970 by an academic from Seattle, to describe a distinct, growing regional identity with an inherent international component (Smith 2008). As Cold-Ravnkilde et al. (2004) point out, the combination of the competitive economic and environmental narrative produced a 'new emphasis on high-tech in the region. Firms such as Microsoft in Seattle, cultural industries related to music, film and television in Vancouver, as well as tourism throughout the region represent the region's growing alternative (to resource extraction) economic base' (Cold-Ravnkilde et al. 2004, p. 68). There is thus a combined focus on the intra-regional (environmental) qualities and the economic opportunities beyond, 'with a focal point on the Pacific Rim and includes value-added industries, manufacturing, defense, transportation, tourism, computer software, entertainment, environmental industries, and biotechnology' (Cold-Ravnkilde et al. 2004). And it is these local–international connections that have encouraged a growing international engagement by the main cities beyond national actions of that kind. They are an important quality and characteristic of this region, which, as in the Øresund region (Chap. 5), uses globalism as a distinct profiling element to locate itself on the international arena. Yet, there are also dangers in this strategy, as Smith (2008) points out: while 'Cascadia', especially with its city-regional image of 'Main Street Cascadia' may seem set on a successful course with its globalist economy-centric agenda, other such attempts have not all been successful in the same way. This reflects their underlying economic and institutional capacity and thus, eventually, credibility and relevance as places of international—or global—relevance. Thus, it is possible to develop a failed 'going global' city brand. Cities such as Baltimore and several failed efforts in Atlanta are illustrative (Smith 2008, p. 77). In Cascadia's case, and similar to that of Øresund, the cross-border nature of the city-region is an important dimension of credible and visible profiling of internationality. 'More peripheral cities—certainly including all in Cascadia—must play a more multi-faceted international—and cross-border—game ... Here a more globalist strategy ... offers the best branding opportunity' (Smith 2008, p. 77).

Along the I5 Corridor, the underlying similarities in values and agendas around the 'enviro-economic' vision of Cascadia (Cold-Ravnkilde et al. 2004, p. 68) have resulted in a thickness of linkages and connections between institutions and organisations, as well as businesses and other non-governmental actors, across the international border for both public sector governance and corporate strategies (Brunet-Jailly 2008). Heightened border control since the events of 9/11 (Cold-Ravnkilde et al. 2004), however, counteract such cross-border connectivity, although the barriers are 'lower' for those from within the region. In response to the inherent contradictions of more border security on the one hand, and the idea of free trade as part of NAFTA, on the other, there 'is the emergence of a multiplicity of cooperative agreements in a multiplicity of policy arenas, which are articulated by overarching policy networks spanning the border and fostering cross-border relations' (Brunet-Jailly 2008, p. 116). As a result, internationality in the Pacific Northwest comprises a multi-scalar engagement at the institutionalised local, state/province and federal government levels and, of course, also outside the public sector. As a consequence, 'In few places in North America is subnational, binational, international activity being played out more fully than in the Canadian-American West/Pacific North West—Cascadia—region; this cross-border activity is being played out at every jurisdictional level, and in both governmental and nongovernmental settings' (Smith 2008, p. 61).

So it may not come as much of a surprise that Seattle, Vancouver or Portland, for instance, pursue their own international agendas (interviews Greater Seattle Trade Alliance, 19 Februqry 2014, Portland Metro, 28 Februqry 2015), focusing in particular on Asia as a market, and source and destination of FDI. Vancouver seeks to promote its image as an innovative, creative and 'liveable' place, with a matching economy, and thus seeks to build an 'expanded international profile of Vancouver as a destination for business and talent' (VEC 2011). This ties in with the small business structure, with start-ups based on innovative products. Yet, this small-scale structure finds it more difficult to 'knock heads together', as the threat of a big company, like Boeing, did in the case of Vancouver's southern neighbour, Seattle some 15 years ago. This may also be the reason why finding and formalising a city-regional approach to boost capacity and international visibility, has proven so difficult (Bula 2015).

For Vancouver itself, a friendly, trendy image may make the place attractive for the 'creative class' to live in, but it also counteracts bigger picture approaches, as they may be seen as undermining this very image. Vancouver's main economic development body, the VEC (Vancouver Economic Commission), sums up these characteristics in its own profiling: 'The Vancouver Economic Commission (VEC) works to position Vancouver as a globally recognised city for innovative, creative and sustainable business', while also promoting the city as 'cutting edge … consistently rated as one of the world's most liveable cities' (http://www.vancouvereconomic.com/about/). In this instance, the role of the mayors matters as driver of collective action, as was pointed out in Portland, further south in the Cascadia region (Planning Dept, Portland, interview 24 February 2015). Yet, how far this translates into explicit internationalisation strategies varies. In Vancouver, it is primarily the business-oriented VEC that articulates such agendas (VEC 2011), For the city, international engagement, as far as its administrative structure is concerned, is restricted to link-ups with five sister cities: Odessa (Ukraine), Yokohama (Japan), Edinburgh (UK), Guangzhou (China) and Los Angeles (United States). No further expansion of that city-to-city network is currently planned (http://vancouver.ca/news-calendar/international-relationships.aspx). Vancouver seems quite content with utilising its 'liveable city' image as a self-promoting advertisement. There is a danger, however, that such self-contentment might weaken innovative projects and policies and damage the city's friendly image as one of its main assets.

In its southern neighbour, Seattle, the corporate voice is much stronger and more visible in the city's policy-making and self-perception. Boeing, Microsoft and Amazon represent the opposite of low-key likeability. And so there is a much more explicit and matter-of-course degree of internationality in the city's policies, such as an Office of Intergovernmental Relations, which also includes an International Affairs Director. The main tasks are: advising the mayor on international matters, including the city's international engagement strategy; overseeing its relationships with its 21 sister cities; promoting international business in partnership with similarly focused local and regional actors (e.g. the Trade Development Alliance of

Greater Seattle, the Washington State China Relations Council, Economic Development Council of Seattle and King County); and managing Seattle's relationship with the Consular Association of Washington and other internationally oriented local organisations, such as the World Affairs Council or OneWorld Now! (http://www.seattle.gov/oir/international-relations). Just comparing the international network of 21 sister cities with Vancouver's five (and no further expansion planned), indicates the different interest in actively 'going international'. And Seattle actively promotes and advertises its international engagements, such as on Facebook (https://www.facebook.com/SeattleInternational/) as part of its reaching out to that level. This international sentiment is now also being picked up in the second city of Puget Sound, some 40 km south of Seattle: in 2014, the mayor of Tacoma installed a new Commission of International Relations in City Hall to 'align resources and make a concerted effort to attract more foreign investment and boost tourism, education, and the arts in Tacoma' as part of a new campaign to increase the city's international visibility and engagement with markets and investment opportunities elsewhere (TDA 2015).

Further south, in neighbouring Portland, similar to Seattle, an Office of Government Relations exists, situated in the Mayor's Office to underpin the importance attributed to intergovernmental relations. The international dimension is subsumed in one of the three sub-units, each of which deals with a specific level of government from state via federal to international, as expressed in the Department's slogan 'The City of Portland's voice in Salem and Washington D.C.' (https://www.portlandoregon.gov/ogr/65019?). 'International' in this context refers to the nine sister cities in Europe, Asia and Mexico. Beyond that, international engagement refers mainly to welcoming mayors from other (foreign) cities and delegations from other countries. Much of this internationality relates to trade delegations and is thus clearly driven by economic players and their interests. In this respect, Portland combines to some extent the large business world found in Seattle, here represented by Nike, and the small business, entrepreneurial world dominating in Vancouver. Particularly concerning big international business, the city is well aware of the mobility of such capital and thus seeks to raise its profile by enhancing and marketing its lifestyle and liveability appeal (just as Vancouver does).Yet, there are indications of an increasingly more pro-active effort at raising the city's profile on the international circuit of business investors. Examples are the recently published Greater Portland

Global Trade and Investment Plan, developed inter alia by the Portland Development Commission, or the consultations with the Brookings Institution's Metropolitan Policy Program (McDearman and Donahue 2015). The plan focuses on FDI and business investment and 'escalates global engagement to realize a stronger regional economy' (http://worldoregon.org/events/programs/headline-and-cultural-forums/launch-the-greater-portland-global-trade-and-investment).

So, individual cities' initiatives are not particularly spectacular, and clearly aimed primarily at the respective state/province and federal governments. Referring to, and marketing, Cascadia as an international region could add to the credibility and uniqueness of these cities by pointing to established 'borderless' working and an international outlook (rather than being in the periphery). Cascadia, like Øresund, therefore exemplifies a synthesis of individual cities' collective action, with collaborative, international regionalisation offering an important added value for the cities, but also the region and its other constituent (less famous) municipalities. It is the inherent international nature of the Cascadia region that provides an image, as well as reality, of outward-looking engagement at the international level. This distinguishes the region from most other city-regions. For Vancouver, Tacoma and Portland, this provides an important credibility bonus in their attempts to claim international interests and ambitions. For Seattle, this context is less important, as the city has raised its international profile on the back of its main economic actors. Here, the balance between regionally, collectively carried internationalism, and individual engagement has shifted in favour of the latter.

Yet, by the same token, the cities and their governmental and non-governmental actors also act jointly internationally as a collective 'virtual region'. Its reach across international borders may seen as underpinning the international character of the region, yet is also subject to changing quality ('harder', 'softer') of that international border through national policies. Manning (1977) seeks to capture this cross-purpose by calling such city-driven responses to globalisation 'intermestic', a combination of 'international' and 'domestic', which cuts across 'more traditional conceptions of international, subnational, local-global and urban multilevel governance relations' (Smith 2008, p. 70). As a result, the policy learning and institutional capacity developed by major city jurisdictions within Cascadia, such as Vancouver, Portland and Seattle, through such international activity were not insignificant factors in subsequent regional developments in Cascadia. Importantly, much of this activity was city-centred (Smith 2008, p. 70).

Nevertheless, globalisation, and so the growing impact of events and processes on cities—without the traditional protective effects of national borders, has encouraged cities to do more themselves about the local and regional effects of globalism. Generally, policy and institutional responses have been relatively slow in recognising the role individual cities can play in the international arena as beacons of regional and national competitiveness and international visibility, especially so at the national level (see above). The final section will summarise individual cities' actions in North America.

6.6   SUMMARISING COMMENTS

The political aspirations and agendas by the cities presented in this chapter reveal a growing tension between established state-centric understandings of 'international' as space and relations, and the changes as part of globalisation that place cities and city-regions in a key position—to the disadvantage of the state. The outcome of this suggests a changing dynamic in the relationship between cities as increasingly powerful economic centres, and the territorially-based state with a greater variety of interests and underlying structural inequalities and tensions. 'So a foreign policy for cities in the twenty-first century will not look like the kind of foreign policy that states have' (Curtis 2015).

However, cities are not yet in a position, nor want to be in it, to act independently of nation states, as they, too, are conditioned by the long-held notion of the territorial state within which they are embedded. Removing themselves from that institutional and legal framework, as well as spatially scalar embeddedness, which also provides international security and sovereignty, may seem a step too far, at least at the moment, and no clear alternatives for governing the international having emerged as yet, even as a concept. Rather, cities gain international status through their economic success, and the nature of the workings of a globalised economy with its emphasis on connectivity, rather than merely location. So, economic competitiveness pushes cities into key positions, often with the express support of their respective states, while territorial competitiveness in a mercantilist understanding comes to be replaced by a much more selective, differentiated re-spatialisation of economic opportunities, favouring a few centres with some interconnections as 'flowing' relationships. It is those relationships through which cities (and regions) can, as sub-national actors, mobilise extra political agency and thus power. By pooling and more broadly projecting interests and relevance, they seek to generate a novel form of trans-scalar global governance. This may involve transcending familiar practices and notions of 'due responsibility', such as embodied in the concept of multi-scalar governance: a neat layering of distinct, separate layers of responsibility.

'The challenge placed before cities is to decide how they want to shape this regime, and what values they want to embed within it' (Curtis 2015, p. 00). However, scope to do so varies, with national capitals having an inherent advantage because of their proximity to national government. 'But global cities that are not national seats of government, such as Chicago or Shanghai, increasingly need to forge foreign policies of their own by co-ordinating the global engagement of its corporations, top academic centres, cultural institutions and civic bodies in ways that benefit the city and its citizens as a whole. Greater strategic direction, more co-operation and better co-ordination of such global engagement would constitute the equivalent of a foreign policy for Chicago' (Daalder 2015). And so, Daalder adds, 'today's international politics is beginning to resemble the Hanseatic League of medieval cities, with global centres trading and working together to address common problems in ways that large nations do not. While not sovereign, global cities are increasingly independent—driving policies that stimulate wider change … And while nations debate over what to do about climate change the largest and most important cities are getting together and doing something about it' (Daalder 2015). One of these initiatives is the C40 group of 75 major cities (see Chap. 4). 'In short, global cities are increasingly driving world affairs—economically, politically, socially and culturally. They are no longer just places to live in. They have emerged as leading actors on the global stage' (Daalder 2015). And much of this lead is based on pragmatic considerations, delivering policy outcomes rather than mere discourse, since the municipal tradition is based on specified duties and an electorate that is 'close by' and which responds more immediately to policies at the next ballot box.

References

Borbely, J.M., 2009. US labor market in 2008: Economy in recession. *Monthly Lab. Rev.*, *132*, p. 3. Available under: http://heinonline.org/HOL/LandingPage?handle=hein.journals/month132&div=22&id=&page=, accessed 4 Mar 16.

Bothwell, R. and Rothwell, R., 1995. *Canada and Quebec: One country, two histories.* British Columbia: UBC Press.

Boudreau, J-A., Hamel, P., Jouve, B. and Keil, R., 2006. Comparing metropolitan governance: The cases of Montreal and Toronto. *Progress in Planning 66,* 7–59.

Brunet-Jailly, E., 2008. Cascadia in comparative perspectives: Canada-US relations and the emergence of cross-border regions. *Canadian Political Science Review,* 2(2), 104–124.

Bula, F., 2015. Co-operation among cities crucial to Vancouver region's economic prospects. In: Globe and Mail, 28 Dec 2015.

Champion, T., 2001. Urbanization, suburbanization, counterurbanization and reurbanization. In: R. Paddison (ed.): *Handbook of Urban Studies.* London: Sage, pp. 143–161.

Chicago Forum on Global Cities., CFGC, 2015a. Global Cities Reach Beyond National Boundaries to Advance International Agendas. 8 Apr 2015, Available under: http://www.chicagoforum.org/press-release/global-cities-reach-beyond-national-boundaries-to-advance-international agendas., accessed 15 Mar 16.

City of Aurora., 2015. Comprehensive Strategic Plan 2015–18, Available under: https://www.auroragov.org/cs/groups/public/documents/document/024722.pdf, accessed 5 Mar 16.

City of Hamilton, 2010. Hamilton Economic Development Strategy 2010–2015, Available under: http://www.investinhamilton.ca/wp-content/uploads/2011/ 06/Hamilton-EcDev-Strategy2010.pdf.

Clarke, S., 2000. Regional and Transnational Discourse: The Politics of Ideas and Economic Development In Cascadia. *International Journal of Economic Development,* 2(3), 360–378.

Cold-Ravnkilde, S.M., J. Singh and R.G. Lee., 2004. Cascadia: The (Re) Construction of a Bi-National Space and Its Residents. *Journal of Borderlands Studies,* 19(1), 59–77.

Curtis, S., 2015. Commentary – A Foreign Policy for Global Cities? The Chicago Forum on Global Cities, 1 Dec 2015. Available under: https://www.chicagoforum.org/blogentry/commentary-%E2%80%93-foreign-policy-global-cities.

Daalder, I., 2015. *(president of the Chicago Council on Global Affairs):* On Global Cities. In: Financial Times, 26 May 15.

DFID, 2010. Cities – the new frontier. Available under: https://www.gov.uk/government/uploads/system/uploads/attachment_data/file/67689/cities-new-frontier.pdf.

Dierwechter, Y., 2008. *Urban Growth Management and Its Discontents. Promises, Practices, and Geopolitics in U.S. City-Regions.* Basingstoke: Palgrave Macmillan.

Ethiosports – Ethiopian-American Mediaservice, http://www.ethiosports.com/2014/08/23/aurora-hosts-first-sister-city-delegation-from-adamaethiopia/.

Florida, R., 2002. The Rise Of The Creative Class: And How It's Transforming Work, Leisure, *Community And Everyday Life*. Basic Books.

Hartley, K., 2015. Global cities in the 21st century: A Chicago model? In: newgeography.com, 28 April, accessed 5 Mar 16.

Hartley, K., 2016. Cosmic Cities: Small but Global. Chicago Council on Global Affairs, 14 Jan 16, Available under: http://www.thechicagocouncil.org/blog-entry/cosmic-cities-small-global, accessed 5 Mar 16.

Herrschel, T., 2013. Competitiveness AND Sustainability: Can 'Smart City Regionalism' Square the Circle? *Urban Studies, 50*(11), 2332–2348.

Herrschel, T., 2014. *Cities, State and Globalisation: City-regional governance in Europe and North America*. London: Routledge.

Hubbard, R. and Paquet, G., 2010. Federalism as a Philosophy of Governance. In: G. Paquet and R. Hubbard (eds.): *The Case for Decentralized Federalism*. Ottawa: University of Ottawa Press, pp. 1–14.

Jackson, D., 2013. Announcing the Global Cities Economic Partnership between Chicago and Mexico City. Available under: https://www.brookings.edu/blog/theavenue/2013/11/14/announcing-the-global-cities-economic-partnership-between-chicagoand-mexico-city/.

Kaplan, E., 2015. Chicago leads the way as a global city. Medill Reports Chicago, Medill News Services, 6 May 2015, http://news.medill.northwestern.edu/chicago/chicago-leads-the-way-as-a-global-city/, accessed 23 Mar 16.

Khanna, P. and Joishy, M., 2011. Mayor of the World: How Bloomberg flexes New York's Diplomatic Muscle. City Lab, no 9, Available under: http://www.citylab.com/politics/2011/09/mayor-world-how-bloomberg-flexes-new-yorks-diplomatic-muscle/167/, accessed 22 Mar 16.

Kresl, P. and Fry, E., 2005. *The urban response to internationalization*. London: Edward Elgar Publishing.

Madison, I. and Brunet-Jailly, E., 2014. The International Activities of Canadian Cities.: Are Canadian Cities challenging the gate-keeper position of the Federal Executive in International Affairs? In: S. Curtis, (ed.): *The Power of Cities in International Relations*, London: Routledge: pp. 107–132.

Manning, B., 1977. The Congress, The Executive and Intermestic Affairs. *International Journal, 55*, 306–24.

Manyika, J., Remes, J., Dobbs, R., Orellana, J. and Schaer, F., 2012. Urban America: US cities in the global economy. Mc Kinsey Global Institute, Available under: http://www.mckinsey.com/global-themes/urbanization/us-cities-in-the-global-economy, accessed 4 Apr 16.

McDearman, B. and Donahue, R., 2015. The *10 lessons from global trade and investment planning in U.S. metro areas*. Washington, DC: Brookings Institution.

NLC (National League of Cities) 2015. Annual Report. Available under: http://www.nlc.org/Documents/About%20NLC/NLC%20FY%202015%20Annual%20Report%20Final.pdf.

Pierre, J., 2011. *The politics of urban governance*. Palgrave Macmillan.

Rodríguez-Núñez, E. and García-Palomares, J.C., 2014. Measuring the vulnerability of public transport networks. *Journal of transport geography, 35*, 50–63.
Saha, D., Fikri, K. and Marchio, N., 2014. FDI in U.S. Metro Areas: The Geography of Jobs in Foreign-Owned Establishments, Report | June 20, 2014, Available under: http://www.brookings.edu/research/reports/2014/06/20-fdi-us-metro-areas, accessed 14 mar 16.
Salomon, A. and Klocksin, K., 2014. Curious City: Sister cities: Chicago's international family. WBEZ 91.5 Chicago. July. Available under: https://www.wbez.org/shows/curious-city/sister-cities-chicagos-international-family/6f2c3b84-a21e-40f8-a0a7-97163164e161, accessed 4 Apr 16.
Sassen, S., 1991. *The global city: New York, London, Tokyo. New York*: Princeton University Press (also later editions, 2001, 2013).
Schafran, A., 2014. Rethinking mega-regions: sub-regional politics in a fragmented metropolis. *Regional Studies, 48*(4), 587–602.
Slack, E and Côté, A., 2014. Comparative urban governance. Review for the UK Government's Foresight Future of Cities Project, Government Office for Sciences, London, Available under: https://www.gov.uk/government/uploads/system/uploads/attachment_data/file/360420/14-810-urban-governance.pdf, accessed 5 June 16.
Smith, P., 2008. Branding Cascadia: Considering Cascadia's Conflicting Conceptualizations: Who Gets To Decide? *Canadian Political Science Review, 2*(2), 57–83.
Soja, E., 2000. *Postmetropolis: Critical Studies of Cities and Regions*. London: Wiley.
Stevenson, D. and Gilbert, R., 2005. Coping with Canadian federalism: the case of the Federation of Canadian Municipalities. *Canadian Public Administration, 48*(4), 528–551.
TDA (Trade Development Alliance of Greater Seattle., 2015. Mayor of Tacoma Launches Campaign for International Relations. Blog by TDA, Available under: https://www.seattletradealliance.com/blog/tda-blog/post/mayor-of-tacoma-launches-campaign-for-international-relations, accessed 30 May 2016.
Tiboris, M., 2015. Nations Pledge at COP21, Cities Must Deliver. CCAG, 14 Dec 15. Available under: http://www.thechicagocouncil.org/blog-entry/nations-pledge-cop21-cities-must-deliver, accessed 15 Mar 16.
VEC (Vancouver Economic Commission), 2011. The Vancouver Economic Action Strategy: An Economic Development Plan for the City, unpublished, available under: http://vancouver.ca/files/cov/vancouver-economic-action-strategy.pdf, accessed 28 May 2016.
Williams, G., 1999. Institutional capacity and metropolitan governance: the Greater Toronto Area. *Cities, 16*(3), 171–180.

CHAPTER 7

Conclusions: Towards Closing the Conceptual Gap?

The starting point of this book was the observation of a growing complexity of actors and their interrelationships in the international arena—a development that has been driven by the pressures of globalisation. Following more than three decades of continuing discourse of globalisation as guarantor of economic growth, the dominant narrative of neo-liberalism and a belief in increasing the efficacy of government through adopting private sector-style, marketised rationales, a growing number of sub-national authorities have begun to venture into new policy fields and arenas to chase presumed opportunities. The larger cities have responded to this pressure to become more entrepreneurial and innovative in their policies. Their scope and capacity to do so varies, owing to different positions of strength: the successful metropolises, especially the so-called global cities, are in a much stronger position to become international actors than smaller, peripheral towns or struggling post-industrial cities. In addition, available instruments and established political cultures and milieux also matter. What all sub-national actors share is the growing willingness—out of conviction in the case of the desire to engage with international work on climate change or sheer economic necessity—to go beyond national borders and familiar political-economic conditions and relationships, and step into the international arena. While this action is the logical consequence of the past decades of ideological discourse and political strategies, it seems that academic debate and, especially disciplinary comfort zones, have been largely unresponsive to these developments, remaining wedded

© The Author(s) 2017
T. Herrschel, P. Newman, *Cities as International Actors*,
DOI 10.1057/978-1-137-39617-4_7

to their established respective focus on, and approaches to, cities (and regions) on the one hand, and the international realm surrounding 'black boxes' of nation states, on the other. The growing dynamics that have brought these two phenomena—cities and internationality—increasingly closer together, to the point of challenging nation states in their presumed sovereignty in the international arena, have not really been captured analytically and fallen into a 'conceptual gap'. Chapter 1 discussed this 'gap' between the inherent topical and conceptual boundaries of the two relevant disciplines, Urban Studies and International Relations. Neither has ventured much beyond their self-defined conceptual horizons, and thus they have been unable to draw on each other's expertise and insights to gain a better understanding of, and explanation for, the unfolding process of the growing 'urbanisation' of global governance. It is a process, as pointed out in Chap. 1, that demonstrates some aspects of the concept of glocalisation, although that was proposed by Swyngedouw (2004) from a perspective of economic globalisation. This argued for the fusion of the local and the global scales in analysing economic globalism, so as to capture the growing role of localness in economic decisions and strategies. At first sight, this seems an inherent contradiction to the notion of an unbounded, in effect unified, global space. This realisation of a clear role for the sub-national, especially cities, needs to find a corresponding response in the analysis of global governance. Yet, while Global Political Economy does recognise the multi-scalar organisation and interaction of the global economy, IR, as the political-institutional 'sister' discipline, has largely stayed away from such a trans-scalar approach, and has, instead, continued to define the 'international' first and foremost as a sum of nation states and their sovereign action, with all other interests subordinate to that. Certainly, this largely applies to the sub-national actors, as conceptualised some twenty years ago by Agnew (1994) as the 'territorial trap' in IR. Yet, this container thinking, as Chap. 2 demonstrates, has shown few signs of abating, as 'realist' approaches continue to dominate IR in its conceptualisation of the 'international' and its governance (Baylis et al. 2013; Nye 2004).

Likewise, in Urban Studies, there have been, again economy-centric, acknowledgements of the urban role in shaping globalism, albeit largely restricted to a select elite group of 'global cities' (Sassen 1991; Abu-Lughod 1999), 'world cities (Knox 1995) or 'global city regions' (Scott 2002), while globalisation has been portrayed much more as a driver of local responses and 'adjustments' to their governance (Amin and Thrift

1995), including as part of a scalar restructuring of the state (Brenner 1998). But while there has been talk about interrelations and 'flows', the nature and operation of these has not been of much interest. 'Flows' and their spatial manifestation (Castells 2006) have largely remained a descriptor of an observed phenomenon, with cities being located on it as 'connectors' (Sassen 2002). Cities have been conceptualised less as actors with their own interest and agency in global governance, and thus their impact on the very nature of internationality has largely gone unrecognised. It is here, as elaborated in Chaps. 1 to 3, that Urban Studies-based perspectives can benefit from drawing on a broad body of theories of the 'international' offered by the discipline of IR. It is through combining these two disciplinary lenses, this book argues, that 'actually existing' internationality, as shaped by policies and political actions of a growing and diversifying number of sub-national actors, can be captured conceptually more accurately than has been the case so far, with a state-centric lens. The resulting picture of how global governance is gaining in actor 'thickness' may provide a more relevant picture of the ways in which global governance is manifesting itself and acting itself out.

From the starting point of a conceptual gap in recognising the rapidly changing nature of the 'international realm' and its governance, Chaps. 2 and 3 explored the forces behind the sub-national challenge to the traditional sovereignty of nation states as the established representatives of national interest in the international realm, and the implications of that for, and manifestation in, the territoriality and institutional structure and operation of the nation state (Brenner 1998). But while both are subject to challenges by a growing agency among sub-national actors to take more care of their own developmental prospects and future, evidence on the ground suggests that they cannot do so without the nation state altogether. Both sub-national and national actors stand in an increasingly evident symbiotic relationship, something that previous state-centric notions of the international arena have largely ignored or were not able to detect. The end of the Cold War allowed economic dynamism and agency to take the lead in shaping, in effect, a territorially and politically frozen global arena, supported by an internationally agreed drive for free trade, governed by the WTO as one of the few globally operating international organisations. With demands for open borders rapidly gaining traction, established certainties about state territory, its control and role as expressing 'sovereignty' were no longer quite as much the focus of political agendas and interests.

Academically, this became evident in the predominantly economic focus of work on globalisation or global city networks. From this perspective it is economic relationships that matter, and less so the political-institutional implications of the more transient, fuzzy understanding of territory as a space of economic interest and opportunity, embracing both the local and international-global level. It is interesting to note that the main attempt to move in the direction of capturing the trans-scalar challenges to governing, the concept of multi-level governance, albeit tied to the particular nature and working of the EU, did not attract broader and more sustained interest as the basis for further theoretical development across the social sciences. Rather, it remained, in essence, a niche product, closely associated with the particularities of the EU and thus considered not really of much relevance to the wider, 'real' world outside. There, a hierarchical approach to conceptualising the state remained largely intact, focusing on clearly separated—both vertically and horizontally—spheres of responsibilities within the confines of the territorial state.

As concluded in Chap. 2, the resulting potentially conflictual relationship between the different geographies and the underlying dynamics and interests, needs to be turned into a mutually dependent symbiosis, even if it may lead to seemingly contradictory policy agendas and narratives. As the examples (Chaps. 5 and 6) demonstrate, territorially based institutionalisation, but also values and practices of governance and policy-making, affect strategic agendas and entrepreneurialism among sub-national actors 'to give it a go', and venture beyond well-worn boundaries and political certainties. Confidence among actors, not least based on local and regional support by the electorate, can provide sufficient innovativeness and political courage to venture into the international arena. This needs to be undertaken in full view of the established international actors, especially the nation states and international organisations, who may be challenged and inspired by the boldness of such aspirational novel action.

As Chap. 4 discussed, three avenues are open to sub-national actors to enter the global arena: first, individual, direct action with maximum exposure, and two more indirect routes via interlocutors in the shape of city/regional networks of shared interest, or international organisations as agents of local internationalisation efforts. The choice depends on a city's political and economic circumstances, especially its existing level of economic internationality as a bedrock on which to build political links, but also, and in particular (Oikonomou 2016), its political-institutional capacities, including statutory powers and legitimacy to act in such a way. This matters, as nation states may be reluctant to welcome, or encourage, such a challenge to their role as sole actors of consequence at the international level. The EU, with its explicit and broad platform for local and regional engagement with the European institutions and modes of governance, offers here a very specific, unique framework of internationality. And the EU-based concept of multi-level governance offers itself as a reference point. Rather than viewing new sub-national entrants as a challenge to established notions of fixed, one-dimensional state-centric internationality, the EU and MLG, offer the basis of a two-dimensional, 'thicker' understanding and conceptualisation of a more dynamic, evolving, trans-scalar global governance. So, Chap. 4 concludes with the observation that using intermediaries in the form of IOs or collaborative networks gives access to increased capacity, competence and thus likely efficacy of such organisations in engaging with global governance practices. Network regimes and the cognitive authority of technocratic IOs suggest easy, simple and predictable uni-directional transfers of policy between scales from the international to the local. Yet local actors may well be able to muster counter-directional influence, and thus push policy priorities and agendas up to the international scale through lobbying and collaborating with other actors, depending, of course, on their status and stature and thus likely recognition as actors who matter and are of interest to others. Collaborative action through networks can provide useful support for individual local actors' interests and ambitions, but that also depends on their resourcing, so as to avoid too much of an asymmetry of influence in comparison with formalised, institutionalised and recognised structures and actors, such as presented by a state administrative hierarchy or the traditional organisation of international governance among nation states. Maximising scope for 'punching above their weight' internationally will entail consequences for practical governance at city and regional level, such as changes to organisational structures, including public participation as a way to generate support for international action, and the associated remit and capacity for exercising leadership. This includes, for instance, resources to fund the provision of dedicated representational offices to networks, so as to allow more efficient lobbying work and administrative organisation through greater visibility and institutional capacity.

The comparative analysis in Chaps. 5 and 6 looks at the practical use by sub-national actors of the three main avenues to international engagement in different national and global settings. This revealed the interaction between national structures, the role of EU policies and institutions in providing a European internationality that is supportive of multi-scalar engagement with international governance, and the role of national governments, especially leadership, in shaping a global governance that takes a more holistic view, and reaches through states to the local level. And this can be effected either through mobilising IOs, or providing platforms and a political milieu that accommodates city and regional ambitions to take a more active role in global governance processes. Europe emerged in that respect much more entrepreneurial than North America with its evidently more conventional operation of nation state-based international politics. While in Europe, representational offices in Brussels offer to cities and regions the possibility of para-diplomatic activities in European internationality, albeit under the watchful eyes of the nation states, in North America, the situation is still much more conventional. There, the local level interacts with the outside world as a matter of principle primarily via the respective national government as recognised representative of all national interests, and individual local interests are subsumed under that general blanket of 'national interest'—again, evoking the image of the territorial-institutional 'container'.

So, to conclude, in this book we have looked critically at the responses of sub-national actors to 'boundless' cross-border or global challenges. As we saw in Chap. 3 an important lesson from IR's understanding of the international arena is that intergovernmental cooperation and networks which engage other private and civil society transnational actors, are structured through mechanisms—regime complexes, institutional and cognitive authority—that may both offer opportunities for sub-state units to develop new international activities and constrain action on the world stage. How well new actors manage on that stage depends on their understanding of the workings of networks, regimes and the authority claims constructed by other international actors.

We have explored the opportunities for cities and regions to build output-oriented authority if they can deliver international goods and contribute to changing global governance. States, sub-national actors and IOs adapt as the operating system of this global governance presents opportunities and sets constraints on individual or collective action. States adapt, for example, through widening their understandings of and claims about national interest (Humphreys 2015). Cities and regions can also take a wider than local view of the changing world. This needs new attitudes and skills. Adaptive states and cities embed the global in the local. Important differences between urban and regional adaptations depend on relative economic fortunes, increasing opportunities and the domestic resources—the powers and resources allocated by states (Hanegraaff et al. 2015)—available. The mobilisation of social movements, NGOs and other private actors similarly depends on context as well as international opportunity and as networking reproduces existing power relations among and inequalities between NGO actors (Dany 2014, p. 433) we might expect similar effects for sub-national governments. As we understand the operating system of global governance we perceive both opportunity and constraint. Important constraints are set by network regimes, leading cities and by the co-option of sub-national actors by international networks.

Nevertheless it is clear that sub-national actors have become significant players in global governance and the global diffusion of influence and authority. As these new players join in we need a broadly based understanding of global governance that includes all formal and informal institutions and the working norms, rules and procedures that guide individual initiatives and collective action. We have emphasised the importance of cooperation and competition and the 'serious questions' (Kuus 2015, p. 436) about transparency and accountability in the complex and changing world of global governance.

Legitimacy and authority generate fundamental debate in political science. The distinction between input and output legitimacy is helpful in contrasting the formal legitimacy of democratic states with legitimacy drawn from the economic and other outputs that cities may deliver as a result of their international orientation. There is a distinction between legitimacy as a property of the rules and processes of governance arrangements, on the one hand, and the legitimation of solutions derived from debate and interaction of a variety of actors, on the other (see Rousselin 2015). And 'legitimate' policy outcomes may well be the result of 'structural asymmetry' (Rousselin 2015, p. 13) among participants, where some cities or regions are more influential than others in networks and have more influence on IOs. In global governance the transparency and accountability of the decision process are important.

Some parallels may become evident between the emerging relationships of cities and their states in the changing nature of state sovereignty in other areas. For example, from the 1980s and 1990s the oversight of banks was geared more towards international competitiveness and creating national financial champions than to limiting risk (Epstein and Rhodes 2016). Over the same period national urban policies weakened in favour of creating competitive cities, preferencing infrastructure and prestige projects over social welfare—regulation of the physical rather than social city. As far as banking is concerned, in the EU in particular, regulatory control did not return to states after the 2008 crash but to banking unions and the enhanced power of supra-national officials. Having created internationally connected competitive cities, states now see their cities increasingly lost to the policy influence of IOs and burgeoning international networks.

REFERENCES

Agnew, J., 1994. The territorial trap: the geographical assumptions of international relations theory. *Review of International Political Economy*, 1(1), 53–80.

Abu-Lughod, J (1999): *New York, Chicago, Los Angeles: America's Global Cities.* University of Minnesota Press.

Amin, A, and Thrift, N (1995): Globalisation, institutional thickness and the local economy. In: P Healey, S. Cameron, S. Davoudi, S. Graham and A. Madani-Pour (eds): Managing Cities: The New Urban Context. Chichester: John Wiley, pp. 91–108

Baylis, J., Smith, S. and Owens, P. (2013): *The globalization of world politics: An introduction to international relations.* Oxford University Press.

Brenner, N., 1998. Global cities, glocal states: global city formation and state territorial restructuring in contemporary Europe. *Review of International Political Economy*, 5(1), pp. 1–37.

Castells, M., 2006. *The space of flows* (pp. 407–459). Oxford: Wiley-Blackwell.

Dany, C 2014 Janus-faced NGO Participation in Global Governance: Structural Constraints for NGO Influence, *Global Governance* 20 , 419–436

Epstein R & Rhodes M (2016) The political dynamics behind Europe's new banking union, *West European Politics*, 39:3, 415–437

Hanegraaff M, Braun C, De Bièvre D, Beyers J. 2015. The Domestic and Global Origins of Transnational Advocacy: Explaining Lobbying Presence During WTO Ministerial Conferences *Comparative Political Studies*, Vol. 48(12) 1591– 1621.

Humphreys A., 2015 From National Interest to Global Reform: Patterns of Reasoning in British Foreign Policy Discourse *BJPIR: 2015 VOL 17, 568–584.* doi: 10.1111/1467-856X.12053

Knox, P.L., 1995. *World cities in a world-system.* Cambridge University Press.

Kuus, M., 2015. Transnational Bureaucracies: How do we know what they know? *Progress in Human Geography*, 39(4), 432–448.

Nye Jr, J.S., 2004. *Power in the global information age: From realism to globalization.* Routledge.

Oikonomou, G. 2016. Bypassing a Centralized State: The Case of the Greek Subnational Mobilization in the European Union, *Regional & Federal Studies*, 26(1), 73–94.

Rousselin, M., 2015. The Power of Legitimation: The Role of Expert Networks in Global Environmental Governance. *Journal of Environmental Policy & Planning*, 1–17.

Sassen, S., 1991. *The global city: New York, London, Tokyo. New York*: Princeton University Press (also later editions, 2001, 2013).

Sassen, S., 2002. *Global networks, linked cities.* Psychology Press.

Scott, A., 2002. *Global city-regions: trends, theory, policy.* Oxford University Press.

Swyngedouw, E., 2004. Globalisation or 'glocalisation'? Networks, Territories and Rescaling. *Cambridge Review of International Affairs*, 17(1), 25–48.

BIBLIOGRAPHY

Adams, N. Cotella G., & Nunes, R. (2014). The Engagement of Territorial
   Knowledge Communities with European Spatial Planning and the Territorial
   Cohesion Debate: A Baltic Perspective, *European Planning Studies*, 22:4,
   712–734.
Agger, A., & Löfgren, K. (2008). Democratic assessment of collaborative planning
   processes. *Planning Theory*, 7(2), 145–164.
Agnew J (2013) Territory, Politics, Governance, *Territory, Politics,Governance*,
   1:1, 1–4, DOI: 10.1080/21622671.2013.765754.
Aldecoa, F., & Keating, M. (Eds.). (1999). *Paradiplomacy in action: the foreign
   relations of subnational governments*. Psychology Press.
Allmendinger, P and Haughton, G (2010): Spatial planning, devolution, and new
   planning spaces *Environment and Planning C: Government and Policy* vol 28,
   803–18.
Allmendinger, Ph and Haughton, G (2009): Soft spaces, fuzzy boundaries, and
   metagovernance: the new spatial planning in the Thames Gateway. In:
   Environment and Planning A, vol 41, 617–633.
Alte Liebe. In: Der Spiegel, no 36, 1986, pp. 50–52, available under: http://
   www.spiegel.de/spiegel/print/d-13518534.html.
Atkinson, R (2001): The emerging 'urban agenda' and the European Spatial
   Development Perspective: towards and EU urban policy? *European Planning
   Studies*, vol 9, no 3, 385–406.
Barca, F., McCann, P., & Rodríguez-Pose, A. (2012). The Case for Regional
   Development Intervention: Place-Based Versus Place-Neutral Approaches.
   Journal of Regional Science, 52(1), 134–152.

© The Author(s) 2017   247
T. Herrschel, P. Newman, *Cities as International Actors*,
DOI 10.1057/978-1-137-39617-4

Barnett, M. N., & Finnemore, M. (1999). The politics, power, and pathologies of international organizations. *International organization*, 53(04), 699–732.

Brenner, N (2004): *New State Spaces: Urban Governance and the Rescaling of Statehood*. Oxford: Oxford University Press.

Brenner, N. (1997): Global, fragmented, hierarchical: Henri Lefebvre's geographies of globalization. *Public Culture*, 10(1), 135–167.

Broome, A; Clegg, L and Rethel, L (2012) Global Governance and the Politics of Crisis, Global Society, 26:1, 3–17.

Brookings Institution (2015): Memorandum of understanding to establish the global cities economic partner-ship between Chicago and Mexico City, on 14 Nov 2013, Mexico City.; available under: http://www.brookings.edu/~/media/Programs/metro/gci-mexico/GCEP-CHI-MEX-MOU_FINAL. pdf?la=en, accessed 15 Mar 16.

Brunet-Jailly, E., & Smith, P. (2008). Introduction: Constructing a Cross Border Cascadia Region. *Canadian Political Science Review*, 2(2), 1–5.

C40 cities, UCLG, ICLEI (2014). *Global Mayors Compact* http://www.uclg. org/sites/default/files/global_mayors_compact.pdf.

Chicago Council on Global Affairs (CCGA) (2015): International Leaders to Initiate New Dialogue in Chicago on Global Cities, press notice of 24 Mar 15, available under http://www.chicagoforum.org/press-release/international-leaders-initiative, accessed 15 Mar 16.

Chicago Forum on Global Cities (CFGC) (2015): International Leaders to Initiate New Dialogue in Chicago on Global Cities.

Chorianopoulos, I and Iosifides, T. (2006). The neoliberal framework of EU urban policy in action: supporting competitiveness and reaping disparities. *Local Economy*, 21(4), 409–422.

Church, A., & Reid, P. (1999). Cross-border co-operation, institutionalization and political space across the English Channel. *Regional Studies*, 33(7), 643–655.

City of Aarhus (website 11 Nov 2003) The Aarhus EU Office – a Danish regional office in Brussels. (https://www.aarhus.dk/da/omkommunen/English/Collaborate-with-the-City/International-Relations/Internationalisation.aspx).

City of Toronto (2000a): Annual Report - City-to-City Outbound Missions (All Wards), adopted 1–4 Aug 2000. Available under: http://www.toronto.ca/leg-docs/2000/agendas/council/cc/cc000801/edp8rpt/cl010.pdf, accessed 14 Mar 16.

City of Toronto (2000b): International Alliance Program, Annual Report - City-to-City Outbound Missions (All Wards). Available under: http://www. toronto.ca/legdocs/2000/agendas/council/cc/cc000801/edp8rpt/cl010. pdf, accessed 5 June 16.

City of Umeå (2008): Curiosity and Passion. The Art of Co-Creation. First bid for ECoC status. Available under: http://umea2014.se/wp-content/uploads/2013/01/ansokan_1_eng.pdf, accessed 3 Apr 16.

City of Umeå (2009): Curiosity and Passion – the Art of Co-Creation. Application for Capital of Culture nomination, Available under http://umea2014.se/wp-content/uploads/2013/01/ansokan_2_eng.pdf, accessed 2 Apr 16.

Coen D., Pegram T. (2015): Commentary Wanted: A Third Generation of Global Governance Research http://www.ucl.ac.uk/global-governance/ggi-publications/thirdgenerationglobalgovernance (accessed 28/10/15).

Drezner, D. W. (2009). The power and peril of international regime complexity. *Perspectives on politics, 7*(01), 65–70.

Dunne, T., Hansen L., and Wight C 2013 The end of International Relations theory? *European Journal of International Relations* 2013 19, 405–425.

FCM (n.d.): Municipal principles for free and fair international trade. Available under: https://www.fcm.ca/Documents/tools/International/Municipal_Principles_For_Free_And_Fair_International_Trade_EN.pdf, accessed 15 Mar 2016.

FLACMA, Federation of Latin American Cities, Municipalities and Municipal Associations, established 17 Nov 1981 Quito, is international in nature and represents state, regions and cities of Latin America, and acts within. UCLG world organization.

Flint, C., Diehl, P., Scheffran, J., Vasquez, J., & Chi, S. (2009). Conceptualizing conflict space: Toward a geography of relational power and embeddedness in the analysis of interstate conflict. *Annals of the Association of American Geographers, 99*(5), 827–835.

Gehring T, & Faude B 2014 A theory of emerging order within institutional complexes: How competition among regulatory international institutions leads to institutional adaptation and division of labor. *Review of International Organisations* 9, 471–498.

Glasbergen, P (2007): Setting the Scene: The Partnership Paradigm in the Making. In: Glasbergen, P; F Biermann and A Mol (eds, 2007): *Partnerships, Governance and Sustainable Development: Reflections on Theory.* Cheltenham: Edward Elgar, pp. 1–28.

Gordon, I. (1999). Internationalisation and urban competition. *Urban Studies, 36*(5–6), 1001–1016.

Haas R (2015) 'World Order: What can be done?' http://www.crassh.cam.ac.uk/gallery/video/richard-haass-world-order-what-can-be-done (accessed 26/10/15).

Happaerts, S., Van den Brande, K. and Bruyninckx, H., 2011. Subnational governments in transnational networks for sustainable development. *International Environmental Agreements: Politics, Law and Economics, 11*(4), 321–339.

Harrison, J. (2006). Re-reading the new regionalism: a sympathetic critique. *Space & Polity, 10*(1), 21–46.

Harrtley, K (2015): Global cities in the 21st century: A Chicago model? Available under: http://www.newgeography.com/content/004908-global-cities-21st-century.

Hartlapp, M., Metz, J and Rauh, C (2014): *Which Policy for Europe? Power and Conflict Inside the European Commission.* Oxford University Press.

Harvey, D. (2010). *Social justice and the city* (Vol. 1). Atlanta: University of Georgia Press.

Haughton G, Allmendinger P, Counsell D and Vigar G (2010): *The new spatial planning: territorial management with soft spaces and fuzzy boundaries.* London: Routledge.

Hauswirth, I., Herrschel, T. and Newman, P. (2003). Incentives and disincentives to city-regional cooperation in the Berlin-Brandenburg conurbation. *European Urban and Regional Studies, 10*(2), 119–134.

Haworth, N., 1997. Multinational corporations and state sovereignty. In G A Wood and LS Leland jr. (eds): *State and Sovereignty: Is the State in Retreat Retreat,* Dunedin: University of Otago Press, pp. 80–88.

Healey, P (2006): Relational complexity and the imaginative power of strategic spatial planning *European Planning Studies,* vol 14, pp. 525–46.

Healey, P. (1999). Institutionalist analysis, communicative planning, and shaping places. *Journal of Planning Education and Research, 19*(2), 111–121.

Herod, A., & Wright, M. W (2002). Placing scale: An introduction. In: A Herod and M Wright (eds): Geographies of power: Placing scale. Oxford: Blackwell, pp. 1–14.

Herrschel, T. and Newman, P. (2004). Continued division through obstructionist institutionalism: the city-region of Berlin and Brandenburg 15 years on. *disP- The Planning Review, 40*(156), 98–104.

Högenauer, Anna-Lena (2015): The Limits of Territorial Interest Representation in the European Union, Territory, Politics, Governance, 3:2, 147–166,

Hospers, G (2006): Borders, Bridges and Branding: The Transformation of the Øresund Region into an Imagined Space. *European Planning Studies* Vol. 14, No. 8, 1015–1033.

http://www.chicagoforum.org/press-release/international-leaders-initiative, accessed 15 Mar 16.

http://www.uclg.org/en/media/news/local-human-local-efficient-local-beautiful-highlights-3rd-world-forum-local-economic.

http://www.umea.se/umeakommun/kommunochpolitik/internationelltarbete/internationalcooperation.4.3343915a13c39d4211980ab.html.

https://www.aarhus.dk/da/omkommunen/English/Collaborate-with-the-City/International-Relations/Internationalisation.aspx.

https://www.aarhus.dk/da/omkommunen/English/Collaborate-with-the-City/International-Relations/Internationalisation-Committee.aspx, accessed 13Feb 2016.

https://www.aarhus.dk/da/omkommunen/English/Visit-Aarhus.aspx.

Sassatelli, M (2008): Europeanization and cultural policy. *European Societies,* Volume 10, Issue 2, 225–245.

Jarvis, D. S. (2000). *International relations and the challenge of postmodernism: Defending the discipline.* Univ of South Carolina Press.

Jeffery C., Wincott D 2010 The Challenge of Territorial Politics: Beyond Methodological Nationalism 167–188 in C Hay ed *New Directions in Political Science. Responding to the Challenges of an Interdependent World,* Basingstoke: Palgrave.

Jonas, A. and Pincetl, S. (2006): Rescaling regions in the state: the new regionalism inCalifornia. *Political Geography,* 25(5), 482–505.

Keating, M. (1999). Regions and international affairs: motives, opportunities and strategies. *Regional & Federal Studies,* 9(1), 1–16.

Kiran, K (2013): Integration by Interpellation: The European Capitals of Culture and the Role of Experts in European Union Cultural Policies. In:*Journal of Common Market Studies,* Volume 51, Issue 3, pages 538–554, May 2013.

Kölling, M (2015) Subnational Governments in the Negotiation of the Multiannual Financial Framework 2014–2020: The Case of Spain, *Regional & Federal Studies,* 25:1, 71–89.

Krasner, S (1985): Structural Causes and Regime Consequences: Regimes as Intervening Variables, In Stephen Krasner, ed., *International Regimes.* Ithaca: Cornell University Press.

Krätke, S. (2001). Strengthening the polycentric urban system in Europe: conclusions from the ESDP. *European Planning Studies,* 9(1), 105–116.

Lecours, A. (2002). Paradiplomacy: reflections on the foreign policy and international relations of regions. *International Negotiation,* 7(1), 91–114.

Lecours, A., & Moreno, L. (2003). Paradiplomacy: A nation-building strategy? A reference to the Basque Country. In: Alain-G. Gagnon, Montserrat Guibernau, and Francois Rocher (eds): *The Conditions of Diversity in Multinational Democracies* Quebec: Institute for Research on Public Policy, pp. 267–294.

Lefèvre, C. & d'Albergo, E. (2007). Why Cities Are Looking Abroad and how They Go About It. *Environment and Planning C,* vol 25, no 3, 317–326.

Macleod, G. and Jones, M. (2007) Territorial, scalar, networked, connected: in what sensea 'regional world'? *Regional Studies,* 41(9), 1177–91.

Makarychev, A. S. (2004). Where the North Meets the East Europe's 'Dimensionalism' and Poland's 'Marginality Strategy'. *Cooperation and Conflict,* 39(3), 299–315.

Mansfield, E and Milner, H. (1999). The new wave of regionalism. *International organization,* 53(3), 589–627.

Marshall, A. (2005). Europeanization at the urban level: Local actors, institutions and the dynamics of multi-level interaction. *Journal of European Public Policy,* 12(4), 668–686.

Metro African (2014): Aurora, Colorado Forms Sister City Partnership With Adama, Ethiopia. In: Metro African, 28 Jun 2014, available under: http://metroafrican.com/2014/06/aurora-colorado-forms-sister-city-partnership-with-adama-ethiopia/, accessed 5 Mar 16).

Metropolis (2014) *Action Plan 2012–14* http://www.metropolis.org/sites/default/files/pdf/plan_accion_2012-2014_en.pdf.

Neil Adams, Giancarlo Cotella & Richard Nunes (2014) The Engagement of Territorial Knowledge Communities with European Spatial Planning and the Territorial Cohesion Debate: A Baltic Perspective, *European Planning Studies*, 22:4, 712–734.

Nick McAteer, Neringa Mozuraityte and Neil McDonald (2012): Ex-post Evaluation of 2012 European Capitals of Culture Final Report for the European Commission DG Education and Culture July 2013 Ecorys UK Ltd http://www.uk.ecorys.com, accessed 22 Mar 16.

NLC (2016): Annual Report 2015, available under http://www.nlc.org/Documents/About%20NLC/NLC%20FY%202015%20Annual%20Report%20Final.pdf, accessed 10 Mar 16.

NLC (2016): National League of Cities Announces 2016 Federal Priorities, 19 Feb 2016.

O'Dowd, L. (2002). Transnational integration and cross-border regions in the European Union. *Transnational Democracy: Political Spaces and Border Crossings, London: Routledge*, pp. 111–128.

Oikonomou, G. (2016). Bypassing a Centralized State: The Case of the Greek Subnational Mobilization in the European Union, *Regional & Federal Studies*, 26(1), 73–94.

Ornelas, E., 2005. Trade creating free trade areas and the undermining of multilateralism. European Economic Review, 49(7), 1717–1735.

Orsini, A., Morin, J. F., & Young, O. (2013). Regime complexes: A buzz, a boom, or a boost for global governance? *Global Governance: A Review of Multilateralism and International Organizations*, 19(1), 27–39.

Pain K., Van Hamme G., 2014 *Changing Urban and Regional Relations in a Globalizing World. Europe as a Global Macro-Region.* Cheltenham: Edward Elgar.

Provan, K. G., & Kenis, P. (2008). Modes of network governance: Structure, management, and effectiveness. *Journal of public administration research and theory, 18*(2), 229–252.

Rodiguez, A (2014): How does Chicago stack up? City seeks to show global corporations it's an evolved place to do business. Are they buying the pitch? In: Chicago Tribune, 26 Jan, 2014.

Sassen, S. (2001) *Global Networks, Linked Cities.* London: Routledge.

Sassen, S., 1999. *Globalization and its discontents: Essays on the new mobility of people and money* (Vol. 9). New York: New Press.

Schaffer J. K. (2012) The boundaries of transnational democracy: alternatives to the all-affected principle, *Review of International Studies* 38, 321–342.

Schmitter P. C. (1996), "Imagining the Future of the Euro-Polity with the Help of New Concepts", in: G. Marks, F. W. Scharpf, P. C. Schmitter & W. Streeck, *Governance in the European Union,* London: Sage, pp. 121–150.

Scott, J. W. (1999). European and North American contexts for cross-border regionalism. *Regional Studies*, *33*(7), 605–617.

Scott A 2012 *A world in Emergence: Cities and Regions in the 21st Century*. Cheltenham: Edward Elgar.

Shen J 2014: Not quite a twin city: Cross-boundary integration in Hong Kong and Shenzhen *Habitat International* 42, 138–146.

Sparke, M. (2000). Excavating the future in Cascadia: Geoeconomics and the imagined geographies of a cross-border region. *BC Studies: The British Columbian Quarterly*, (127), 5–44.

Steunson, D. and Gilbert, R., 2005. Coping with Canadian federalism: the case of the Federation of Canadian Municipalities. *Canadian Public Administration*, *48*(4), 528–551.

Swyngedouw, E., 2004. Globalisation or 'glocalisation'? Networks, Territories and Rescaling. In: *Cambridge Review of International Affairs*, *17*(1), 25–48.

Tallberg, J; Sommerer, Th; Squatrito, T and Jönsson C (2013) *The Opening Up of International Organizations: Transnational Access in Global Governance*. New York, NY: Cambridge University Press.

Thompson, G. (2003). *Between hierarchies and markets: The logic and limits of network forms of organization*. Oxford University Press.

Tickell, A., & Peck, J. A. (1995). Social regulation after Fordism: regulation theory, neo-liberalism and the global-local nexus. *Economy and Society*, *24*(3), 357–386.

Toronto City Council (2000): International Alliance Program, Umea 2014: (http://umea2014.se/en/about-umea2014/, accessed 11 April 14).

Umeå municipal website: Town twinning and international cooperation localities—http://www.umea.se/umeakommun/kommunochpolitik/internationelltarbete/natverkochvanorter/vanorterochsamarbetsorter.4.bbd1b101a585d7048000173977.html, accessed 3 Apr 16.

Walsh, C (2012) Spatial planning and territorial governance: managing urban development in a rapid growth context, Urban Research & Practice, 5:1, 44–61.

Weiss, T and Ramesh, T (2010): Global Governance and the UN: An Unfinished Journey. Bloomington, IN: Indiana University Press.

Whittle, A., & Spicer, A. (2008). Is actor network theory critique? *Organization Studies*, *29*(4), 611–629.

Zadek, S (2008) "Global collaborative governance: there is no alternative", Corporate Governance: The international journal of business in society, Vol. 8, no 4, 374–388

INDEX